You're Not Paranoid.
They're Actually Trying
To Drive You Crazy.

They don't mean to do it. They'll even deny that they're doing it. This new survival guide goes beyond good intentions and denials, and is designed to help *you* help *them* to STOP IT.

"Crazymaking: how to recognize it and decode it, and how to end it . . . an interesting book and it could even help change lives if taken seriously by people who complain that their jobs, children or husbands/wives are driving them crazy."

—LOS ANGELES TIMES

STOP! YOU'RE DRIVING ME CRAZY

Dr. George R. Bach
& Ronald M. Deutsch

BERKLEY BOOKS, NEW YORK

This Berkley book contains the complete
text of the original hardcover edition.
It has been completely reset in a type face
designed for easy reading, and was printed
from new film.

STOP! YOU'RE DRIVING
ME CRAZY

A Berkley Book / published by arrangement with
the author

PRINTING HISTORY
Berkley / Putnam edition / November 1979
Berkley edition / April 1981

ISBN: 0-425-04738-5

A BERKLEY BOOK ® TM 757,375
Berkley Books are published by Berkley Publishing Corporation,
200 Madison Avenue, New York, New York 10016.
PRINTED IN THE UNITED STATES OF AMERICA

ACKNOWLEDGMENTS

The senior author, Dr. Bach, is now in his thirty-sixth year of university-connected and private practice of psychotherapy. Practically every consultation hour brings up the paradoxical human problem: Persons who consciously like, love, or at least respect each other unconsciously tend to undermine rather than build up the morale and mental well-being of their friend, lover, or spouse. Why? And how do people unwittingly inflict nerve-racking stress on each other? It is a mystery to all concerned.

From thousands of stress reports during individual and group psychotherapy sessions, a linkage emerged between pathogenic communication patterns and indirect, so-called passive aggression. For the opportunity to find the key to this paradox, we acknowledge our indebtedness to the patients who openly shared their struggles for sanity, and chose our CAG (Creative Aggression) approach to let us "coach" their fight for growth.

Insights gained from decades of clinical therapeutic work led to preventive educational programs and techniques (exercises) designed to recognize, stop, and/or decode what we termed *crazymaking* in everyday life.

We are grateful to the thousands of adult participants

in our university courses and at the Bach Institute's workshops and seminars for showing us why and how presumably normal, intelligent people engage almost as much in the crazymaking process as patients undergoing psychiatric treatment are prone to do. With this population of healthy, everyday crazymakers, we tested the practical value of our self-help, preventive approach to crazymaking described in this book. A heartfelt thank you to these adult students.

Among the regular faculty of these seminars on crazymaking CAG lab leaders, Luree Nicholson deserves special recognition for contributing original ideas, techniques, and editorial suggestions throughout the many years of preparation of this book. Dr. Roger Bach helped shape the structure of the text, Dr. Herb Goldberg kept a constant, constructively critical eye on the evolving manuscript and guarded through hours of meaningful dialogues the senior author's sanity from contagion by the subject he was working on. Further intellectual and emotional support was received from Dr. Lew Yablonsky, Dr. Zev Wanderer, and Dr. Vance Kondon. Dr. Bruce Parsons improved the terminology of crazymaking ploys. During conferences and personal visits, Gregory Bateson, to whom this work is dedicated, initially inspired this project and supported its progress and completion during many memorable personal encounters. Francis Greenburger, the literary agent, in a dedicated and caring way beyond the call of duty, guided it wisely through some production crises.

The following CAG lab leaders contributed valuable feedback from their conducting of crazymaking laboratories: Carrol Bacheller, Cathy Bond, Ed and Ester Bourgh, Lewis and Brandy Engel, Eric Field, Joe Ignoto, Florian Latka, Inge and Haja Molter, Michael Paula, Dominik Salfi, and Sascha Schneider.

Psychological concepts were clarified in discerning discussions with Dr. Gretchen Anderson, Dr. Ernst Beier, Dr. Irenaus Eibl-Eibesfeldt, Dr. Cedric Emmery, Dr. Seymour Feshbach, Dr. Don Goldsmith, Dr. Birger Goos, Dr. Steve Harrison, Dr. Ulrich Hoegg, Dr. Gert

Lorusso, Dr. Ted Lorusso, Dr. Georgia Paradisi, and Dr. Maria Selvini Palazolli.

Joan Hotschkiss, Peggy Bach, and Stephanie Bach read early versions of the manuscript and offered valuable suggestions.

As the logic of crazymaking and of this book began to emerge, and it became necessary to find and fictionalize the many human examples that are used to explain it, the recall, imagination and psychological insight of Diana Deutsch became invaluable assets. She also, with patience and understanding, provided again and again the soothing settings in which two authors, often driven to the brink by their maddening material, would stop before they drove each other crazy.

*For
Gregory Bateson,
pioneer in
the study of pathogenic
communications,
who encouraged us to
examine them in the context
of everyday life*

CONTENTS

PART III
The Fight for Sanity

STOP!
YOU'RE DRIVING ME
CRAZY

PART I

The Crazymaking Experience

CHAPTER ONE

The Crazymaking Experience

"My husband is driving me crazy."

"This job is driving me crazy."

"The kids are driving me crazy."

When we say that someone or something drives us crazy, we speak more truth than we know.

For, contrary to what we may think, we are not exaggerating. We are saying just what we mean. We are feeling one of the most urgent and meaningful warning signs in the whole catalog of human emotion. And for just a moment—or for the entire duration of a relationship—our very sanity is at risk.

The seriousness of the threat depends mainly on how important the crazymaker is to us. A pay phone that swallows our money and then goes dead or a stranger who blithely steals our turn at the bank window may drive us a little crazy. Yet there is no real harm unless we do to the telephone or the line-crasher what, for a moment, we would like to do.

On the other hand, when we feel driven crazy by the people who matter most, emotional danger flags are flying.

Few of us are even aware that these danger signals are there. But fewer still realize what they mean.

This failure of understanding can be tragic. For typical crazymaking by intimates is rarely what it appears to be—a strangely maddening annoyance born of seeming carelessness, forgetfulness, or accident.

Instead, it is usually an urgent message about a concealed problem, a problem that is central to the relationship. But it is a message in code.

Unless we can read that code, we cannot recognize the problem or deal with it. The result is that the crazymaking will continue to recur. And as it recurs, it will steadily erode the relationship. It can destroy the trust and goodwill we need with lovers and co-workers, with parents and children.

The central purpose of this book is to show you how to recognize and read crazymaking code. It is to show you how to understand and deal with these disguised messages of trouble. For only if we can reveal the hidden fears and conflicts that underlie crazymaking can we stop the destructiveness and grow.

Before we can use crazymaking as a psychological key that can open up some of the most puzzling and disturbing aspects of our close relationships, we need to understand a little about how the phenomenon works. It helps to begin by first looking at crazymaking of a genuinely trivial kind, at incidents such as these:

After thirty minutes of waiting for your dinner, you finally get the attention of the waitress. And she says, "Oh, I thought I'd already served your order."

You've run out of gas on a rainy night and walked a mile to the lights of a service station. And the attendant says, "Sorry, but we don't have a gasoline can. Anyway, I'm closing in five minutes."

You've reached the airport after a breathless rush through heavy traffic. The passenger agent pushes a few buttons marked Sure-Reserve on his computer, nods his head at the read-out, and says, "I'm afraid we have no record of a reservation for you. And the flight is full."

Typically, your feeling of upset and confusion in such situations is out of proporation to what has happened. The realities, while certainly annoying, are usually not catastrophic. You have to go a little further to find gas, wait a little longer for food, or find another flight.

But you may tend to *feel* as if something terrible and shocking has happened. You may blow up or burst into tears, depending on the circumstances and your personal style. Or feelings of shock and disbelief may leave you immobilized for a moment, stumbling for words, perhaps even trembling with anger or frustration, unable to think what to do.

In that moment you are literally deprived to some extent of your sanity—which is defined as a soundness of thought, feeling, and judgment. And that is why we say such experiences drive us "up the wall," "bananas," "ape," "nuts," "wild," "out of our skulls," "*crazy*."

On reflection we may be embarrassed a bit by our reactions in such situations. We may shout at attendants, stalk out of restaurants, or make unreasonable threats or demands. Since we do not understand what has happened to us, we may try to excuse ourselves as overtired, under pressure, on edge, off guard. We say, "I don't know what got into me."

Something really did hit us, hard. But what?

The answer is important—not so much to understand these trivial episodes of life in a complex society but because when we are similarly derailed by people who mean more to us, the effects can go deep indeed. Psychotherapists often see instances in which seemingly small crazymaking matters—perhaps a lost key or a forgotten errand, a bill left unpaid, a word left unsaid—can trigger explosions as big as a lost job, a runaway child, or a broken marriage.

So when crazymaking occurs with the important people in our lives—and we will see that inevitably it does—we need to understand a number of things about it. First of all it helps to know why crazymaking has so much impact on us, why it makes us feel so bad. And if we analyze a number of occurrences, we find a clue to the crazymaking pattern.

Invariably a false expectation is created.

Then—zap!—it is destroyed.

We are led to believe that a person or a thing can be counted on to perform in a certain way. And then that belief is suddenly contradicted.

In this way, things can be effective crazymakers. For example, your new twenty-five-inch television set turns into so many green, wavy lines on Super Bowl Sunday. Or your brand-new marvel of German automotive precision breaks down in the fast lane of the freeway. But even in such circumstances, it is well to remember that the machines do not create their own false expectations. They are created for them by people.

Our expectations of strangers are often based on seeing them much in the same way we see things. We expect bus drivers to drive buses, information clerks to give information, and so on. And we feel a little crazy when they don't play the roles they are supposed to play. Our expectation is of the role, rather than of the person, whom we may not really see at all.

That is why you expect that once the waitress has taken your order, food will eventually arrive. In our crazymaking example, the waitress has reinforced that expectation with her set speech of greeting: "My name is Miriam and I'll be taking care of you folks this evening. Just tell me if there's anything you need."

So it is doubly disturbing when she proves to have forgotten you. For you not only have your expectations of waitresses, but you also have a promise. She has made you feel that she is aware of you as a person and is concerned about your comfort.

Then she not only fails to perform as a waitress, but in saying that she thought she had already served you, she makes it clear that she was not really much aware of you or much concerned about you.

However, to get a glimpse of how understanding can alter such experiences, let us add just one factor to the story. All is as before, but after she delivers her crazymaking line, she shakes her head sadly and says:

"I'm awfully sorry. I've been doing terrible things like this all day—ever since I heard this morning that my father died."

Immediately the crazymaking effect abates. You have clear information that breaks it up. On the one hand your expectation is greatly reduced. You don't expect a person in a state of shock to perform dependably. And on the other hand you can see how she was distracted from her awareness of *your* need by her own.

The necessary conditions for crazymaking are gone. Her behavior no longer surprises you. And your anger and upset are replaced by sympathy for a harsh wound.

Understanding and managing crazymaking experiences with intimates can be far more subtle and complex. But the principles involved are much the same.

This little incident can also suggest how such upsets can be turned to positive purposes. For example, once you understand, you see the waitress as a person, not just as a Thing that brings food. You notice now, for example, that her eyes are red and swollen, that her face is drawn.

And you may change your behavior, too. You say thank you when she brings each course. And perhaps when she apologizes again as she brings your check, saying that all she can think about is how she can afford to get home for the funeral, you ask your dinner companion: "Would it be really foolish to leave a ten-dollar tip on a twenty-dollar check?"

When we can understand crazymaking, there is more than the relief of a painful situation. There is a constructive change in the relationship as well, a change that gives both partners more.

However, the simple frustration of expectations is not enough to explain crazymaking. For example, suppose you have planned a picnic. The weather forecast is for scattered clouds. But to your dismay it begins to rain.

You are disappointed. But you do not have a crazymaking experience.

Why not? Because your expectation had not reached the level of firm belief. It had not reached the level of trust. Experience teaches us not to count on the weather or the prognostications of the Weather Bureau.

Similarly, you are not greatly upset if you dial a long-distance call and it does not go through. You have also learned that telephones are not sure things.

On the other hand there is one part of telephone service that you do depend on. Every month you get a bill. And if you pay it the phone goes on working.

But suppose that one month you send the check, and ten days later your phone is disconnected. You receive a curt notice which says that service has been cut off for nonpayment. That can be crazymaking. You rage at the customer representative. You write to your congressman.

One simple rule is that the deeper our trust in people, the greater the crazymaking effect when it is broken. For trust is one of our earliest emotional lessons. It is fundamental in our emotional lives. Current theory is that an infant's love begins with trust. So obviously, when our trivial crazymaking examples are mirrored in our dealings with intimates, the effect is much greater. For instance, at breakfast, Martha asks her husband, "What time will you be home tonight, dear?"

"We're having the monthly sales meeting," says Dick. "I'll probably be late—maybe about nine o'clock."

"Anything special you'd like for dinner?"

"Just something plain. You know how touchy my digestion gets when I'm too tired and hungry."

That night, as Dick opens the door, he finds Martha in her coat, about to leave. "I'll be back by eleven, dear," she says brightly. "I'm going over to Alice's to watch that TV special on women in medicine. My, you look tired! You've had dinner, haven't you?"

It is not hard to see why Dick is upset by this greeting. As with all crazymaking, at first he is a little stunned, bewildered by the failure of his sure expectation that a stomach-soothing supper would be waiting for him when he got home.

He sputters for a minute. And then he begins to get angry. But his anger is cut off.

"Now I'm sure you said," says Martha, "that you were going to eat dinner downtown. Remember—you said you wanted something plain, and you said you didn't want to wait too long to eat because it was hard on your digestion.''

"I said some of that," replies Dick. "But I definitely said I was coming home for supper." He sulks, hurt.

"Now, dear," Martha asks patiently, "are you sure you really said it in so many words?"

Dick tries to think. He can't remember, and this makes him angrier. "Damn it," says Dick, "I know I told you. What do I have to do, write you a memo?"

"Well, people can be unclear, you know. And people can misunderstand." She looks wounded.

"Goddamnit, I distinctly remember that you asked me what I wanted for supper!"

"That was before you said you'd be late," his wife responds. Her eyes are beginning to moisten. She looks away. Then, without a word, she removes her coat. And, silently, she takes it to the closet.

Dick watches her. "Well, OK," he says, feeling a little bad. "So I yelled at you. It's been a long day, and then there's a thing like this. You just end up feeling that nobody gives a damn.''

Martha turns quickly. "How can you say that?" she demands tearfully. "How can you think it? For eight years I've tried to be a good wife. I've tried to take care of you. I've tried to cook nice things. And you don't think I care about you! You think I'd just let you starve.''

"Look, I didn't say that, I said—"

Martha's shoulders slump. "Well, it's probably all my fault. But I didn't do it deliberately. Can't a person make one mistake in eight years?"

Soon Dick is feeling guilty and soothing Martha. And Martha is poaching eggs and toasting bread to soothe him. She brings him cocoa and cake in bed, and then they end by making love, not well, but better than usual.

Note that the crazymaking incident itself has never really been explained. It has not been dealt with. Note too that Martha has had a crazymaking experience of her own—Dick's expression of the feeling that no one gave a damn, in the face of her years of careful caretaking.

Most important of all, the two have had no way to deal with their shocks and hurt feelings. Seeing that they faced a confrontation, both backed up. The situation just seemed too insignificant to be worth a fight. So they merely swallowed their feelings and smoothed the imminent battle over.

Next morning the unpleasantness seems to be forgotten. Dick is solicitous. When Martha starts to take the trash cans out, Dick stops her. They are too heavy for her. It is his job to do such things, he says.

They kiss affectionately as Dick leaves. And it is only after the trash collectors have passed that Martha notices he has forgotten to put the trash out. "Honestly, Mother," Martha says on the phone later. "I know Dick means well. But sometimes he drives me crazy."

The fact is that Dick has not been able to bury his crazymaking distress of the night before. He has tried, but his resentment has emerged again. Without realizing he was doing it, he has evened the score.

Dick and Martha have long been engaged in this circle of crazymaking. And the steady round of shocks of disappointment has begun to erode their marriage. For it has weakened their trust in each other.

When trust is repeatedly broken in small ways, we cannot help becoming a little tense and suspicious. There is a defensiveness which shows itself in many ways. The persons involved no longer communicate very openly. Instead, it is a rather formal communication that seeks to avoid opening old wounds and narrows itself to saying only what one thinks the other wants to hear.

With the loss of openly communicated feeling, Dick and Martha have lost true intimacy. For example, their sex life, which was once quite free and good, has deteriorated. Often, when they begin to make love, something seems to intervene. They seem aware of little annoyances which would once have gone unnoticed.

At one typical bedtime, Dick begins to stroke Martha's back gently.

MARTHA: Ah, that feels good.

DICK: [*Expectations rising*] Really? I like to do it.

MARTHA: Mmmm. It turns me on.

DICK: [*Expectantly*] It turns me on doing it.

MARTHA: So gentle. So sweet.

DICK: I feel very gentle tonight.

MARTHA: It makes me remember how gentle you used to be.

DICK: [*His mood breaks with a little jolt. Used to be? He stops stroking but can't quite say anything.*]

MARTHA: Don't stop.

DICK: What do you mean . . . how gentle I *used* to be?

MARTHA: [*Now* her *mood is broken.*] I didn't mean anything. It just came out, that's all. But there was a time when you didn't get so sensitive about every word. . . .

DICK: [*Trying to salvage the situation*] Look, forget it. I just want to please you, that's all.

MARTHA: OK. Just let's not fight. Just go ahead.

DICK: [*Feeling frustrated and a little violent*] Damn it, Martha, I love you as much as ever. [*He reaches toward her fiercely and turns her toward him.*] I want you.

MARTHA: [*Turning on to his unusual show of passion*] I want you, too.

DICK: [*Expectations zooming, he lunges toward her.*] Martha!

MARTHA: Ouch! Take it easy.

DICK: [*Expectation destroyed*] What's the matter?

MARTHA: Well, you didn't used to weigh so much, either. You hurt my arm.

DICK: [*Put off by the weight remark*] Look, I got carried away. I'm sorry. We fat people are clumsy.

MARTHA: I didn't mean to say that.

DICK: Is that why you forgot my dinner the other night? A subtle hint?

MARTHA: Oh, stop it, Dick. I said I didn't mean it.

DICK: I'm sorry. Look, I really want to make love.

MARTHA: Then please just do it. I don't want you to say I'm not taking care of you that way either.

DICK: *What?*

This time Dick and Martha do not make love. They smooth it over in the morning. And then, for some quite unexplainable reason, after eight years Martha forgets and turns his eggs over.

With repeated crazymaking, a tension grows in the relationship. It is a kind of bracing for the next blow. And it manifests itself especially in bed. Dick's growing tension has even led to his becoming sexually premature—which has created still more sexual tension, still more alertness to disappointment or injury, in Martha.

Some of this tension is due to the special way in which crazymaking disappoints expectations. For a simple psychological mechanism is involved, which can be shattering. We call this mechanism *the double message.* And much of the emotional power of crazymaking may be attributed to it.

We can see the effect of the double message at several points in Martha and Dick's story. In the initial incident, when Dick's supper was forgotten, the two messages which were delivered simultaneously went like this:

Message One: Tell when you'll be home and what you want to eat and I will provide it for you. I will take care of you.

Message Two: I know you're worried about your digestion, but I don't care. I'm doing my thing.

Such a conflicting double message is maddening. And the same elements appear when Dick forgets to take the trash cans out. He sends these messages:

Message One: I want to protect you by doing the heavy work. So I will take care of the trash.

Message Two: If you want the trash cans out, take them. You don't take care of me, so I don't take care of you.

The effect of such double messages was made clear in some early animal experiments. The animals were taught that while a bell was ringing they could get food by pushing a bar. Then they were taught that while a buzzer sounded, if they pushed the bar, they would get a small electric shock.

Then one day the experimenters set off both bell and buzzer at the same time. The message to the animals was that pushing the bar would yield both reward and punishment.

The result was pathetic. The animals did not know what to do. They became distraught. They became confused and trembling creatures, paralyzed by the conflicting impulses of an experimental neurosis.

It is appalling but true that most of us reproduce this experiment—usually without realizing it—with the people who are closest to us.

We don't necessarily really mean to hurt. Dick and Martha love each other. But they are caught in the crazymaking trap.

Martha, for example, is genuinely unaware that Dick is coming home to supper. Her unconscious mind tricks her into real misunderstanding. And Dick really does mean to put the trash out but forgets. He is upset about this when he recalls the incident at lunchtime. He phones and apologizes profusely, but he will probably forget and do the same thing again next week.

But whether or not Dick and Martha are trying to hurt each other, they are succeeding. And if they are trying to send messages to one another, what are they trying to say? Plainly those messages are neither clearly sent nor clearly received.

Above all, why are the messages not sent openly instead of in the devious and painful language of crazymaking's curious code?

This is perhaps the core question of this book. For at the Institute of Group Psychotherapy, in decades of dealing with human relationships of every kind, it has been found that the most important requirement for healthy and growing relationships is that the people involved have clear information about one another.

If information is exchanged in a cloudy, mystifying form, any relationship is soon in trouble. Crazymaking is a danger sign that this is happening. For at its heart, we shall see, crazymaking is an almost universal way of communicating indirectly. Its code is a way of concealing the true meaning of its message.

Once we can crack that code, on the other hand, we have a tool for making direct communication possible. Then we can become free to ask others for what we want of them, free to see and hear what they want of us. Then we can satisfy and be satisfied. We can let ourselves and our relationships grow.

So let us look more closely, to learn the purposes of crazymaking, the real content of its cryptic messages. For only then can we understand the groundless fears which make the code seem necessary. And only then can we see how those fears may be laid to rest.

CHAPTER TWO

The Madness Behind the Method

Only a few days of the visit have passed, but already Charlotte and her mother have begun to drive each other a little crazy—just as they did when Charlotte still lived at home.

Before she made the long trip home to show her mother the new baby, Charlotte wrote proud letters about her reducing diet and how well she was doing on it. After the baby was born, Charlotte had found herself some fifteen pounds overweight. An attractive young woman—and very concerned about her appearance—Charlotte was quite disturbed to find herself a little fat.

Now, after months of self-denial, she has lost thirteen of the unwanted pounds. In fact, to all but her own critical eyes, she has regained her former elegant figure. Nevertheless she still diets diligently.

But at the first breakfast, on the same plate with Charlotte's single boiled egg and dry toast, Mother had put just a few little sausages. "I know, dear," said Mother in response to Charlotte's questioning look. "But this is just a special welcome home. It's that homemade sausage from Klipstein's that you used to love."

At dinner, Mother respects Charlotte's request for baked fish. But it swims in a seasoned cream sauce. And there is dessert—Charlotte's old favorite, chocolate mousse. "Do you remember how you used to lick the pan, dear?"

Charlotte knows her mother has planned and worked to please her with these treats. And she doesn't want to hurt her feelings. But after four days of such loving efforts, when Mother says, "Now, a little of my pecan pie never hurt anyone," Charlotte suddenly stares at her, wordlessly. Then she bursts into tears, throws down her fork, and runs from the house, not to return for at least an hour.

Is this just an example of love and good intention gone awry? Not likely. For it follows some of the most basic principles of crazymaking.

First, expectations, carried to the level of trust, are destroyed. And then the trusting expectation is broken by a classic crazymaking double message.

Charlotte gets these conflicting messages from her mother:

Message One: I am willing to go to a lot of trouble to please you by giving you what you want.

Message Two: I know that losing weight means a lot to you. But I want to cook for you. I want to do my thing regardless of how you feel about it.

And there is another principle of intimate crazymaking involved. It is that the incident becomes mutual. Both Mother and Charlotte end by feeling like victims. And each sees the other as the destroyer of a strong expectation. Mother gets another pair of conflicting messages:

Message One: I understand that you communicate your love by doing things for me. I accept your offerings of food with pleasure because I accept your love.

Message Two: I know my diet blocks you from giving me love your way. But I don't care. My waistline matters more to me than you do.

And still one more crazymaking principle is seen here. The trigger for the incident is seemingly trivial, a slice of pecan pie. It is too unimportant to explain the strong feelings. So later it becomes easy to deny that the experience was real. It seems sensible just to smooth the upset over. For how can there have been such a fuss over such a little thing?

The irritation seems petty indeed in comparison to the importance of the relationship. And typically, the victim decides that it is not worthwhile to risk the relationship by so insignificant a conflict. We shall see, however, that this apparently commonsense judgment is actually the most dangerous self-deception of crazy-making.

For instance, that evening Charlotte phones her husband long distance. She feels bad and needs to talk to someone who understands.

HUSBAND: Hey, what's the matter? You sound all upset.

CHARLOTTE: I—[*She starts to cry.*] I—guess I am—

HUSBAND: What happened? Is little Bobby all right?

CHARLOTTE: Bobby's fine. It's Mother. She—she's driving me crazy.

HUSBAND: What did she do?

CHARLOTTE: She—[*Blowing her nose*] She—gave me a piece of pecan pie.

Mother, in turn, is tempted to go to her confidante next door for sympathy. But when she rehearses what she wants to say, she shakes her head. How will it sound, after all? "My daughter is driving me crazy. She doesn't want my love anymore. How do I know? She wouldn't eat her dessert!"

If the surface problem, like the pecan pie, can't explain the emotional power of crazymaking, what can? Why do people who care about each other send the maddening double message? How can we understand what it means?

The answer is essentially simple. First, people are not usually aware that they are sending two conflicting messages. And second, both sides of the double message are real. So if we want to understand crazymaking, we must accept both as largely true.

Let us see how this works. The new boss tells you his pet idea for increasing business. You think it is terrible, but you are afraid to say so. Then he says he needs your help. He asks you to prepare a list of your clients who might be interested in the idea, and you feel that you have to agree.

So you are split. You like the boss. He likes you. Your relationship looks as though it should lead to your advancement and to friendship. So you don't want to risk any trouble.

On the other hand, you are fairly certain that his idea is doomed to fail. And when it does, you don't want either your clients or your own higher management to think that you approved of it.

What to do? Since the biggest immediate risk is a conflict with your boss, you grit your teeth and agree to make the list he asked for.

You choke down your reservations. You really mean to do what he asked. But the reservations will not stay down. Your reluctance is buried. But it is not gone.

Openly, you continue to send the *acceptable* message, the one he wants to hear. Each time he reminds you about the list, you say it is a good idea and that you will help. But inwardly you drag your heels. You keep forgetting to do the chore. Or you seem to be too busy to work on it. Or you begin the list and then misplace it.

So your failure to perform becomes the second half of a double message. It is the *unacceptable* half. You are saying no while you are saying yes. You are creating a false expectation and then destroying it. The result is crazymaking.

The unacceptable half of a double message is often delivered by "mistakes" and "forgetting," or by a kind of "absentmindedness" or "carelessness." In a sense, your conscious mind looks the other way—while you manage to say, indirectly, what you really want to say.

It is in this way that Mother "doesn't think" when she offers Charlotte fattening treats. Similarly, it "doesn't occur" to Charlotte that Mother's best way of showing love is to cook generously and richly. It is the same with Dick and Martha. Martha "forgets" that Dick is coming home to a late supper. Dick means to take out the trash, but "forgets."

Such convenient and well-aimed lapses make it possible for crazymaking to madden those close to us while the crazymaker remains innocent and unaware. And they permit the wound to become repeated. For as long as the unacceptable feeling survives—and it survives a long time if it is not openly expressed—crazymaking will continue to make it known, vaguely and indirectly.

For example, by late evening, after their crazymaking experience, both Charlotte and Mother feel foolish and guilty about it. They assure each other that they meant no harm. ("I didn't mean it" and "I didn't realize" are often symptoms of crazymaking.)

They hug each other in tears. They decide to smooth the incident over and accuse themselves of being overly sensitive—Mother because the weather is hot, Charlotte because of the time of the month, and both because they are worried about little Bobby's diaper rash.

They decide to have an intimate late-night talk as they used to in the old days. So Charlotte goes upstairs to get some photos of her new house to show Mother. And Mother, while waiting for Charlotte, decides to create a cozy setting. So she goes into her kitchen—to make a pot of coffee and warm up the pecan pie.

The crazymaking is doomed to continue.

Start a discussion of crazymaking in any group, and the stories tend to take on remarkable patterns:

"Henry always forgets and plans a business trip right on my birthday."

"My secretary is the best—except for one thing. Darned if she doesn't bring me a pile of stuff to sign just when I'm trying to get away from the office early on Friday afternoon."

"Wouldn't you think, after a year of living together, that Mary could remember how it bugs me when she doesn't put the car keys back on the hook by the door?"

"Kids are so out of it. That's why they drive you

crazy. My Joey is the most thoughtful boy, really. But no matter how many times I tell him, he can't seem to remember to wipe his muddy shoes on the mat before he comes into the kitchen.''

"I can't figure out why Jean always puts every ashtray back into the cupboard, why she can't leave just one out in the living room.''

Each of these complaints derives from the obscure portion of a double message.

The open half of the message is always clear and understandable. It is always something that the recipient wants to hear. It is invariably a message of goodwill, acceptance, agreement, love, concern, loyalty.

But the second half of the double message is always foggy. It is indirect. And it is always especially hard for us to hear and understand, because it is something we don't want to hear. In many cases, it suggests a conflict in the relationship. It casts a disturbing shadow of doubt, not only over the goodwill expressed in the open message, but often over the relationship itself.

That contradiction is what is so maddening. But if we are to understand crazymaking, we must be ready to acknowledge that the contradiction, and the underlying conflict, exist. We must face their reality.

Why does the secretary make it hard for her boss to catch the early train on Friday? She likes him and likes her job. She is loyal and hardworking. But she is also resentful. Because repeatedly he dumps the end-of-the-week dirty work in her lap and takes off—while she must remain at the office until 7 P.M. to get it done. She feels that he uses his power unfairly.

But she is afraid to speak out, so she uses the indirect protest of crazymaking instead.

Why does Henry take business trips on his wife's birthday—and on his own, too? He loves her, and he expresses his birthday good wishes with expensive presents. But he does not want to be there when she opens them.

For they have developed a round-and-round pattern of crazymaking about age. It begins with the fact that

Henry is much older than she. Afraid of losing her, he tends to keep her dependent. Unaware, he does this by making all the decisions, on the basis of his greater age and experience.

She resents this but is afraid to express it openly. So she indirectly turns Henry's age to a liability—by "harmless teasing" about his bald spot, his need for glasses, his growing paunch. Birthdays tend to bring out this crazymaking on both sides. Henry tries to avoid it.

Why can't Joey remember to wipe his shoes? Because Mother has three younger children. And she also has a great fear of seeming incompetent to manage her home and her brood while she keeps up a very active civic life for which she doesn't really have time.

Her always-shining kitchen floor is a symbol that she can cope with it all. But to cope, she must run a tight ship. The children are not allowed much freedom of play in the house. And Joey is repeatedly recruited to watch the younger children while Mother does the washing and waxing.

Joey feels this is unfair. But when he has tried to say so, he has been accused of being selfish and uncooperative. He is told that if he is not willing to help Mother, he must not love her. So how can he protest? With muddy shoes.

Why does Mary forget to put the car keys on the hook? Because her live-together partner convinced her that they could save money by selling her car and both using his. But now he still hogs the car as his own.

He makes her feel that she must ask permission before using it, and he hesitates before granting it. So she feels cheated. But she hopes they will marry. And she wants to show him how pleasant married life will be. So she bites her tongue. But the resentment is still there. And somehow she can never remember where she put the car keys. In this way he must come to her before he can use the car. And the balance of power is indirectly restored.

Why does Jean put away the ashtrays so her husband always finds himself with a dangling cigarette ash and no place to put it? She has begged him to stop smoking. She is sure it will shorten his life. He agrees but makes no effort. (Note that the crazymaking really begins here, with his double message.)

If Jean reminds him of his promise, he calls her a nag. Several times he has angrily stalked out of the house. So she tells him, but indirectly, by putting the ashtrays away. Of course, he too avoids conflict. He is afraid to say directly that he is not going to stop smoking. We can observe that he does not look for an ashtray *before* he lights his cigarette. And we can also observe that the ash is long before he notices that the ashtray is absent. Somehow that long ash always falls on a clean table or floor.

In all these double messages, the negative and obscure half is of very real importance to the sender. It has force. It can be choked down, but it does not stay down. It remains, smoldering. It does get out. It is expressed, but in the curious cipher we call *crazymaking code*.

Often, to help mask the obscure message even more, the open message is sent with especially positive strength. And the effect is to make the crazymaking experience even worse.

For example, as Joey tracks dirt across the kitchen floor, it is with his cutest, most engaging smile, with his arms out for a hug and a worshipful, "Boy, it sure smells good in here!"

The two messages go out simultaneously—to clash like bumper cars at a carnival. And after the jolt, which message should one respond to?

Joey, we should point out, is not being scheming or diabolical. It is just that down deep he knows that his dirty shoes are making a forbidden protest. At the same time he is both afraid to make the protest—or he would do it openly—and anxious to show that he does love his mother and has basic goodwill toward her. The sugar-coating of the open message becomes an important safety measure.

Nevertheless, the fact remains that the two messages

not only contradict each other, but deny each other. And it becomes almost impossible to respond to either in a whole-hearted way.

Look back to our experimental animals. The bell signals feeding. But when the buzzer (signaling punishment) sounds at the same time, the bell cannot be believed as the sign of a rewarding experience. And the ringing of the bell denies the punishment which the buzzer implies.

In part, it is in this way that crazymaking with intimates derails us so badly. It puts a vague question mark beside our loves, our friendships, our loyalties.

Moreover, the fogginess of the cryptic part of the message makes it even harder to respond. Did we really get a message at all? Or did we imagine it? Was it really intentional or an accident? Since we don't want to believe in the unpleasantness, we are all too willing to see it as bad luck, bad timing, or simply an inadvertency.

In fact, a blunt "Why did you do that?" is likely to bring an innocent "Who, me?" It is likely to bring a prompt disavowal of any harmful intent. And if the injury is clear, there will be a torrent of regrets and apologies.

Thus there is a tendency of both parties to disavow the crazymaking experience, to deny it and smooth over its ill effects. And this is one reason why it can go on interminably. How can one put a stop to something that never happened or that was merely accident? The denial of crazymaking, and the result of that denial, is evidenced by the number of times you've heard people say to their children or their spouses, "I've told you a hundred times—"

They probably have. Yet the offense recurs.

And just as the crazymaker's real feelings spill out without his or her full awareness, so does the victim tend to react. He denies that he has been injured, or at least that the hurt has meaning. But the wound festers.

Once again the message of reaction cannot be sent

directly because the person feels it will not be acceptable. It is likely to produce a conflict that is not wanted.

So when Joey opens his arms to Mother as he tracks across her floor, she bites her tongue. What sort of mother can ignore her child's gesture of love for the sake of discipline? But inwardly she knows that she is being injured, no matter how she may deny the importance. Inwardly she at least feels the smart of indifference to her interests.

That is why she too "forgets." She doesn't mean to do it. But when the phone rings with an invitation to a Sunday brunch, she promptly accepts. "If I can't get a sitter," she says to her friend, "Joey can watch the little ones. He doesn't mind."

But Mother has "forgotten" to look at her calendar. That is where Sunday is marked as the day of Joey's most important Little League game.

Does such a reaction imply a mean pettiness, a thirst for revenge? Not at all. That the methods of crazymaking are cruel does not mean that the people who use them are cruel. They are merely human. The irony is that usually they hold back their direct reactions out of kindness, out of a genuine and understandable wish to keep peace and goodwill.

Yet this very effort toward kindness and tranquillity, this very fear of hurting and displeasing those about whom we care, is what ultimately inflicts pain and bewilderment. And sadly, tragically even, once the pattern of indirection begins, it tends to be perpetuated.

Crazymaking becomes a thorn passed from one to the other, back and forth. It becomes a crucial aspect of the *style* of a relationship.

With the growth of that style, the relationship must deteriorate. For the pain of the crazymaking experience is not well tolerated. The more often it happens, the more we struggle to avoid it.

In this process we begin to channel our open communications into only those areas that are safe. More and more we avoid all conflict, all areas of controversy.

And as this happens, more and more of what we really feel and want to express comes out indirectly, hurtfully.

Eventually we feel choked and confined in such a relationship. At the Bach Institute of Group Psychotherapy, therapeutic groups for the recently divorced explore new, crazy-free patterns of communication. And while there is much talk about the pain, the fear, the sense of loss involved, there is also one positive note sounded. "In a way," it usually goes, "I feel so *free* now. I can be myself. I can be me."

These people are expressing their release from the strangling effects of indirect communication—their escape from crazymaking.

But breaking the relationship is not the only way to get out of the crazymaking trap. There are much less drastic possibilities and much more effective ones. For if we have once adopted the crazymaking style in the false hope of thus preserving an important relationship, it will do no good to sacrifice the relationship. The tendency will be to protect any new alliance in the very same way.

To deal with crazymaking realistically, we must understand the most basic reason for it. We must deal with the almost universal fear which gives it life.

CHAPTER THREE

The Fear That Makes Crazymaking

Only a rare person wants to be a true crazymaker.

For only someone perverse indeed sets out to madden and confuse the important relationships in his life. And fortunately there are few people so perverse.

Yet from time to time all of us become crazymakers—not by choice, but by what seems like necessity. Because, given the right conditions, crazymaking often appears to be the only way to deal with a basic human fear—and a painful dilemma to which it leads.

To understand this fear, and the dilemma, it helps to look back to childhood. For the fear that triggers crazymaking is first encountered in infancy. And by early childhood, most youngsters, as their parents will attest, have become proficient crazymakers.

Marian is a single parent. She has invited Paul to what she hopes will be a quiet and intimate supper. And she has prepared her son, Tommy, who is four, to go to bed early, make no fuss, and stay there.

She has both promised a treat if he behaves well and threatened severe punishment if he does not.

"Do you love Mommy?" she asks Tommy in a last-minute rehearsal, just before Paul is due to arrive.

Tommy nods his head vigorously. Then, in further affirmation, he tries to hug her.

"Well," says Marian, pushing him back from her to

be sure he is paying attention. "Mommy loves you, too. She doesn't have to work tomorrow. So, if you're a good boy, we'll go to the zoo and eat popcorn and see the animals.

"But if you're a bad boy, Mommy will know that you don't really love her, and that will make her sad—and very angry with you. And no zoo. No popcorn."

Marian has planned the evening meticulously, from the low lights in the dining room to the fresh sheets on the bed. Paul is someone special, and this is her first chance to show him her domestic skills.

She is also aware of a handicap. She would like to remarry. And the prospect of living with another man's child is not especially alluring for most single men.

Paul is at the table now, and Marian has just poured the dressing into the crisply chilled salad greens when the first call comes from Tommy's room. Anxiously seeing this as a possible signal of trouble to come, she hurries to cut it off, and enters Tommy's room fiercely. "Tommy," she begins, "tonight is very important to me. You have to be quiet. I told you what would happen if—"

"I'm thirsty, Mom," says Tommy sweetly. "I want a drink."

Marian grits her teeth. She is suspicious, but she can't very well deny water to a thirsty child. Thinking that the salad is wilting, she gets the water and watches skeptically as Tommy takes it. He gulps it eagerly as if to show that his need is real and then he curls up under the covers with a polite "Thanks, Mom."

Paul has just poured the wine into her glass, then given her an approving kiss for having chosen it so well, when Tommy calls again. "Now I told you—" she whispers through clenched teeth as she enters the room.

"I'm cold, Mom," says Tommy pathetically. "I need more blanket."

Marian puts a temperature-taking hand on his arm and finds it is chilly. "What's wrong with me?" she asks herself guiltily as she gets the blanket. "He's only a baby, after all." And she tucks the blanket in very gently. But then, remembering the broiling steaks, she gives Tommy a perfunctory kiss and turns to hurry for the kitchen.

"Mom!" Tommy calls as she is closing the door.

She swings the door open again, and in a hushed but angry voice says, "Damn it, Tommy, go to sleep!"

"Mom—" he says hesitantly.

"Well, quick—what do you want?"

"I love you, Mom."

Guilt wells up again, right through her mental image of blackening steaks. "I love you too," she sighs, torn between love and frustrated anger. "But Mommy has to go now. She *has* to. Please be a good boy and go to sleep. Please. I love you."

And again she closes the door.

"Mom!"

"Jesus!" she explodes, struggling to keep her impatience under control and her voice to a hoarse whisper. "Tommy, if you don't this minute—"

"I want to hug you, Mom," says the small, sleepy voice.

And so it goes. In the kitchen, maddened almost to tears as she tries to salvage the meat, Marian thinks to herself, "That child drives me crazy!"

Indeed he does. Tommy has expertly set up a conflict of feeling which is almost intolerable. Love, tinged with guilt, on one side. Irate frustration on the other. Marian is neatly torn between motherly selflessness and an equally powerful and understandable need to be a separate person. Moreover, Tommy's systematic sabotage of her mood and her dinner is carried out within all the limits she has set.

He hasn't cried. He hasn't left his bed. He hasn't demanded stories. He has merely been thirsty and cold and affectionate.

Marian is angry. But she cannot accept her anger, let alone express it. Not only because Tommy has followed her rules, but because close beneath the surface she feels that the divorce was her fault and that it has done Tommy an injury. She feels it clearly every day when she puts Tommy into nursery school and goes to work.

She feels that in asserting her own wishes she has deprived Tommy. And the present evening is a mirror of this basic conflict.

Of course Tommy has no idea of this. He is merely reacting to his own simple feelings. But they, too, conflict—and create his crazymaking.

Tommy feels rejected and alone. From his bed he can see traces of light. He can smell good food. A trace of Marian's perfume is still on his cheek and it adds to his loneliness. He hears music and talk and laughter. And he wants to be a part of that cozier world.

But he can't say so. The prohibition has been laid out in the strongest terms. He knows that his mother is willing to resort to punishment. And, more than this, his behavior has been made a test of his love. If he says what he feels, what he wants, he will lose the zoo and the popcorn—he will risk both loss of his mother's love and the incursion of violence and pain.

Yet Tommy's feelings are strong, too strong to be buried, even though fear blocks their open expression. They still press to be expressed, but in a safe way. So he becomes sensitive to any physical discomforts. (Adults always accept these and meet them.) And he concentrates on his loving feelings. (Adults never refuse them.) He delivers both these messages simultaneously, and with the sweetness Mother likes.

And, at age four, Tommy has become an expert crazymaker.

He has been pushed into the role by fear, the fear that is at the root of intimate crazymaking—*the fear of open aggression*.

Most people are put off by the very word *aggression*. For it is perhaps the most misunderstood word in our language.

The mere mention of the word makes many people a little anxious, by conjuring images of anger, violence, invasion, and assault. And they feel their own aggression may lead to being disliked, rejected, isolated, or even injured in retaliation.

But to psychologists, aggression is merely a basic of human behavior. And aggression may not intend to hurt. It may be only the necessary assertion of oneself—the necessary expression of what one is or feels or wants.*

To the psychologist, "Please pass the salt" is an aggressive statement. So is "I'm sleepy" or "I am a friendly person" or even "I love you." And so is "Excuse me, but you're standing on my toe!"

Aggression merely describes how we get what we need or want—emotional or material or spiritual—from the world and the people in it. It is the way the gentlest of us survives. It is as necessary and as natural as an infant's reach for the breast.

Yet to some extent, and in some ways, all of us learn to fear aggression.

For we learn early that when we express our wishes and feelings in a direct, open way, there is a risk. We may be rejected. We may come into conflict with the wishes and feelings of others. We may be hurt. We may drive others away. ·

So we soon discover how, when we perceive any risk, to hedge it. We cannot make our aggressive impulses disappear, even if, fearing them, we manage to drive them out of our conscious awareness. Instead we seek a safe path, an indirect path, by which they may come out.

We learn to mask our aggressions, to translate them into code and symbol, in any number of ways and at many levels of obscurity. For example, at a very simple level, Fred and Elaine are spending their first weekend together in the mountains. Elaine is an athletic, robust girl. And Fred is a lifelong city-dweller.

They are hiking in the snow, uphill, and Fred is not only getting winded but he is cold. Elaine is trudging happily up the path and Fred can see that he will soon have trouble keeping up. He does not want to appear weak or unmasculine in her eyes. Nor does he want to break the present cheerful mood. To say "I'm cold"

---

* There is some semantic controversy about whether personal assertion should be included in the term aggression. But modern psychology trends strongly in this direction.

seems to him to risk all this. So, instead, he shivers. The shiver is real, but Fred gives it a little emphasis.

Now he can watch Elaine's reaction. If she sneers and says, "Don't tell me you're cold," he can smile, grit his teeth, deny it, and go on. But if she is only concerned for him, if she puts a sympathetic arm around him and says, "A little cold, honey?" then he can become open.

He shivers again. "You're not cold, are you?" says Elaine with a tinge of annoyance in her voice.

"Oh, no," says Fred. "Maybe just a touch. But a little good cold air never hurt anyone. I think I feel it a bit because there's a little polyester in my underwear; all-cotton is so much better."

"Race you to the top of the hill," says Elaine.

Fred and Elaine will continue their relationship for months, but they will not go to the mountains again. Not that Fred will ever complain. He will share the romantic memory she expresses of their walks in the snow, and say how fine it was. He will even, because he is afraid to risk saying no, agree to more wintry country weekends. But he won't go. At the last minute, if necessary, something will come up at his office—once when Elaine has just bought a whole new outfit. "That job of Fred's," she will complain to a friend. "It drives me crazy!"

The office "crises" are, of course, a form of indirect aggression. They let Fred refuse without taking responsibility for the refusal. These coded messages, however, would not be crazymaking in themselves. They only become so because they go out together with the conflicting open message: "I really want to go and I really intend to go."

The sugar-coated open message is an indispensable part of crazymaking. And it, too, arises in an understandable way. For if we fear a bad reaction to an unacceptable message, it is natural to send along a simultaneous assurance that we mean no harm, that we feel goodwill, to prevent the other person from becoming angry or rejecting us.

The device is easy to see at its simplest. Mary's boss says, "Now, Mary, you know how much we like you and how valuable we think your work has been. But we've lost two accounts in the last week, and things are pretty tight—''

So, when people fear aggression, either their own or that of others, they tend first to make their assertions in coded, indirect ways. And at the same time they openly send goodwill messages, hoping to ward off any painful response.

A number of factors tend to increase that fear. It is heightened as the relationship grows closer, as the other person becomes more powerful, and as there is a greater dependency upon the relationship. As these factors grow, so grows the fear of open assertion—and with it the tendency to turn instead to crazymaking.

This is one reason why people in power—celebrities, the wealthy, public officials, etc.—are likely to be special targets for crazymaking. And it is one reason why such people tend to become cynical about others.

For example, Larry has been told that the sign on his shop violates a city ordinance because it is too intensely lighted. It must be changed.

Larry recalls that the mayor of his small town went to school with him. The two have never been good friends, but Larry phones the mayor and invites him to lunch. Afraid that he will be rejected if he tells the mayor his real objectives, Larry says that what he wants is advice about an alumni committee which he is chairing.

At lunch Larry softens the mayor with a drink, then dwells on the good times of their old college days. The two become nostalgic and the mayor relaxes. He has been under a lot of criticism lately, and Larry's friendliness is warming. The mayor begins to confide in Larry about some of the pains of public office.

Larry responds with great reassurance about the fine job the mayor has done, sympathizes about the lack of public understanding of his programs, and expresses outrage at the opposition by the mayor's opponents. The two order another drink to have with lunch. "Most people just don't understand what the pressure is like," says the mayor, "even in a little town like ours. The nasty calls at night, people snubbing your wife and kids—''

"I don't know why you put up with it," says Larry. "It's so damned ungrateful, so miserable."

"It's good to know that you have one friend," says the mayor.

"Yessir," says Larry. "You just don't get any real understanding, not even from your own staff."

"The city staff?"

"Well, I hate to tell you this," says Larry, grabbing an opportunity, "but take your program against street crime. Complete good sense. Ought to be copied by every city in America. So simple. Just little things like getting more light on the streets at night.

"But what does your own Building Department do? You know that little sign of mine? Complete good taste. Cost $15,000. Lights the street for fifty yards. Well, you won't believe this, but your Building Department says it's too *bright*. Too bright! They've given me an order to—"

At last, with a jolt, the mayor catches on.

That night at dinner, the mayor's wife asks how the lunch with Larry was. "Oh, that," says the mayor, slicing the roast with a vicious cut. "I don't even know why I went. I never did like that son of a bitch. He drives me crazy!"

Power differences—like those between Larry and the mayor—are probably the primary teachers of crazy-making. For it seems dangerous to be openly assertive with persons who hold all the cards. Why should such persons be willing to do what you wish, especially if your wishes in any way conflict with theirs?

Nowhere is that difference so apparent as it is in the relationship between parent and child. To the child, it may seem that the parent has overwhelming power of decision, that the parent can do whatever he or she pleases, and that the child depends entirely on the parent's goodwill and indulgence. The child feels utterly dependent. The parent seems utterly powerful. Direct conflict seems to the child to end in certain loss. So the child resorts to crazymaking and its derailing double message. It seems to work on an immediate basis. And the long-term price escapes the child.

For example, in the case of Tommy, the small boy who is sabotaging his mother's romantic evening, he gets the immediate result he seeks. He gets his mother to return to him repeatedly. In a sense he competes successfully with her lover and manages to hamstring her anger as he does so.

Tommy obtains his mother's attention. He also gets to the zoo the next day. He receives not one but two bags of popcorn, and even a stuffed giraffe.

But Tommy does not understand the full result of his behavior. For one thing, Marian is nervous and irritable the whole day, making Tommy very uncomfortable and uneasy. And, somehow, situations recur in which Tommy fails. He is given the chocolate ice cream cone he asks for and is allowed to walk with it in the sun. But then Marian scolds him severely for the inevitable brown spots on his shirt and pants. She forgets to give him a paper tissue for his pocket, then snarls when he tidies his nose with his sleeve. She promises a ride on the merry-go-round, but decides it turns too fast for him. She has a headache and frequently sits down on benches, while Tommy waits, fidgeting, wanting to see the lions.

Marian has been in her irritable state ever since the flaming dessert went out while she hunted for Tommy's lost teddy bear. She has been especially irritable ever since 12:17 A.M. At that moment she and Paul had re-established their romantic mood, and also established a gasping, rhythmic counterpoint of movement in her bedroom, when both were suddenly startled by a terrible squeal of pain from the hall. Tommy had started for the bathroom in the dark and had bumped his toe.

What explains Marian's behavior? The simple truth that crazymaking begets crazymaking. Marian has been blocked from expressing her anger with Tommy. But while she thinks she has put it out of her mind, it is too painful. It will out. It demands to be expressed. And since the direct expression is not tolerable, her anger must emerge indirectly—under the cover of a basic goodwill—and as the result of "accidents."

There is also a second result of Tommy's crazymaking. It, too, is characteristic. And it results from the simple fact that whenever they can people try to avoid the repetition of crazymaking experiences.

The night before, Paul had generously suggested that Tommy might share the camping week that he and Marian had been planning. "It would be good for him," said Paul. "And kids get so worn out in the mountains that they sleep like logs." He grinned. "I could show him how to fish. It could be a kick, teaching him things."

But now, as she walks through the zoo, Marian is thinking how to ask her mother to take Tommy for a week.

In this way crazymaking often results in the precise effect that the crazymaker was trying to avoid—his rejection. And when crazymaking becomes habitual, when it becomes part of a person's lifestyle, a gradual, destructive escalation of the problem may begin.

The crazymaking, which was intended to avoid conflict and confrontation, which was used to escape from the necessity of disappointing or refusing an important other person, causes the crazymaker to be rejected. This is a confirmation of his fears. It convinces him that he was right, that any kind of conflict is dangerous. So the fears grow greater. And the avoidance of aggression of any kind becomes more and more a dependable pattern.

Eventually the whole communications style of the individual, or of the relationship, becomes indirect. It can reach a point at which the crazymaker becomes quite impossible to live or work with. In the case of a relationship that takes on this style, it may well become untenable.

This resultant isolation—either of two people from each other, or of an individual from the world around him—is the ultimate price of crazymaking. It is worthwhile examining. For it is the only real alternative to the direct assertion of oneself.

CHAPTER FOUR

The Price of Crazymaking

One of the many paradoxes of crazymaking is that the chronic crazymaker often appears at first to be among the most lovable of people.

The reason is simple. He has gone repeatedly through the circles of crazymaking. His fear of aggression has led him to express himself by indirection. This in turn has led to his rejection and increased his fear, and so on.

The net effect is that he is now addicted to the acceptable. And the price he and others pay is high.

Jim Harvey is the perennial Nice Guy, a people pleaser. He seems a natural for public relations since he rarely says no. He smiles a lot and gives the answers others hope for. The trouble is, he cannot always back up his yes-saying with performance.

This maddening characteristic has cost him one job after another. Lately, his salary has dwindled. And he was out of work for three months before he finally found a spot in a huge food company and settled for a rather minor role, considering his experience.

Jim is in charge of display materials and booths for Sweet Screws, "the cereal with the peppermint twist."

"I hope you have something special, Jim, for the annual Sugar Coaters of America meeting," his boss says.

"Oh, I do," says Jim with a smile. "We're just

finalizing the plans now for your approval. I know you'll like it.''

Actually he has not come up with anything unusual. Then he meets Julie, a clever young designer. She has fresh ideas. ''But you can see they won't be cheap to do,'' she warns.

''No problem,'' smiles Jim, putting out of his mind the fact that the year's display budget is close to the brink.

''My own time estimate,'' says Julie, ''looks big, but you can see how much detailed work there will be.''

''No problem,'' smiles Jim. ''We're not a small company. We want quality and we expect to pay for it. Just give me a rough estimate on everything and we'll work out the details later.''

Jim's boss likes the idea. ''But it looks expensive.'' He is worried. ''Things are kind of tight right now.''

Jim smiles. ''Don't worry. Julie's my buddy.'' He winks. ''We'll get a good deal.''

When the project has to be rushed, Jim takes Julie to an expense-account lunch and talks a lot about future work. ''You could be a regular for us, you know,'' he says. And Julie sets aside her other clients.

Jim repeats the rosy picture of more work when Julie is preparing her bill, and she trims back a bit. But it is still larger than Jim had hoped.

Three months later Julie is still trying to understand why only part of her bill has been paid. Jim has her rewrite her invoices ''to comply with company policy.'' He tells her he has authorized payment and that there must be a foul-up in the computer somewhere. Finally Julie has to face the fact that Jim is not leveling with her, that he has put through only part of her bill. She calls his boss.

For Julie the experience has been crazymaking. But as soon as she abandons her false expectations of Jim, as soon as she abandons her false expectations of big future jobs, the crazymaking stops. She demands and is paid.

For Jim's boss, who has suffered repeated incidents of Jim's underbudgeting and overspending, and has had to explain a number of Jim's overenthusiastic promises, the crazymaking is also ended soon. He arranges to have Jim transferred to the Cincinnati branch.

Before Jim leaves, he smilingly assures everyone that he will keep in touch with them. He is especially assuring to the girl in the secretarial pool with whom he has been sleeping. He promises to get her transferred to Cincinnati if he can. He says he will do it even before he arranges for his wife and children to make the move.

Since most people in the office are familiar with Jim's style, they do not take his promises seriously. But the girl in the secretarial pool—who has a number of acne scars and very few dates—needs to believe him.

Habitual crazymakers such as Jim can inflict much distress. But most people will not suffer it long, since they do not have any reason to put up with it.

Keep in mind that not only does strong dependency on a relationship spur the fears that lead to crazymaking, but these fears also incline people to accept the dependency.

Whenever crazymaking has become chronic in a relationship, you can be sure that it is not only the crazymaker who fears open aggression, it is also his victim.

For the person who is the chronic target of crazymaking is colluding with the crazymaker. He or she is shutting out all but the sugar-coated, desirable half of the double message. Such a victim simply denies the coded, negative aspect of the double message, convincing him or herself that it is an accident or a mistake.

This denial of anything that would throw the sugar-coated message into doubt is doubly destructive. For it unrealistically builds trusting expectations. When the conflicting messages finally begin to get through, they do so with a shattering shock effect.

In this way a close, long-term relationship with an habitual crazymaker can become painful indeed. Lily,

THE PRICE OF CRAZYMAKING 39

the girl in the secretarial pool, has been learning this in
her relationship with Jim.

Lily does not have a pretty face. And having been
raised by grandparents who were withdrawn and quite
inexpressive, she has a colorless manner.

But she has an ample and bosomy figure. She also has
a submissive, acquiescent quality which bespeaks her
loneliness and hunger to be attractive—and to attract
Jim.

Jim's chronic crazymaking has long since made his
sexual life with his wife mutually unsatisfying. So he has
looked elsewhere. What he has looked for has mainly
been the illusion of closeness through physical contact,
without the demand for real closeness, which has to en-
tail direct expression of real feelings.

It began one night when Lily had worked late with
him. He had sent out for Chinese food, and his sympathetic façade, and the smiling agreement which
seemed like understanding, had started Lily talking.
Soon after reading the message in her fortune cookie
("Someone Understands"), she was weeping softly in
his lap. And he was helping her with her fasteners.

Jim did not of course openly assert his real wishes for
the relationship. Above all he did not say that what he
wanted from Lily was trouble-free sex and as little more
as possible. So he never corrected any of Lily's romantic
assumptions. In Lily's mind they had a secret love affair. Only his wife and children prevented them from
spending a great deal of time together.

Lily's one open demand, made wistfully and tentatively, was the wish that they could spend more time
with each other. Jim saw her only on Saturdays, and
briefly, at her apartment. She talked about how nice it
would be if they could go to dinner or dance or see a
movie.

Jim said he was working on it. Each time they slipped
into bed he would tell her about little places out of
town, small hotels and intimate country restaurants.
But nothing ever happened. Jim continued to appear

only on Saturday afternoon after his golf game. "I have to play a round to make it look good," he would explain. "I can't go home without a card and a little grass on my cuffs."

But Lily gradually began to feel resentful. Jim would show up at any time on Saturday and expect her to be there. "You understand," he would say, "sometimes the course is crowded and I have to wait. Sometimes I run into business contacts and have to have a drink."

Finally, when he arrived late one Saturday, Lily was wearing a congealed white facial mask. "I didn't think you were coming," she said. The next Saturday she was in curlers. "I didn't think you'd be so early." In each case Jim had to wait half an hour while Lily disengaged herself.

The next Saturday he was late again and opened the door to find her playing gin rummy with the girl next door. Jim paled, but she introduced him as her cousin. Then, as time passed, and Jim kept looking at his watch, Lily seemed to make no effort to get rid of her neighbor. "I was afraid I'd make her suspicious," she said.

These were not really conscious efforts on Lily's part. They were indirect aggressions. They were crazymaking responses. They were buried feelings—suppressed out of fear that any aggression might drive Jim away—but emerging nevertheless in code.

Lily was also beginning to make little "slips." Twice at the office she had answered, "Yes, dear." Then she had sent a birthday card to his house. "I didn't think anyone would open your personal mail." And she began to make annoying errors in her typing.

Always the slips were sugar-coated, of course, blocking Jim from becoming openly annoyed. "When I'm working close to you, sometimes I can't stop wanting to touch you," she would say. Or, "I thought of you on your birthday with no one to love you, and I wanted you to have a little of me with you."

"But that card," Jim protested mildly. "It said, 'I

want to give you a little something for your birthday—ME.' ''

''But I thought that was what you wanted,'' replied Lily sweetly. And Jim, wanting to be agreeable, was silent. But he was beginning to be uncomfortable.

''It's really an ideal setup,'' Jim confides to the man sitting next to him on the airplane. ''She never says no, not to anything.'' He winks. ''But she keeps doing these little things that make me very jumpy. Like last weekend. We were in the sack and really getting it on, I mean almost to the point, and suddenly she asks me if you can go off the Pill for a few days and not get into trouble. Well, I almost flipped. Then she said she hadn't done it, she was just wondering, since we only got together once a week. Man, after that, I wasn't good for anything for half an hour. What I mean is, how can such an ideal girl drive you crazy?''

Why do crazymaking relationships seem to become increasingly more painful? Why do they steadily push people apart?

A fundamental reason lies in a classic precept of psychology—that frustration leads to hostility, to an aggression of anger and violence.

When fear of aggression forces someone to suppress his or her true feelings so that they cannot be directly expressed, a feeling of frustration grows. But more than this, when an important message is sent in code, it is hard to read its message clearly. So it is hard to respond appropriately.

To take a simple example, suppose that for the last four weeks you have been seeing the doctor about an intestinal complaint. You seem to be only a little better each week, yet the doctor just tells you to keep taking the same medication. You don't want to annoy him by challenging him, but you are beginning to worry. On the fourth visit, when he says, ''Keep up the medication and make an appointment for next week,'' you want to say, ''But it doesn't seem to be doing much good.''

You don't say it, however. You don't want to offend.

Instead you say, indirectly, "Is there anything else I could take to help things along?" And he merely shakes his head.

But had you asked directly, he might have said, "Don't worry. It usually takes about six weeks to get full control of these infections."

Crazymaking is commonplace in medical relationships, for fairly obvious reasons. Fearfulness may be high. And the patient is in an extremely dependent position. The doctor, especially in a hospital, has a kind of parental power. Moreover, medical people often resort to what end up being crazymaking tactics, fearing that open communication may be too painful.

For example, in a more serious vein, you have had a heart attack and become unconscious. You wake up in an intensive-care unit, surrounded by wires and machines. "What—what happened?" you say, almost afraid to ask.

"Now, you're perfectly fine," smiles the nurse. "Don't worry about a thing. You're going to be all right."

Such bland reassurance, received simultaneously with the indirect but very clearly threatening message that is conveyed by the situation is crazymaking indeed!

In intimate relationships the back-and-forth flow of indirect messages (covered over with reassurance) becomes increasingly more frustrating. And anger and resentment pile up beneath what is often a calm, sweet surface.

For the indirect messages are too unclear for you to know how to comply, even if you wanted to. And the other person does not know how to respond to your coded communication. So neither of you can satisfy the other or be satisfied.

The tendency when you don't know what is wanted of you but want to protect the relationship, is to follow one of two basic lines. One is to convince yourself that the indirect message was never intentionally sent at all, that it means nothing. The other is to give *something* in the hope of pacifying the person.

The latter strategy leads to some of the most pathetic relationships. Joan feels rejected by her husband, but she doesn't want to say so. Part of her reaction is to work endlessly at making a beautiful home, constantly sewing new curtains, finding furniture bargains and refinishing, even doing her own upholstery after taking a class. She does this to attract her husband, Peter, to the house and to show her dedication to their marriage. But he continues to work late and take on extra jobs.

Peter, sensitive and unsure, reads Joan's homemaking as another sign of dissatisfaction. He sees it as a message that he does not provide enough money so that things can be done for her. He does extra work to make more.

When Joan says, "I keep looking at the living room draperies. Don't they look a little faded to you?" Peter hears a challenge. "You know, there's a fabric sale at Macy's," she continues, "and I wonder—"

"Tomorrow's Saturday," says Peter. "Maybe we should go and see about having some draperies professionally made."

What Joan hears is a rejection of her efforts. So the two spend the next day buying custom-made draperies that neither really wants. Neither can explain why they both seem irritable all day. But when they are home, Joan goes to the garage to antique a dressing table and Peter begins to call some friends about poker.

Too often, chronic crazymaking increases in its abrasiveness and frustration until the only way out seems to be a total escape. And what is really going on in the relationship becomes obscured by layer after layer of complex, indirect communication.

Crazymaking becomes a clearly dominating characteristic of most marriages as they approach divorce. And when the hope of covering up and smoothing over is almost gone—so that the old, powerful fear of separating is nearly ended—there are violent explosions.

For the real messages of the marriage—long sent in frustrating, maddening code—now burst out clearly, and with all the force of the years. And the same is true of all other similar relationships.

With Jim, Lily's growing crazymaking has undermined the relationship until it has become too uncomfortable. After his transfer she calls him three times. Each time, being an agreeable person, he apologizes profusely for not being able to talk. But he never calls back.

Not, at least, until a certain day some six weeks later. That is the day on which his wife, having delayed her move to Cincinnati a dozen times on different pretexts—the children's school, the difficulty of packing alone, the problem of deciding which furniture to take—finally admits that she is not going to join him at all.

That evening Jim calls Lily. He needs to know he has someone. He tells her how he has missed her, how busy he has been. He asks her to come spend the weekend with him. When she does not respond, he even says he and his wife are splitting.

Lily listens as usual, saying virtually nothing. Then, finally, as he is telling her which plane to take, she blurts out almost in a whisper: "I don't want to see you anymore. You drive me crazy!" And she hangs up.

Jim's crazymaking, along with both Lily's and his wife's acceptance of it, are at quite extreme levels, which evidence serious and incapacitating emotional problems. The stories are told here because the extremes make the principles stand out more boldly.

But less extreme crazymaking can follow these same lines more subtly. And when it persists, when it becomes an integral part of relationships between people who are more psychologically sound, it can be no less destructive.

For with the repeated pain of chronic crazymaking, there comes a kind of sensitization. A defensiveness grows. And with this cautious effort to avoid the hurts of crazymaking, a sadly crippling effect appears.

For example, Adam and Norma have both been divorced for about a year when they meet. Both had been in marriages in which the crazymaking had become chronic. Both are gentle people whose dream is love without any conflict, so at first they are delighted to see how painlessly they spend their time together, how nicely they accommodate each other to avoid confrontations and cross-purposes.

For three weeks they have one date after another. Each, bearing the scars of indirect aggression, watches for the signs uneasily. But neither sees any. So they are joyful, grateful, but waiting skeptically for crazymaking to come.

They walk together, go to the movies, lunch, dance. And there is no bickering and no double message. There is, however, no sex. And it was in bed that each of them had suffered some of the worst wounds, the worst sense of incompetence to satisfy and be satisfied.

But now Adam and Norma are in her apartment, having spent another happy evening together. Norma has gone into the kitchen to brew coffee, and Adam has followed her, and suddenly they are standing close and their arms are around each other, and their hands and bodies are searching eagerly. All at once both seem to let go, tentatively trusting again.

Adam draws her back to the couch in the living room, and then they are both fervid, both feeling free. They are locked together, clothing wildly disarrayed, reaching.

It is all an exciting blur, a free, splendid blur. They feel released, free of restraint, accepted, and all their mutual hunger to be close pours out.

"Oh, Adam!"

"Oh, Norma!"

"Oh, God, you're a wonderful man!"

"Oh, what a beautiful woman!"

"Oh Adam!" She draws his face to her breasts.

"Oh, Norma!" He buries his face.

"Ouch!"

"Norma? Norma, what?"

It is as if an icy wind has suddenly blown.

"Nothing, darling. Nothing, just your beard. Don't stop—" She senses his withdrawal. "Don't!"

"I didn't mean to hurt you," he says, leaning back.

"Oh, but you didn't hurt me. I mean, not really. I mean, it's really OK."

"I guess I got carried away," he says, sitting up. "I guess I lost control." He fumbles for a cigarette and lights it.

She reaches out toward him with one hand, almost touching his back, but not quite. And then she withdraws. "Maybe I should go and get the coffee."

"Yes—yes, I'd like some coffee."

Both move very slowly, leaden, depressed.

"You know," says Adam, "I had no idea how late it was. I—I have some early meetings in the morning."

"Do you have to go?" says Norma. "I mean, the coffee is all ready." She adjusts her clothing.

"Well, I just didn't realize how late it was."

"I understand."

Adam stands. "I'll call you." He smiles weakly. "I'd better get going."

Both Adam and Norma have become sensitized to crazymaking. Both have experienced it in one of the most commonly damaging ways, sexually.

Norma's former husband had used sex for indirect aggression by convincing her that she was not capable of normal response. He made love to her brusquely, perfunctorily, and then complained that she did not respond in the two minutes' duration of the act.

Adam's former wife was not sexually responsive, and she blamed him.

Somehow he always seemed to do something wrong. His approach should have been more gradual and seductive, for it took longer for a woman to be prepared. He should have thought to close the window, because he should have known that the draft would distract her. He should have known better than to eat salad dressing with garlic if he wanted to make love.

But the demands of both these crazymaking ex-partners were not real. Norma and Adam had been set up. They were doomed to fail, no matter how hard they tried. Norma could not have been lusty enough to satisfy her ex-husband. Adam could not have been delicate enough to satisfy his ex-wife.

Neither, however, had seen through this sexual crazymaking. Neither recognized it for what it was—a way to make them feel inadequate and in debt.

The pain of this sexual crazymaking had sensitized both Adam and Norma to the least sign that it was coming. In their former marriages, both had begun to avoid sex as much as they could. For they would always end by feeling bad.

This was one reason why they delayed making love to each other. But when they had finally begun, it was different. It was incredibly better. For just as they had made each other feel accepted and understood in other ways, so they did in bed.

And so it was that the brush of Adam's late-day beard became an alarm signal. It reminded Norma of her ex-husband's roughness and brevity. And her anxious reaction reminded Adam of his wife's repeated rejections.

Ordinarily, between two lovers so taken with each other, so small a distraction would scarcely have been noticed. But for two longtime crazymaking victims, it had been enough to destroy the moment, to bring all the old anxieties into the open.

So it is that long exposure to crazymaking can spur a crippling defensiveness, a sad and sensitive pessimism. And that defensiveness can become a powerful barrier to new relationships of every kind.

For, as with Adam and Norma, crazymaking can teach an expectation of failure that is self-fulfilling. After a history of crazymaking experiences, we can become convinced that lovers will exploit, that children will manipulate, that we ourselves will prove to be inadequate.

These convictions of eventual pain and failure are the archenemies of mental health. And it is in this way that crazymaking accomplishes just what its name implies. It deprives us of sanity. It cheats us of confidence in our own feelings and judgments of what is real.

It cheats us of our rights to sanity.

For of all the human rights, probably none is less often mentioned than one's right to one's own mind and heart, to one's own perceptions of the world and of the people in it.

At first glance the human rights to sanity may seem so obvious that there is no point in discussing them. Yet ask any psychotherapist. One of his hardest tasks is to make his patients recognize that they have such rights, to teach how they are violated and how they may be protected.

Crazymaking is the primary invasion of those rights.

Why do we permit this invasion? In part because we are not clearly aware of our rights to sanity. And in part because we do not really recognize when we surrender these rights—or when they are stolen from us.

So it is that our first need is to understand that we have certain rights to sanity, to know when they are being abridged—and how.

Let us see.

PART II

The Sabotage of Sanity

CHAPTER FIVE

The Right to Know

In a recent university class, students were asked to list some of the psychological rights that make up the overall right to sanity. Within just a few minutes they had compiled more than sixty. Voted most important by a majority of the class was what students called *the right to know, or the right to clear information*.

In a sense this right is as broad as all of crazymaking. For, as we have seen, the fogginess of the information we receive in a crazymaking experience is what makes it maddening. The two messages conflict, and one of them is coded. Often, especially in intimate crazymaking, we want to respond with a heartfelt "What are you *saying* to me?"

We will see that nearly all the tactics of crazymaking are partly designed to obscure information. And we will see that they are also designed to keep us from demanding or obtaining clarification.

So, whenever we experience crazymaking, to some extent our right to clear information is being abridged. Particularly in intimate crazymaking, most of the time we are being asked to choose how we will behave toward a person who is very important to us—without really understanding what the person thinks or feels, what he or she needs or wants, what is expected of us, and what effects our actions have on him or her.

It is like trying to cross a highway blindfolded, or, at least, while wearing glasses with smudged and distorting lenses. No one has a right to ask this of us. Yet this is precisely what the crazymaker is doing.

One of the commonest demands of such crazymaking is that we read the minds of others. As an example, the program committee of the League of Women Voters is meeting to set final arrangements for a lecture. They have invited a distinguished economist.

"Now," says Barbara, the chairman, "all we need is someone to meet him at the airport, get him to his hotel, and take him to dinner. Any volunteers?"

Barbara sees this assignment as a plum. But there is silence. Six pairs of eyes avoid one another and fall toward notepads. Barbara wonders, "Do they want to do it, but don't want to ask for the job? Or are they silent because no one wants to drive forty miles to the airport?"

She probes for a clue. But she does not ask directly. It might not be tactful. "The League will pay the expenses," she tries.

Still no answer. "Well, is there anyone who *doesn't* want to do it? Are you all willing?"

There are slight head nods. Marian mouths an almost audible "Yes." Barbara leaps to this clue and appoints Marian. "You don't mind, Marian?" she asks.

"No, I don't mind," says Marian.

Later, Barbara is driving home with another committee member, Cora. "Is there some reason," asks Cora, "why you didn't appoint me?"

"To do what?" asks Barbara.

"To pick him up at the airport."

"Well, why didn't you say you wanted to?"

"I couldn't say anything. I knew everyone wanted to do it. And you are supposed to be my best friend. It would have been unfair. I didn't want to embarrass you. But you should have known that I wanted to go. I read every book of his the minute it comes out. You know that. You should have known what it would have meant to me to spend hours with him. Who else on that committee got their masters in economics?"

Barbara feels exasperated but says nothing for several minutes. "I *hate* chairing committees," she says at last. "It drives me *crazy*."

Then, on the morning of the lecture, Barbara calls Marian to make sure the lecturer has arrived. "How did it go?" she asks Marian.

"OK."

Sensing something wrong, Barbara asks, "Was it really OK?"

"Well, frankly, I can't understand why you picked me for that job. You know perfectly well how awful it is for me around dinnertime, with all the kids. And you know how Dick is about getting stuck with feeding the kids and putting them to bed. You must have known that Dick would blow up—"

"But—but you said it was all right," protests Barbara.

"What else could I say when you put me on the spot in front of everyone like that? I don't know anything about money and I couldn't care less. For three hours I didn't understand a thing he said. Really, Barb, how *could* you?"

For many people the fear of aggression is especially magnified in groups. They become particularly cautious.

For, consider. The person who fears to be assertive wants to send only acceptable messages. This can be hard enough to do with one recipient, and can require much coding and indirection.

But in a group such a person feels that his or her messages must be put so that they are acceptable to a number of others. Small wonder that so many meetings become frustrating exercises in crazymaking. For the open messages can become little more than nods and smiles and agreeable banalities.

And at the same time the indirect messages can become so obscure as to be quite unreadable. A common result is the desperate, bewildered, but tightly controlled look one often sees on the face of the person who is chairing the committee. For he or she must translate all the code into some sense of purpose and decision. It is not surprising that so many committees produce wishywashy positions and actions which may be tempered to the point of no meaning.

The heightened fears of aggression in groups, and the resultant crazymaking, help to explain a number of well-known phenomena of group behaviors. For example, we can easily see how one or two assertive people can control the thrust and content of a meeting. And it is easy to see how someone who presents his or her interests and ideas openly and assertively in such a setting may be labeled as "selfish" or "dominating."

Another similarly based phenomenon is the curiously powerful anxiety that many people feel about speaking to groups—even when all they have to do is read a prepared talk. When we understand the fear of aggression, the deep-seated feeling that one must present only what is acceptable, we can understand how an audience of a hundred people can make normally steady hands tremble and normally strong voices quaver.

The experience of public speaking is not only scary, it is also crazymaking. For it may be hard for the speaker who is not experienced to get any clear information about how the audience is reacting to him. He has no guidance. He must simply plunge ahead. Lincoln's biographers say that when he had finished delivering his Gettysburg address, he was badly upset because he thought the crowd was disappointed or disapproving. For they did not react. They were awed and simply stood silent. For Lincoln, making those classic remarks was a crazymaking experience.

Having to act without clear information about what others think or feel is not only upsetting, it also often leads to pathos, to ironic mistakes. It is pathetic that whereas meeting the economist at the airport was an awkward bore for Marian, it would have been exciting for Cora.

And such incidents begin to have a much greater degree of pathos when they take place with intimates.

We can obtain some insights by looking at what goes on between mothers and their babies, who often cannot communicate clearly for the most understandable reasons.

Ellen is awakened at 3 A.M. by the crying of her seven-month-old baby. Ordinarily he sleeps through the night. Sleepily she goes to his crib. What is wrong? He merely cries, so she must guess.

Like most mothers Ellen accepts the guessing without being upset. For she expects it.

In her usual routine she checks to see if the baby is wet. He is, but not very, and she suspects that this is not why he has awakened. Besides, he continues to cry through the changing—and after.

Hunger is her next guess. She carries him into the kitchen and holds up a bottle. He reaches for it. So she forces herself to mix formula and warm it—all the while rocking him in one arm—and settles into a kitchen chair to feed him.

But he takes just a few swallows and then turns his head away. And cries.

Is he ill? He seems a little warm, but not very. Colic? She feels his belly. Is it just a little more rigid than usual?

Maybe he has had a dream? She seems to remember reading that babies dream. Frustrated, uneasy, she resorts to rocking him, walking back and forth through the house, and he quiets, though occasionally he makes little sounds. At last his eyes begin to close. Relieved, she keeps up the walking and rocking until he seems to be asleep. Carefully, she takes him to his crib, sets him down gently, covers him, and gets just one step away before there is a piercing yell.

Ellen never does solve the problem. Two hours later, when she tries the bottle again, he drinks it. And now he does fall asleep.

Such experiences of parenthood are commonplace. And almost any parent will agree that they are crazymaking.

Why? At first glance the incident does not seem to

conform to our crazymaking rules. True, the baby's crying is the message in code. And it is mystifying. But where is the conflicting communication to make the double message?

The answer to this question is essential to a full understanding of crazymaking. For, as is often the case, half the message may not actually be sent at all. Yet it exists.

For the second message is generated in the mind of the receiver. The receiver *assumes* it, taking it from such cues as the nature of the other person, the situation he or she is in, and the character of the relationship with the other.

In this case Ellen assumes that mothers are expected to meet the needs of babies, that they should be able to, even though babies cannot express those needs clearly. And this is the origin of the phenomenon we call *mind reading*.

The baby's survival requires that the mother be able to act for it. She must be able to provide a blanket without being told that the baby is cold, to give food, comfort, and whatever else is needed, either by intuition or by detective work.

From the mother's usually good performance, the baby learns to believe that she can know intuitively what his discomforts are and how to relieve them. And from this idea two beliefs grow and are carried into adulthood, to varying extent.

The first belief is that Mother—and by extension all persons who take care of us in some way, from the stewardess on the airplane to the spouse who nurses us when we are ill—knows what we want and should supply it without being asked.

The second is that when we ourselves play a kind of motherly role—that is, when we are taking care of someone else, regardless of whether we are male or female—we should know what they need and should not require expressions of wish or need.

Both these beliefs, once we leave the cradle, are mainly fantasy. But they persist, to form a deadly trap. For they can lead us to false expectations of others and of ourselves which are common sources of crazy-making.

For example, the very fact of her baby's discomfort is an open message to Ellen, although one that originates in her own mind. It says, "You should know what he wants and you should give it to him." The message is acceptable because Ellen sees it as an obligation inherent in the relationship between mother and child.

The second half of the double message is, of course, in code only because the baby cannot speak. And while it would not normally be crazymaking, it is now—for the simple reason that Ellen is unable to read it and respond to it. This inability conflicts with the demand she makes on herself.

As Ellen experiences conflicting feelings, an underlying hostility begins to grow. Inevitably, some of that hostility is directed toward the baby, though Ellen denies it. "What do you want?" she finally says to the baby after an hour of frustration. "I got out of bed. I'm trying, but nothing works. For God's sake, what do you *want*?"

She can't be angry with a helpless baby. And anyway, how could she be angry with the baby when it is she who fails?

But the anger is there and looking for an outlet. So, as she climbs back into bed, exhausted, she is irritable. Greg, her husband, rouses. Inadvertently he says exactly the wrong thing. "What did the baby want?" he asks sleepily.

She is silently angry. And part of her feeling is the same false belief in mind reading. After all, Greg takes care of her in many ways. And for some reason she feels that he ought to *know* better. His question feels outrageous—and a little like criticism.

"What was wrong?" he asks. For he wants to show his interest and he assumes that she *knows* he is sympathetic.

When Ellen still says nothing, Greg, sensing that she is upset, starts to put his arms around her. "Oh, for

God's sake!" she snaps, shoving his arms away. "Do I have to take care of you now, too?"

Some assumptions about other people are fair and sensible. Often they are matters of common sense or of longstanding agreements.

For example, Ellen can assume that when Greg comes home from work he will be hungry. And he can assume, because they have so defined their roles, that she will have prepared something to eat. Neither of these assumptions can be classed as mind reading.

But suppose when he comes home Ellen says, "Dinner in fifteen minutes."

Greg looks at her in surprise. "Well, why did you cook dinner?" he asks.

She is derailed and confused. "Well, I—"

"I told you George was coming into town to see me this afternoon. You know how rarely I see him. You should have known we'd take him to dinner. How come you're not dressed?"

Greg has made an unjustified assumption, and it is crazymaking for Ellen. His demand is that she be able to read his mind. And Ellen's irritability now is of the same variety.

When we make assumptions about others, we must be careful to see that they are realistic. Otherwise a lack of clear information can drive them or us crazy.

We tend to make fewer unrealistic assumptions about people who are not close. We depend on those assumptions. And if they are not fulfilled, it can be crazymaking. The reason is that we see them, not as people, but in terms of their roles.

For example, we assume that when we step up to a counter, the clerk will help us. If the clerk continues to talk on the telephone or total up a receipt book, ignoring us, it can be crazymaking.

Usually we neither want nor need much information about people who play only functional roles in our lives. When we say "How are you today?" to the mailman, we do not really want an account of his chronic indigestion.

But we need much more information about those who are close to us. Indeed, the closer the relationship, the more the making of assumptions risks a crazymaking situation.

Yet, sadly, most people tend to believe that the closer someone is, the better we know them, the more assumptions can be made. For example, consider Ellen, going back to bed after the long effort to quiet her baby. She is tired and worn to an edge of anger generated by frustration. That edge is honed by the picture of her comfortably bedded husband, whose apparent comfort represents indifference.

In truth, he has been wakeful. He has heard the crying. He has wondered what was wrong. But he has not got up because, in the past, Ellen has regarded his offers of help as interference if not as doubt of her ability to handle the baby properly.

When Greg puts his arms around Ellen, he is expressing his sympathy for her, his awareness that she must be tired and worn. He wants to comfort her. But he doesn't say anything. He assumes that she will know.

To Ellen, however, the gesture means just one thing. After six years of marriage there have been fewer and fewer affectionate gestures. Affection in bed has come to mean just one thing to her: a demand for sex. Having felt pulled at for hours, her impression is that she is now expected to satisfy Greg, too. So she strikes out at him.

Again Ellen has received a double message which was not sent: indifference to her distress coupled with a call for sexual service. It is crazymaking for her. And it is crazymaking for him to have his sympathy harshly repulsed.

Is such mutual crazymaking, which is founded on a lack of clear information, just an unhappy accident? Is it just an inadvertent result of laziness?

Not often. For we find that usually such situations can be traced to underlying problems. The making of such assumptions is usually a way to avoid the fear of being openly aggressive.

Let us see how mutual crazymaking can begin with

seemingly harmless assumptions in a more complex way. And let us see what lies behind such "innocent" misunderstanding.

For some time, the electronics firm Jason works for has been losing government contracts. And finally Jason and the other senior engineers are offered a choice. They can take a stiff cut in pay and hang on until things improve or they can look for other jobs.

Jason and Margaret talk it over. First, another job may be hard to find. The whole industry is in a slump. And Jason has ten years invested in his company. If he quits he will lose seniority and many benefits. But most important, he loves his specialized work. He is not likely to replace it.

So they decide that Jason should stay on. It means cutting expenses to the bone. Margaret gives up her art classes, takes their youngest out of nursery school, and begins to look for new ways to cook hamburger.

For six months now Margaret hasn't had a babysitter, a night out, or so much as a new blouse. And Jason has sold his sports car, given up his weekly poker games, and brown-bags his lunches.

It is hard to take a step back. But there is one compensation. The mutual sacrifice has brought Jason and Margaret closer than they have been for years.

But their feelings of satisfaction have different meanings for each of them. For each merely assumes that the other is pleased in the same way. And both are wrong.

While he was still making top money, Jason began to choke down feelings that he had become a kind of meal ticket. For to Jason, a woman's interest in her family was expressed by her service to them and her attention to her home. But Margaret's interest seemed to center on local politics.

There were more and more TV dinners as Margaret spent her days in meetings and working on campaigns. She began to take political science classes two nights a week, and she never baked anymore.

Most important to Jason, however, was the fact that

she no longer looked to him for decisions as much. Outwardly he encouraged this. But inwardly, when she did not ask his suggestions before choosing a new car, Jason felt let down. She had begun to make most purchases without consulting him, and the more he earned, the more she spent. And she no longer questioned him about his work and his feelings about it. She just seemed to assume that he would continue to succeed and to be interested only in building her own life.

But with the new retrenchment, all had changed. When Margaret supported his decision to stay with the job he loved, despite the cut in pay, Jason felt again that she supported him, that she put his wishes above all. Her staying at home and scrimping signified to him his restoration as the traditional family head and decision maker.

He liked it. But he never expressed how he felt.

And Margaret never told him how she felt. But her motives and feelings were different from those Jason supposed.

For the more successful and well paid Jason had become, the more she felt useless and parasitical. They ate out a lot. Jason frequently stayed late at the office and took many business trips. A maid came in to do the heavy cleaning. And when, to try to restore some of their old feeling of working together, she suggested joint household jobs to him, he would say, "Can't you hire someone to do that?" In fact, he even began to say this about the do-it-yourself work she tried to undertake alone.

It was to try to feel worthwhile again that Margaret began to involve herself in politics and took classes. It was to fight her growing feeling of helpless dependency that, once Jason suggested she buy a new car, she bought it herself, without asking any advice.

Neither brought up their discomforts because neither wanted to risk asking the basic question: "Am I still as important to you?" But as their reduced income forced a return to some of the old patterns of teamwork, kept them together more, sharing the same kinds of activities, both felt reassured. Each had a separate reason for feeling more valued, more needed and wanted. Each assumed that the other shared it. But again, neither wanted to risk checking it out.

Margaret, for example, felt restored to partnership. Her efforts were keeping them afloat. She was important. And, above all, Jason seemed to acknowledge her equal status.

For evidence Margaret had the fact that if they so much as wanted a take-out pizza, they talked it over. "What do you think?" Jason asked. "Can we splurge tonight?"

"If you want to," said Margaret. "You work so hard. You deserve a little reward."

But while Margaret read partnership into this little episode, Jason saw it quite differently. His question had been asked out of politeness. And the way Margaret had phrased her answer gave him just what he wanted to hear—that the choices and privileges were his.

Such differences of vision are, sadly, commonplaces of intimate relationships. But we can predict that sooner or later some reality will intervene to force the true feelings into the open.

And we can predict more. We can say that the revelation of the difference between what we assume about our intimates and what they really feel will be a dramatically crazymaking experience.

For one key truth about intimate crazymaking is that it can go on for years without actual conscious recognition. As in this case there is a strong tendency to see only what we want to see and hear only what we want to hear from someone on whose closeness we depend. In a sense, we keep collecting bits of evidence to prove what we want to be true.

There are small contradictions all the time. But we screen them out. This is easy to do if neither we nor our partner is willing to risk an open assertion or an open question—and instead sends any contradictory message indirectly, in the foggy language of crazymaking code.

Jason and Margaret each create the open, acceptable

half of the double message in their own minds, much as a mother does with a baby. And when the real meaning of each other's indirect message becomes clear, when the code is broken, there is a shock. For the impact is powered by months or years of denied crazymaking.

It happened on their wedding anniversary. Margaret had made up her mind. Jason had always played the host on their anniversaries. He had surprised her with expensive gifts, little trips, elegant restaurants. And she had felt like the guest, the passive receiver.

This year she would please and pamper him instead. Weren't they equals? They might be down on their luck, but she would contrive a celebration. It would be her gift.

She planned for weeks, scrimping to save every penny. His pleasure and surprise and pride in her would make it worthwhile. She managed a good roast and some French wine. Using the equipment of the woman next door, she even made some candles. And though she had done little sewing, she found a bargain in cloth and painstakingly stitched a new shirt for him.

The first shock came when Jason arrived home. "I found a babysitter," he said expansively, "and we're going out for a super dinner. For one night screw the budget!"

Margaret felt the jolt but denied it and rallied. "Let me show you something." She smiled and led him to the dining room. "This year," she said, "it's my turn. We're going to have a prime rib and a good Saint-Emilion. And look at the candles. Aren't they beautiful? Can you possibly guess who made them?"

Now it was Jason's turn to feel jolted. He was being set aside from the role of leader and provider. But he, too, denied his distress. He knew that he still had a card up his sleeve.

And as they finished the last of the wine, he grinned sheepishly and reached into his pocket. It was a small box, but very elegantly wrapped. Margaret felt a quiet foreboding as she opened it.

It was a pearl necklace, the one she had admired for

months in the window of the local jeweler.

When Margaret looked up again, there were tears in her eyes. At first Jason assumed that she was touched. But then he saw there was a puzzled quality to her look. He took it that she was merely overwhelmed by his generosity. "I just wanted you to know," he said, "that I love you."

But Margaret's look was not gratitude. It was accusation. After a long moment of silence she began to shake her head slowly, as if to deny what she saw. Then suddenly she threw the box to the floor, buried her face in her arms, and began to weep uncontrollably.

"It's enough to drive you crazy," Jason said to his best friend at work the next day. "You know what it's been like doing without, feeling like a slob who can't even buy his wife a night out. And I was so sure she backed me all the way. And then I wanted to do one lousy thing to show her that I appreciated the sacrifices she's made for me. I was so sure she'd understand—that I was taking a wad of what I'd earned and splurging it on her. I was so sure she would just put her arms around me and—Jesus, but it drives me *crazy*!"

And Margaret, of course, felt equally distraught. "How could he do that to me?" she demanded of her sister. "I looked at that goddamned necklace and all I could see was every hamburger casserole, every floor I'd scrubbed, every hole in every pair of panty hose I own. And for what? So he could be the King of Arabia and shower me with jewels—with the money *I'd* saved? It made me feel like he didn't give a damn about me, just about his own fat ego."

Mind reading is usually spurred by one of three basic crazymaking strategies that cause information problems: *underloading, overloading*, and *fogging*. In the story of Jason and Margaret, we have an example of mind reading being occasioned by simple lack of information, by noncommunication. But the crazymaker can create the same effect either by giving confusing information or, paradoxically, by giving too much information.

Often these strategies are used to accomplish specific purposes, when a person fears to say directly what those purposes are. For example, when she is five months pregnant, Laura quits her job and feels her new dependency acutely. Not only is she no longer a wage earner, but she is dismayed to see how easily she tires.

Mark, for his part, is traditionally protective. He begins by buying new machines to ease the workload around the house. On the day when the washer and dryer arrive, Laura is especially pale and fatigued, for she has been clearing a space in the basement for them.

Right after dinner Laura feels terribly sleepy. "Well, why don't you take a nap?" says Mark.

"I can't," says Laura, trying to establish the importance of her work at home. "I have to do the laundry. I've been accumulating it for two weeks, waiting for the new machines."

"Tell you what," says Mark brightly. "I'll do a couple of loads. It can't be that hard, can it?"

"No," says Laura. "But you have to sort everything and I haven't done that yet."

"Well, can't I do it? What do I do?"

"It's my job," says Laura. "But if you really want to—just put a couple of loads of white things together."

"And then you just put the soap in and push the button?"

"Well, some of your T-shirts and a couple of the towels may need bleach."

Laura is not consciously aware of it, but she has *underloaded* Mark, given him too little information to be successful. Some time later, when she wakes from her nap, Mark is looking a little puzzled as he tries to fold the two loads he has done.

Laura looks. "Oh my God, Mark!" she bursts out. "What did you do? You didn't put the heavy towels together with the drip-dry, did you?"

"You said to put the whites together."

"But the drip-dry stuff is wrecked. Did you use hot rinse temperature or something? And chlorine bleach— you must have used chlorine bleach on the synthetics.

Look! My best blouse is ruined. It looks like an accordion—and the elastic on the underwear—you never use bleach on elastic. And you used hot temperature on the dryer, and—''

It will be a long time before Mark tries to help with clothes washing again. He is thoroughly convinced that it is a highly technical business. Laura has used crazymaking to assert her importance. She has given the open message that Mark can do the job, but then conveyed the indirect message, ''Stay out of my work and respect how hard it is,'' by giving him inadequate information.

Overloading could have been used for the same sort of purpose—the very common but usually indirect business of balancing importance and authority in a relationship. In their courtship, and then in their first year of marriage, Deborah has been earning most of the money. Will has been finishing his degree in economics and still receives a poor salary as an executive trainee with a brokerage firm. Deborah has been selling for a fashion manufacturer, and her commissions have been snowballing.

Feeling a little parasitical, Will has been reluctant to do any spending. As they furnished their apartment, he simply deferred on all decisions to Deborah, since it was her money they were spending. So she has gradually taken on the decision-making role, choosing how much to spend on rent, whether to buy steak or hamburger, and so on.

Will feels that his one bastion is investing. He has taken Deborah's savings and traded them in and out of well-chosen common stocks with real expertise. Then Deborah says, ''I've been thinking. I've made all this money and I don't even know how. I'd really like to take part and help decide.''

Of course Will can hardly reject her. It's her money.

''Now I think Consolidated has peaked and we ought to sell it,'' he says.

''It's been going up steadily. Shouldn't I hold on?''

''No, I think it's probably going to sell off. Let me

show you why. First, when we bought it, the price-earnings ratio was only seven to one. You can see that it's a little better than ten now. With the dollar devaluation and the fact that Consolidated has had to float some debentures in the European market, I think we can see some falloff in the net. They're paying too much for money. Look at their annual report and you can see how much debt service must be costing. Anyway, we've got a strong market signal. Notice the volume decline in the last week, against the overall Dow-Jones volume. . . .''

By the time Will is through, Deborah will leave the investing alone. Will has defended his one area of power. He has asserted it by overloading. And we should observe that, with all the information he is pouring onto Deborah, his real message is merely implied: "Leave this one thing strictly to me. Allow me the one moneymaking thing that I can do and you can't."

All these people use indirect, coded messages because they are afraid to be aggressive in their demands for importance of one kind and another. They fear that any direct assertion would produce conflict and that they would be overwhelmed. How can Will, for example, hope to get away with saying, clearly, "I want you to leave to me what I do with your money. I don't want you to manage it."

Indeed, Will cannot really even accept that this is his real message. It sounds unfair and unreasonable. So he must believe that Deborah is incapable of managing her money. He overloads her until she says, "Oh, it's all too much for me! You've done such a good job, Will. You take care of it."

The third broad form of informational crazymaking —what we call *fogging*—leaves the interpretation open to the recipient. And it can involve some very subtle purposes and interplay. But it still occurs for the same basic reason. It is a way to avoid the open aggressiveness of a clear statement. If the real message is divined correctly, but turns out not to be acceptable, it can be denied.

The crazymaking of foggy information is seen especially often in sexual relationships. For sexual self-revelation often carries a high degree of anxiety.

In the past year Ned has been doing a lot of reading about sexual technique. Brought up very conservatively, he had little sexual experience before he met and began to live with Sandra. Sandra was also very unsure of herself sexually. Quite inhibited, she was satisfied only by very careful physical manipulation. She supplied quite a lot of literature to Ned to improve their sex life.

"You see," she explained, "at last we know that clitoral orgasm is just as satisfying as vaginal orgasm. I do fine when you build up to it very slowly, and then when you—you know—touch me a lot—*there*. And anyway, you're so excitable. Once you start to—you know—*do* it, you're all through pretty fast. And it says right here that it's perfectly normal if you—you know—help me *finish*. And then I'm in a really good mood—ready for you, and I'm perfectly happy to have you finish, too, you know, *inside*."

Ned and Sandra have recently split up, following which Ned met Frances. Frances was not nearly so reticent about sex. Though she excited Ned enormously, it worried him when she encouraged him into bed with her on their third date.

In fact, it worried him. Was she promiscuous? He had never had an experience of quite this kind. Not only had she accepted him as a lover so quickly, but she had actually seemed to hurry him into intercourse eagerly. He was excited by the whole thing, but somehow it was upsetting.

(Here we see the diversity of crazymaking. For, ironically, it is just as crazymaking to have a negative expectation broken, an expectation of discomfort or failure, as it is to be disappointed in the expectation of success.)

Sandra had been a passive lover. She said she did not want to stimulate him overmuch. But Frances was somewhat aggressive. She made love to him.

This alone was somewhat crazymaking for Ned. And

he was afraid that he would be premature, that he would turn Frances off by being poor in bed. Frances was ready for intercourse quickly. Not wanting to say so directly, she had tried to give Ned little hints, drawing him to her. But Ned merely read these as meaning that she liked what he was doing with his manual manipulation. He didn't seem to realize that she had already reached orgasm twice and wanted him very badly.

When she had felt terribly teased, and had finally done everything except mount *him*, he at last entered her. It did not last very long. But in his passion he did not realize that she had reached orgasm with him.

She was going to tell him how good it had been when he apologized, sure that he had left her unsatisfied. And she was going to tell him that she was very well satisfied indeed, when he went further.

"Look," he said. "I want you to know I don't usually get carried away like that. I mean, I know it isn't fair, that a woman as sensitive as you are needs preparation. I just got so—turned on. I sort of lost control."

"But you were fine," said Frances. "It was good! I'm happy that I excited you. I wanted to. You excited me."

"You're so unselfish," said Ned. "But I'd like to—be with you again. You're some kind of lady. I mean, this first time—well, it got a little frantic. But it means just as much to me to make you happy as it does to please myself. I just want you to know that."

He reinforces the idea. "And you really are sensitive. I don't want to be clumsy or rough with you. I don't feel that. I love your gentleness, your femininity—"

Frances gets the idea. She is indeed gentle and feminine. But she has strong sexual feelings, and she is very drawn to Ned. She does not want to upset his image of her.

During the next couple of weeks they make love several times. Frances grows impatient during Ned's long sexual ceremonials, his repeats of the careful, technical foreplay he has been taught by Sandra and her books. "It drives me crazy," she tells her best friend. "He hasn't any need for it. All he has to do is put his arms around me, and I'm ready. But what can I say?"

Meanwhile, Frances' regular ultimate satisfaction absolutely delights Ned. It makes him relax about sex for the first time. But it also convinces him that what he is doing is right. So he continues to send her a crazymaking double message—first, that he is enthralled by her sexual competence, but second, that she must play a role of being slowly and gradually persuaded to intercourse.

The two have all the makings of a good love affair. But Ned's double message is complemented by one from Frances—that seems to approve his tantalizing, drawnout approach, but that also denies the need for it.

The sending of the fogging messages is a way for both to avoid risking the open statement of their real sexual wishes and pleasures. But it is soon broken down.

After some weeks they go to a party. They have become very serious about each other.

The people at the party are mostly conservatives from Ned's law office. Frances is quite liberal, and she begins to argue with some of the conservative positions expressed. Although she asserts her ideas very mildly, mainly with statements such as "Of course, there's another point of view," Ned keeps explaining her points away.

For example: "Frances," he says, "is really great at seeing both sides of a question. I mean, she isn't saying she disagrees, just looking at the whole matter."

"But I *do* disagree," Frances protested.

They fight all the way back to her apartment, he saying she has deliberately embarrassed him, she retorting that he has no right to keep her from expressing herself. Again, neither is accepting the information the other is sending. He really does not want to hear that her views are so liberal. She really does not want to hear that he allows her so little freedom of expression.

But by the time Ned is about to leave her at her door,

they have cooled off enough for him to kiss her. And ten minutes later they are in bed.

Because of their argument, Ned feels that he must be especially careful in lovemaking, especially persuasive. He holds himself away from her and tries a very delicate Japanese massage he has read about.

Actually, the fight has made them both more excitable than usual. But both struggle to deny this, to keep things calm, because they feel that the other expects it.

Finally Frances can stand it no longer. "Come close to me," she suggests.

"Does this feel good?" he asks.

"Oh, yes, it makes me want to hold you."

He continues the Japanese massage. "Please," she says, "I want you close!" But he goes on, thinking he should. "You're driving me crazy," she says, and reaches for him.

"Take it slow," he tells her soothingly. "I'm too excited. I—"

"I'm so excited, Ned. Please. No more!" He ignores her. "For heaven's sake," she finally explodes. "*Fuck* me!"

Ned is startled. He has never heard a woman use the word this way. He moves to obey, but he is shocked. It is crazymaking for him.

"What's the matter?" she asks. "What's wrong?" For he is suddenly incapable of obliging.

Frances' fear of asserting her feelings is overcome by her great frustration. "It's because of what I said, isn't it?"

"No, no," Ned protests. "I know you were just excited. I know you didn't mean to say that. You just got carried away."

All the suppression of the last few weeks overwhelms Frances. "I *did* mean to say it, damn it! That's exactly what I meant, and exactly what I wanted."

"Well, yes, sure, but—"

"But nothing!" Frances bursts out. "I am sick of not

saying what I mean. I am sick of being interpreted. Yes, I'm sensitive. Yes, I'm a lady. But I am also sick of being diddled to death every night—''

"Diddled?" Ned is mind-blown. He has been so sure that it was his carefully contrived foreplay that has made their relationship good. She has as much as told him so, or at least so it seems to him. His faith and his pride shatter. He feels cheated, unmanned. Wordless and depressed, he gets up and starts to dress.

Frances turns over and cries into her pillow. She reads his message clearly now. Be what he expects her to be—or else.

"I'll call you tomorrow," says Ned very softly, still dazed by the breakdown of his illusion. "We'd just fight more now. You're upset. You're saying things you don't mean because you're angry—''

"I'm saying what I mean," she says fervently, turning over to look at him. "I want to *fuck*. What are you going to do about it?"

At last Ned gives a clear answer. He turns and walks to the door. He does not come back.

When we are blocked from giving clear information, there is as much invasion of our sanity as when we are not given it. The fear of communicating directly and the fear of receiving direct communications dispose equally to crazymaking. And, equally, they dispose us to accepting crazymaking, to tolerating it, and thus giving up one of our chief rights to sanity, our right to know.

The need for clear information reappears again and again, as a part of almost every right of sanity, and as a part of almost every tactic of crazymaking. The means by which information is interfered with are almost limitless.

But these tactics become particularly crazymaking when they block us from clear information about our own feelings. For, as in the story of Ned and Frances, the fear of asserting ourselves can drive us to try to censor more than just what we *hear* and what we *say*—it can trap us into the crazymaking of trying to warp or deny what we *feel*.

CHAPTER SIX

The Right to Feel

There is probably no subtler enterprise than trying to explain why people experience feelings as they do. So it is fortunate that such explanations are usually not necessary.

From childhood, we tend to trust our feelings. We tend to accept that we like vanilla more than chocolate, but that on a given day chocolate may seem irresistibly appealing. We may not know why, but we know when we feel sad, angry, or sexually excited.

Most of us have a basic expectation that our feelings will prove to be real, that they *are* real. An attempt to convince us that they are not real can easily make us angry. A successful attempt can drive us crazy.

Yet, given the right conditions, the fear of aggressing can persuade people to sacrifice their feelings for the promise of a seeming peace and goodwill. But such efforts to sacrifice feelings are eventually doomed to failure, and in the long run they lead to disaster.

It is common for parents to try, as a matter of convenience, to persuade their children to deny their feelings. For example, Donald's mother has promised him that today he may play with Billy. But Mother did not realize that today, after the party of the night before, she would have a bad headache and an acute sensitivity to noise.

If Donald is to play with Billy, she must go and fetch Billy, who lives a mile away, and they must play in *her* house. And her neighbor has just called and asked if Donald wouldn't like to come next door and play with Susie for a few hours, which sounds like a godsend.

"How would you like to go and play with Susie?" she asks.

"I don't like Susie," says four-year-old Donald.

"Yes, you do," insists Mother. "Remember how much fun you had with her puppets? And her mom has some ice cream."

"I want to play with Billy. You said I could play with Billy."

"But last time you played with Billy, do you remember, he hit you with his Batman helicopter and you cried? It would be much nicer to play with Susie."

"I want to play with *Billy*."

Mother will continue to insist, until Donald becomes upset and angry. After all, he is the victim of crazymaking. Then Mother can, in conscience, threaten to punish him—for getting angry and crying. Intimidated, Donald eventually says he would like to play with Susie. In other words, Mother succeeds in making him deny his real feelings by a simple device. She increases his fear of asserting what he feels.

Adults may use more complex means of invading one another's rights to their own feelings. But the principle is the same. We call it *mind raping*.

Essentially, mind raping is carried out by interpreting what we say or do in a way that serves the purposes of the mind raper. For example, Anne and Vincent are at a party that includes a number of people from her office, including Quentin. Anne has worked closely with Quentin for several years, and they have a camaraderie which annoys Vince. Recently, the two have become even closer, because Quentin has been under the stress of a separation and has begun to confide in her.

Anne has returned some confidences, and with the expression of important feelings, their old friendship has acquired some strong new overtones. They can manage the situation easily at the office, but now they are dancing together, and the physical closeness and a little alcohol lead both to open up some fantasies.

"You know," says Quentin into her ear, "you've been a lifesaver these past weeks, listening to me. Don't misunderstand, but if you weren't a thoroughly married woman, I'd be edging you toward the door right now and out behind a tree."

"If I weren't a thoroughly married woman," says Anne, enjoying the flirtation, "I might not even kick or scream."

Later, on the way home, Vince says, "You certainly stayed close enough to Quentin."

"He's going through some bad times," Anne responds. "He's needed a friend. I like him."

"Well, I know you think you mean what you're saying, but I think you ought to face the truth."

"The truth?"

"That you resent him. You have, you know, ever since he got the promotion and the raise. Remember? You said you knew all along they would give it to him because he was male and supporting a family."

"Honestly, Vince, I don't resent Quentin."

"You think you know just as much about marketing, don't you?"

"Yes, but that has nothing to do with it. He always respects my opinions. He never puts me down."

"But he got the money and the title. It's just logic, since you really feel that you're as good as he is."

"Well, I don't resent him. I just feel sorry for him."

"Oh, I believe you *think* you feel sorry for him. But the truth is obvious to an outside observer. I know it's hard for you to accept, but you're really experiencing a kind of triumph when he tells you his troubles. You feel as good as he is professionally. And now his personal problems prove that you really have an edge. It's a typical feminine technique, playing mother to establish superiority."

"You're wrong, Vince."

"Oh, you may think so. But triumph is intoxicating.

You have to deny it; you're too kind a person. But look out. It's a situation that could be a real turn-on for you. You do it with me, you know. When you feel you've beaten me at something, you'll offer me sex as a compensation."

The crazymaking experience of being mind raped is almost enough to make Anne blurt out her real feelings about Quentin. But she bites her tongue. The fear of an open conflict is greater than the pain of the crazymaking. So she suffers it.

For his part, Vince uses the crazymaking to assert his own feelings indirectly. He does not want to say what he suspects, that Anne is becoming infatuated with Quentin. He doesn't want to risk hearing that this is true. So he even crafts his mind rape so that if she does admit her feeling it will be meaningless.

Vince's crazymaking does not make Anne deny her feelings to herself. But it traps her by making it hard to let them show in any way. For if they do show, she is damned no matter which way they are interpreted. In this way the crazymaking accomplishes its purpose—at a serious price, however, to the relationship.

Mind raping can be much more insidious as a crazymaker when it is carried out by escalation. For it can begin so subtly that it seems relatively harmless, not worth defending oneself against, until one finds oneself trapped in a series of inner conflicts, trying hard to deny what one feels. In this form it can be genuinely dangerous.

Ted and Evelyn are at breakfast when she says, "You know, your birthday is coming up in two weeks."

Ted says nothing.

"It's hard to believe you're going to be forty."

"I know," says Ted, his newspaper wriggling as he shifts uncomfortably in his chair.

"That's quite a landmark. Does it bother you?"

"Yes," says Ted after an uncomfortable pause.

"I think we should do something really special, to help," says Evelyn. "Is there anything you'd like to do?"

"Get bombed and forget the whole thing."

"Ted, be serious. I want the day to be special for you."

Ted puts his paper down irritably. He does not want to talk about his birthday. He is having trouble dealing with this very symbolic event. And Evelyn's insistence is mildly crazymaking. For while the discussion is irritating, her open message is one of support and goodwill. She is annoying him and soothing him at one time.

Ted tries to stop the situation by being direct. "Look, dear," he says kindly, "I know you mean well. But this birthday thing does bug me for some reason. Can't we leave it alone?"

Evelyn's response is a strong clue to her indirect aggression, however. For she simply ignores Ted's open assertion. She does not accept his feelings.

"Now, really, dear," she says. "Since you can't prevent a birthday, isn't it better for you to make it special?"

Seeing that his assertion is rejected, Ted realizes that if he continues to press it, conflict will result. But he tries it once more. "I'd really just as soon write it off, just not make a big deal about it. Like I'm just one day older. Like nothing is really changing except one page on the calendar."

Evelyn's insistence now begins to make the mind rape clear as she challenges Ted's feelings once more. "Well, isn't that hiding from the truth? Isn't it more mature to face becoming forty? You know—celebrate the day and meet middle age head-on."

At the words "middle age" Ted winces and looks at his watch. "Maybe you're right. I'll think about it. Right now I've got to run."

Ted has avoided an aggression that looked as if it would lead to conflict, and permitted a crazymaking experience to develop. The experience is not unusual in this relationship. And it does not stop here.

Evelyn has long used an invasion of Ted's feelings as a way to feel more secure in their relationship. For she has never been certain whether he married her because he wanted to or because she was pregnant and their religion forbade abortion.

She suspects the worst. She always wondered, when Ted was younger, whether he might leave her. The approach of his fortieth birthday is reassuring to her. And without quite realizing why, she wants Ted to be very much aware of this traditional time of passage.

So Evelyn, mainly in an unconscious way, sends a double message. Openly, it says that she is concerned about his feelings and wants to help him with them. And, of course, her concern, her caring, disarm Ted. They make it hard for him to do anything about the message in crazymaking code.

It says, "I want you to have a sense of entering another time of life. I don't want you to brush this aside. I want you to see and deal with this problem *my way, not yours*."

Ted intuitively suspects the crazymaking. It makes him irritable. He wants to say, "Leave me alone." But he can't. Evelyn is trying to help, isn't she? And she has convinced him in the past that he has a tendency to avoid confronting reality. She often helps him to see what is real—or at least what she perceives as real.

So Ted feels he has no right to the annoyance he is experiencing. To fight for his vision of the birthday would seem an ungrateful and exaggerated reaction.

But as he thinks about it driving to work, he wonders why this annoyance seems to keep smoldering into anger in his mind. He does not realize that he is suffering one of the special consequences of the crazymaking mind rape. He has been deprived of his own inner defense against a threat. Instead, Evelyn is demanding that he use *her* defense.

Each of us has his or her own way of dealing with the stresses of life. Right or wrong, good or bad, they are our own. And if they are stripped away, we feel endangered.

For our own defenses are what we know how to use. The situation is not unlike that of a man who is going to fight a duel with pistols, which are weapons he understands and uses well. But at the last moment his trusted second says, "Here's your sword. I know you have never used one in a fight, but I think it's a better weapon."

To understand how such crazymaking escalates, let us pursue this incident. The next morning Ted is shaving when Evelyn asks him, "Have you given any more thought to your birthday?"

"Ouch!"

"What?"

"I cut myself. Damn. I can't find the styptic pencil. Have you seen it?"

"I didn't know you had one."

"Well, I think I used to. Can you help me look for it? I want to finish shaving."

By this partially unconscious means, Ted tries to forestall the unpleasant subject—both to defend himself against facing the problem of his birthday again and to defend himself against Evelyn's continued invasion. He has "forgotten" that he did have a styptic pencil but left it in a hotel room two years before. He has changed the subject, we might say, by "accident."

This accident is crazymaking for Evelyn. It is a tactic we call *derailing*, a popular indirect way of forestalling someone else's aggression. We will see more of this. What is significant for the moment is that in this manner Ted indicates that he does not intend to defend his right to his own feelings openly.

Such a stratagem is to be expected. For as we have observed, crazymaking between intimates is virtually never a one-way street. Almost without exception the victim is also the villain.

At breakfast, however, Evelyn repeats her question. "Look," Ted says without looking at his watch. "It's getting late. I don't have time—"

"But have you thought about it?"

"Sort of." Ted makes a last try. "For some reason I think I'd just like the day to myself—go to the beach and sit on a rock or take a walk.''

"By *yourself*?" Evelyn's implication of hurt rejection is very clear.

This is exactly what Ted has in mind, but he does not want to hurt her feelings. "No, no," he says. "I meant maybe just the two of us—kick off our shoes and relax."

"And that's all? What about dinner or theater or something? You know I always love to bake you a beautiful cake."

"I appreciate the thought," says Ted, "but not this year. I'd really be perfectly happy with a hot dog or a taco—just no party."

"But I couldn't take along any presents or anything."

"Don't want any." Ted smiles as he grows a little more confident about his idea and as he begins to identify his own feelings and sees how he can shape the day to meet them. "Say, you know what I could do? I could buy my own present. You know that long lens I've always wanted? If there weren't any presents or big dinners or expensive tickets, I'd have a good part of the price of the lens." He brightens. "I like the idea. You know, I was just reading an article the other day on using telephoto for portraits—how it softens the image, washes out the background—"

"I don't want to interrupt you," says Evelyn with a characteristic crazymaking ploy designed to interrupt him. "But won't you be late for the office?"

Evelyn has become uncomfortable, uneasy, as Ted mobilizes his feelings and gets in touch with them. And she quickly maneuvers a new opening. "So you don't care what we do for your birthday?" she asks. He nods. "Well, why won't you let me take care of the details then. You know how much I'd like to surprise you a little."

"Sure, honey," says Ted, feeling magnanimous. "Go ahead."

It is Friday evening, the night before his birthday. He comes home and enters the kitchen to find it crowded with packages. "Don't come in!" Evelyn calls out. But it is too late. "Darn!" She sighs. "Now my surprise is spoiled."

"What's all this?" asks Ted, looking around alarmed.

"A little birthday party for tomorrow night."

Ted is swept by crazymaking confusion. "But—but I thought we were going to—I mean, we said we wouldn't—"

"Now don't get upset. We're doing just what you wanted. I've got it all planned. We'll start early tomorrow morning and take a nice little picnic to that park at City Beach. And while you're taking your walk, all by yourself the way you wanted to, I can do last-minute shopping. Then we can be back here early enough for me to get everything ready. I'll do the decorations tonight, and the cake is baked, and—"

Ted says little for the next few hours. What can he say? The food and wine are bought. The invitations are out. Evelyn has worked and planned hard—for him.

What kind of ingrate would say what Ted now feels. "I don't want a party. The idea of a lot of people swilling my booze and making jokes about my getting old turns me off. City Beach is not my idea of a beach. I just want rocks and sand and water. And what about my lens? What did all this stuff cost, anyway? I can't buy the lens now. I can't handle this day the way I wanted to."

With Ted's pleasant expectation goes his defense against the somber reminder of middle age. He has not formulated that defense very clearly. But he wants the boyish feeling that open beach has always given him, to know that he can still experience it. He wants the quiet, to get his head clear, to stem some of the confusion.

The last thing Ted wants is to be crowded by a bunch of people acting out their middle age. He wants to look at people of any age, but free in the water and the sun. He does not want to talk to greying men preoccupied with taxes and insurance and retirement plans. He wants to hold on to an inner self that has no age.

But now he has lost this focus. And anyway, he can't

tell Evelyn that her care and attention are making him uncomfortable. How can he turn off her expression of love?

That next night the party proves to be all that Ted feared. It is large. Evelyn has included some old college friends who look portly and are growing bald. And there are some people from the office.

Ted opens presents for half an hour. Some are meant to be funny. There is even a Youth Kit, with diet pills and a long-hair wig. It makes everyone laugh.

Ted is usually a very moderate drinker. But he finds himself gulping his drinks, not sipping. Finally he slips away to the garden. The stars are all bright and the moon is full, and somehow this helps to clear his head. For a moment he hesitates. Then he lies down in the cool grass and studies the sky. He has brought a bottle of wine with him and, calmer, he sips at it. He is just finding something that has been missing all day when he hears Evelyn calling his name.

He closes his eyes and drains the bottle. Twenty minutes later he passes out discreetly in his bedroom.

The next morning Evelyn says to him, "Well, at least you had a good time. Now, tell me—wasn't that a lot better than some hot dogs on the beach?"

Ted's birthday suggests some ways in which crazymaking is escalated slowly, through a series of situations in which it is made difficult for the victim to resist, in which it is hard to assert even one's rights to one's own feelings.

Repeatedly, we see a kind of delicate balance, a balance of decision. The decision to be made is really always the same. And it is intrinsically simple. It is whether to assert the personal right to sanity or to surrender it.

The balance is really defined by fear, the fear of being directly aggressive. And the question is, which of two basic fears is greater?

Is it the fear of what may happen if one is openly aggressive? Or is it the fear of what may happen if one is *not* openly aggressive?

At the beginning of Ted's story, neither of these fears has much strength. For the initial question—"Wouldn't you like to do something special on your birthday?"—does not seem very earthshaking. But when Ted fails to press his assertion of his feelings about the day, he opens the door to steady escalation. He effectively gives Evelyn permission to make his emotional decisions for him, to tell him how to feel.

Once the first concession is made, the die is cast. For with each new step there is more at stake. The risk of assertion grows greater. By the time Ted opens the kitchen door and discovers the preparations for the party, it would take a major upheaval to get control of the day once more.

But in the beginning, Ted could have asserted his feelings with a minimum of injury. He had only to say something like, "The only comfortable way for me to handle this bad spot in my life is to do what feels right to me. If you want to come along with me, fine. But you'll have to trust what my emotions tell me."

When Ted fails to do this, a false expectation is created for Evelyn—that he will not mind if she helps him to do his thinking and feeling. From this point, some of Ted's rights to his own sanity are forfeit. He has implicitly declared them to be up for grabs.

Clearly, this is not the first time such a concession has been made. Crazymaking does not suddenly appear after fifteen years of marriage, nor do the conditions that encourage or even require it. For fifteen years Evelyn has known that if she presses, Ted will allow her to interpret his feelings.

For example, when they bought their house, Ted was reluctant at first. He said that he really didn't want to move into the suburbs. He liked the city better.

"Now you know you don't really mean that," Evelyn had told him. "After all, you always say that you like gardens and quiet, don't you?"

Then, when Evelyn had found a house she liked, it was more than Ted wanted to pay. "Those big payments are going to make me nervous," he said to

Evelyn. "They're going to make me uptight. I know I'll start worrying about losing my job."

"You won't really worry," Evelyn told him. "You know perfectly well that Mr. Brandon thinks you're the boy wonder. You're bound to move up. In a few years the payments will seem like nothing at all."

Finally, Ted disliked the fact that the suburb was well known to be ultraconservative, and Ted tended to be politically rather liberal.

"I don't want to live surrounded by a bunch of people I disagree with all the time," he had said. "I'll feel awkward. They'll be asking why I don't go to church every Sunday. They'll be making nasty cracks about the people I'll be voting for."

"Oh, Ted, you know how tolerant you are," said Evelyn. "And you know how much you like to hear different opinions. This will be interesting for you. It will give you a new perspective. You'll love it. You can feel superior."

Is it overstating the case to say that such incursions actually challenged Ted's mental health? Not at all. For good mental health requires that we perceive the realities of our lives as clearly and accurately as possible. Crazymaking can, if we allow it, force us to deny those realities, to deny what we see and hear and feel. And if we deny what we perceive, we cannot possibly deal with the world and the people in it realistically.

Evelyn does not realize what she does to Ted, or why. In her own mind she is only performing her duty as his partner. She thinks that she is helping him to cope.

She is really, of course, coping with her own fears—fears of being openly assertive, along with fears that if Ted makes open assertions she will not like them. On his part Ted increases those fears. He does so by denying clear information to Evelyn so that she does not know where she stands with him. So her crazymaking, by mind raping, is partly a response to his crazymaking, which he carries out by depriving her of her right to know.

For example, on the night of his fortieth birthday, as

he lay in the backyard grass, Ted recalled an incident that made him feel sorry for himself. A few months before there had been an important proposal that had to be prepared quickly. Ted worked straight through at the office, for forty-eight hours.

Then he had come home, feeling wired tight on coffee and cigarettes and tension. He had showered and slipped into bed. And then he had gently wakened Evelyn.

Scarcely opening her eyes, she had said, "Is something wrong, Ted?"

"No," he answered. "I just wanted you to know that I was home."

"Now, Ted," she reproved, at once reading his mind and mind raping him. "You haven't had any sleep for two days. You know perfectly well that you're really too tired to make love."

One can see why Ted might have felt sorry for himself. But note his own behavior. He began the game. He did not say anything about how he felt or what he wanted, not clearly or directly. He expected Evelyn to divine his wishes and take care of them. He spoke to her in code. And, actually, she read his code message very well.

So it is hardly surprising that she felt free to take the next typical maternal step. She used whatever clues were available to guide her in telling him how he felt and deciding for him how he should express it.

Moreover, in one sense, her mind raping was nothing more than her own crazymaking code. She did not want to make love, but she did not want to say no. So she could reject Ted by telling him that he did not really want what he was indirectly asking for. It was this that made the experience so maddeningly memorable for Ted.

Like most crazymaking couples, Ted and Evelyn also used a certain amount of what we call *mind ripping*. This is another common crazymaking tactic that invades our right to our own feelings and their expression—and that simultaneously serves as a kind of mind reading.

Mind ripping occurs when a person behaves as though reacting to a message we have sent. The only problem is, we haven't sent the message.

As a simple example, you are hosting a dinner party. Everyone has lingered long over coffee and liqueurs in the living roon. Merely out of curiosity you glance at your watch. Immediately, Sam, across the room, stands up. "Better get your coat, Paula," he says. "We're keeping our hosts up much too late."

These three crazymaking, processes—mind reading, mind raping, and mind ripping—are obviously closely related. It can be hard to draw the lines among them. And one is often used to support the other. Used together, under the right conditions, they form a formidable triad. And once they have insinuated themselves into the style of an intimate relationship, they can foreclose some of the simplest kinds of communication. They can perpetuate discomfort and isolation.

As an example, Judith and Charles are driving home from the mountains. Heavy fog rolls in as Judith drives. Charles is napping. For he has had a few drinks with his dinner and is now very sleepy.

When they take a sharp turn, Charles rouses. Then he opens his eyes wide as he sees the fog. "Boy," he says, "this fog is really something, isn't it? Better pull over and let me drive."

Judith feels she must not only do as he says, but smile fondly and say thank you. Yet she is aware that Charles is just a little blurry with alcohol, that his eyes require strong glasses, that he has had three traffic citations and two minor accidents in the last year.

The situation is crazymaking for her because on the one hand she feels she must let Charles drive, and on the other hand believes herself to be more competent. The situation forces her to deny her real perception, along with her feeling that Charles is conveying the illusion of protecting her while actually endangering her.

Such denials, however, are such a routine of her life that she does not even know why, as they start down the road, she feels so uncomfortable. Then suddenly they see the lights of a roadhouse. "Could we stop for a little while and get a cup of coffee?" she asks Charles.

"Why?"

"I don't know why. But for some strange reason I feel a little carsick."

Judith's carsickness is at least partly a physical effect of her crazymaking experience. In a sense she cannot quite stomach her forced denials.

Why does she surrender her rights to her perceptions? Essentially because she is afraid to assert them. And this fear is based mainly upon her idea of her relationship with Charles. For he has taken on the image of protector and leader. And she has the image of protected follower.

In some important ways these images are real. After ten years of marriage Judith feels she needs Charles' protection. She feels that she could not sustain her home and children without it.

So she feels that Charles must be confirmed in this role, consistently. She is afraid to assert her equality, let alone her superiority, for fear that this will weaken his awareness of her dependency, his fond image of himself as her guardian.

What she does not know is that there are times when he would gladly relinquish his role. Right now is one of them. He knows that his eyes are heavy and his reflexes are less than sharp. More than anything he would like to go back to his nap. In one corner of his mind, when he says that he will drive, he vaguely hopes that she will say, "I can handle this and I'd like to."

There are many times when the constant playing of the role is crazymaking. Charles is a lawyer. And he would like to admit that he knows no more about what a mechanic ought to do or a plumber ought to charge than Judith does.

But he is afraid to say so. Just as Judith thinks that he wants her to be the grateful protected one, so does Charles believe that she wants him to be always in command.

Liberated women might be quick to say here that both

these people are locked into culturally determined, sexist conventions. Certainly there is a cultural influence, and it is strong. But psychologically this view must be considered naive and simplistic.

What Judith and Charles respond to first is what they *think* the other expects of them. They need each other. They are afraid to disappoint each other. Charles would go a long way before he would risk losing his role as what Judith, in tender, bedded moments, calls "her man." And Judith wants to do nothing to disrupt Charles' satisfied and loving view of her as "his woman."

The trouble is that, because neither will risk expressing real feelings in an assertive way, neither knows exactly what is needed to maintain the core of their relationship. So they play out their expected roles like cardboard characters.

It would be much easier, much less painful, much more rewarding, to give up the mind reading, mind ripping, and mind raping that must go on to underwrite their highly formalized relationship. But it would not feel safe. So each sacrifices a goodly portion of his or her own rights to sanity in order to perpetuate the uncomfortable myth.

They sacrifice some of their rights to give and receive clear information, their rights to feel and to express what they feel—and something more.

Their rights to have impact.

CHAPTER SEVEN

The Right to Impact

A fundamental requirement for sanity is to have assurance that we exist—and that our existence makes some difference to the world and to some of the people in it.

To a certain extent we can confirm our existence by our effect on the physical world; by digging a hole or cutting down a tree and saying, "I did that." The literature of isolation—the stories of mountain men, shipwrecked sailors, and the like—portrays the isolated person as very busy in the attempt to stay sane, making, building, doing far beyond his practical needs.

But eventually it becomes hard to believe in the reality and meaning of our existence without the help of other people.

Other people confirm our existence by showing us in word or deed that we have *impact* on them. They do this by responding to what we say or do, or even by just noticing that we are there.

At the simplest level we need to hear from others words like "Good morning," "Pardon me," or perhaps a polite "Do you mind if I smoke?"

But to feel whole, we also need more personal reactions, which recognize a little more than our bare existence. We need to hear "I see you got a haircut," "Nice work," "May I join you?" or possibly "You hurt my feelings."

At a deeper level we also need to have some intimate impact upon people who matter most to us—beginning with "You turn me on," or "You make me angry," and leading to, especially, "You make me feel loved" and "I love you."

And if we are desperate enough, frightened enough, lonely enough, we may even be willing to settle for "You drive me crazy."

But whatever the level, whatever the actual message we get, without other people's response to our existence we soon begin to feel worthless, impotent, and unreal. We become nonpeople.

Accounts of brainwashing during the Korean and Viet Nam wars show us that an important stratagem in this vicious process was to deny impact. The denial paved the way for all that followed.

A prisoner tries to talk to a guard, and the guard seems not to hear. The prisoner says urgently that he needs food or water, or that he is ill, and there is no reaction. Not even a simple "No."

Living in a very small world, the prisoner is forced into a heavily dependent state which is made to center on just one or two keepers. They become his only possible source of real impact. Only through them can he prove his existence. And the only way he can have impact on them is to give them the precise words and actions that they decree are acceptable.

The prisoner is accused, falsely, and told he must admit the accusations. At first he protests. He pleads and tries to argue the truth. But he is flatly ignored. His pleas and arguments have no impact. There is no dispute or discussion. The charges are merely restated, along with the demand for confession. Nothing else will be heard.

Any other assertion of wish, thought, or feeling falls on deaf ears. In fact, any such aggression is treated as a deviation from prescribed behavior. It is not only ignored; it may be accompanied by further deprivation.

Thus, the fear of aggression is heightened. Expressions of self are choked off until the prisoner becomes a nonperson. Only one narrow channel is left open. Only through this channel can the victim have impact. Capitulation.

The process is both effective and inhuman and may well seem unrelated to the everyday behavior of intimates. But the truth is that much of the basic method of brainwashing incorporates common intimate tactics.

These tactics between intimates are no less effective than they are between captor and captive. Indeed, in intimate roles, one may quickly note some parallels to the captor-captive relationship. And they are no less inhuman.

Let us see how the denial of impact is used in intimate crazymaking, and why.

The model for all impact denial is the machine. Your car has broken down on the deserted highway. You walk half a mile and find a pay telephone. You have one dime. You put it in the machine and dial. A voice answers, "I'm sorry, but we are unable to complete your call as dialed. This is a recording." Then there is silence. And your dime does not come back. You can talk to the dead machine or pound it with your shoe, but you will have no impact.

Our machine culture has taught us the pain of denied impact through contact with the computer. A letter goes out:

DEAR MARTIN BROTHERS DEPARTMENT STORE:
   Enclosed is a bill I have received from you for one Wicked Woman Girdle at $19.95, size Large. I am a 37-year-old bachelor. I do not wear girdles. I do not give them as gifts. If I did give them as gifts, I would probably not give them to someone who needed a Large.
   Please correct this error and credit my account. I enclose my check for $74.55, my actual bill for this month.
Sincerely,
JAMES THOMAS

The computer sends Mr. Thomas a reply:

Dear Mr. Thomas:
   Of course, we all make mistakes. But we must advise that you have underpaid your Martin Brothers bill for May.

Terms of your account call for *payment in full* each month. If you are unable to pay this full amount, please contact our Credit Office. Remember, your credit is your most valuable asset.

The amount of $19.95 should be paid at once, to avoid late charges.

> Cordially yours,
> MARTIN BROTHERS
> (Your *Personal* Store)

Observe the double-message aspect of such letters. Ironically, most businesses which use computer communications advertise the personal quality of their service. In fact, the company makes a totally unresponsive answer to what Mr. Thomas has written. That answer can be read: "We don't give a damn about you. We just want your money."

Computer crazymaking, like much impact crazymaking, can be stopped for the moment by capitulation. That is, the message, like that of the brainwashers, is really: You can have impact on me only by doing what I want you to do.

The typical cartoon or television situation comedy breakfast scene between husband and wife embodies this principle. The wife seeks to have impact and the husband hides behind his newspaper. The husband responds to all statements with a polite "That's nice." From the information that a letter has come from Mother to the statement that a faucet leaks or Mrs. Smith has died.

The husband is using a kind of impact filter. It screens away everything except something that interests him—perhaps the word that the wife has prepared Eggs Benedict for breakfast.

This comedy, in real life, is usually more complex, and has more purpose. And like virtually all crazymaking, its techniques are learned very early.

What we call *selective impact* may be seen very clearly in children, especially in their behavior in such nicely contrived situations as Headache Park—The Magical Land of Family Fun. The child is so highly motivated by slick promotion that his ordinary fears of direct aggression are minimized. Then he is also confused by noise, color, and hectic movement—so that he clings to a few dominant ideas. The parent is prepared for capitulation by the same tumult and fatigue.

It is six o'clock. Father is starved. "Let's get something to eat," he says with a brave half-smile.

"Look, there it is!" squeals Davey. "The Super Mouse House! Just like on TV! Come on, Dad!"

"Look, you've been on everything. Daddy is hungry. He has got to sit down—"

"The Super Mouse House! Let's go!"

"Davey, there's a line a block long. I just can't—"

"Boy!"—he is still pulling vigorously at his father's hand—"look at the lights! Boy!"

"Davey"—firmly—"we are going to have supper now. You can have one of those Mouse Dogs, like you said you wanted."

"Come on!" Urgency appears in Davey's face.

"All right. After we have supper. Maybe the line will be shorter. Anyway, we're out of tickets and I'll have to go back and buy some. But not now."

Any parent knows how the scene escalates from this time. Logic, threats, pleading have no impact. Father's most violent aggressive instincts are held down by the fact that this is a special day, long planned and anticipated. Father already has fifty dollars invested in making it special. A bad, hysterical scene is brewing.

Psychologically, there are several kinds of crazymaking going on. The central element, however, is simple. Davey's open message is joy, seeing the ride he has heard so much about. It is excited anticipation. This was precisely Father's hopeful expectation. The effort has been to please.

But inherent in the situation and plain in Davey's strained, exhausted expression is an indirect message. "If I can't go, if you delay me, I am going to come apart."

Father is whipped. He feels that he cannot comply. So he tries every possible statement of his feelings and of common sense to restrain Davey. But there is only one thing Davey is going to hear, only one way Father is going to have impact—by getting into line.

Chances are the alert reader can see other double messages here, contradictory and maddening. For example, he may be able to see the cold manipulation inherent in the park, at flat odds with the warmy-cheery decoration. In part, Father is made crazy because he is forced to help maintain the illusion, even as he sees through it.

Father's crazymaking experience is over by nightfall. But other common crazymaking by children is routine. For example, Helen feels that marriage and motherhood are depriving her of all but a selective impact. She has begun to feel, with two-year-old Ginny, like merely a maternal machine.

Reading the magazines, Helen decides that she might find some renewal of her sense of impact as a person by reviving her poetry. So she plans carefully. She lays out Ginny's toys and says:

"Now Mommy and Ginny are going to play by themselves for just a little while, just twenty minutes. Mommy is going to write on her paper, just like she used to do when she was in college. And if Ginny is a good girl and plays nicely in her room, Ginny is going to have a lovely surprise. Mommy has banana cake for Ginny—*if* Ginny is a good girl and plays quietly for just a little while."

"OK," says Ginny, creating the expectation that Helen's strategy has worked.

Two minutes later Helen has set down the first line, the one she thought of in bed last night, when there is a tug at her elbow. "Mommy, I want my cake."

Mother may yell, stand on her head, even strike, but it will do no good. There will be no impact except by the giving of cake. Helen capitulates, gives the cake. But in another two minutes there is a cry for milk. And so on.

Helen is denied the impact she feels she might have by writing a little each day. (Remember, the poem is a communication. It calls for impact on some person who will read and say, at least, "I didn't know you wrote poetry." Or perhaps even "Say, that's pretty good!")

Ginny is selectively limiting the impact she will allow because of a very basic human demand. It goes beyond cake, beyond milk. It is the demand for reactions—a steady, unabating stream of behaviors—that assure her of one thing. Her *centricity* in Helen's life, her centralness to her mother's existence.

Adults need less assurance that they have such impact—the impact of centricity—on an important other. But it is one of the most powerful of all needs for sanity, for feeling whole. Yet despite the importance of this requirement it is often expressed indirectly.

In truth, we may say that it is often expressed indirectly *because* of its importance. For the things that matter to us most often create our strongest fears. We may not dare to ask for what we want most, because we are not sure of the answer. What if it is *no*?

Ginny could not formulate the question (*Am I central in your life?*) directly. Her father, Ken, could. But he neither quite faces nor asks it. And since Ginny's birth he has felt the question more and more acutely. He cannot help feeling displaced by the baby. Certainly, nowadays much of Helen's time and energy goes to attending to Ginny, not to him.

This results in more crazymaking all around. For as Helen's demand for impact as a person grows in importance, and as Ken's demand for impact that shows his centralness to Helen grows, both express them more indirectly.

For example, one simple way in which Helen can validate her existence as an adult is to have sexual impact on Ken. Unfortunately, in expectation of the baby, the two bought a larger house. The bills grew. Ken started working later at the office, then doing extra work at home. So they have had less evening time together, and less sex.

At the same time, Helen's preoccupation with the baby has raised those doubts in Ken's mind about his centricity with her. This has heightened his fear about expressing his affection directly and openly, for he has greater fear that he will be rejected.

So the two, who used to approach each other with an easy kind of freedom, are now cautious, indirect. There are some pathetic incidents.

For example, Ken begins a month-long spate of night work. After two weeks Helen buys, impulsively, a very diaphanous and revealing short nightgown. At ten she peeks into Ken's study. "Am I interrupting?" she asks.

"Oh, no," says Ken, untruthfully but unwilling to put Helen off in any way.

"Well, I bought myself a present today. I hope you won't mind?" She enters the room, drawing her shoulders back to maximize the effect. Ken, in their courtship, had rhapsodized about her breasts.

"No, that's great," says Ken, with a sinking feeling that the charge accounts are going up again, but unwilling, once more, to say anything that sounds like rejection. "That's very nice," he tells her. "Very pretty."

Helen moves close to his desk. "It was on sale," she says, "less than half price. I mean, well, look at this beautiful lace." She leans over the desk. He looks and nods. "Feel how soft it is all around the neck."

He reaches out and touches. "It certainly is soft—beautiful." He is not very interested in clothes and Helen knows it. But he is accommodating again. She says she wants him to appreciate the lace, so he fingers it and examines it carefully. He has a strong urge to let his hand slip under the gown and cup her breast, but he suppresses it. She might feel that he was not paying proper attention to her purchase.

Discouraged somewhat, Helen steps back and pirouettes a little. The gown is a little flared. It comes only to just below the hips. When she turns, it flies up a few inches.

"Say, that's nice," Ken says with appreciation, thinking it would do no harm to stop work for an hour but reluctant to say so. "It's very—short, isn't it?"

"It's a shortie gown. It comes with little pants. But you used to say you didn't like me to wear them. So I guess they'll just be wasted."

"Oh," says Ken, misunderstanding entirely, wanting still to say what is expected, to concentrate on the gown. "Well, listen, that's all right. You can wear them if you want to. Why shouldn't you?"

Ken and Helen have just experienced some crazymaking of an ironic kind. Helen has tried to have sexual impact. In her mind she ends by failing.

Actually, her impact succeeded. Ken wanted to touch. But the open message he got was that his interest was to focus on the nightgown, not the body.

The stage had been set earlier, when Ken had come home. He had hurried into the kitchen. He had been thinking very affectionate thoughts, so much so that he scarcely noticed that Ginny was crying in her high chair and a pot was boiling over. Blithely, he had wrapped his arms around Helen.

This irritated Helen for at least two reasons. For one thing it seemed to deny what she thought was her obvious immediate problems—crying and boiling pot—and for another, it presented the sexual assurance she needed just when she couldn't accept it.

Moreover, Helen had stolen three hours that afternoon to begin a class at the university. Ken knew it. He had hoped it would help her feel less trapped, feel happier, and have more to give him. Instead she seemed more irritable. It did not occur to him that it had put pressure on her to take care of her household work in time.

Backing up to avoid conflict, even that which might result from asking the wrong questions, Ken had fallen back upon standard dialogue. "What's for dinner?" he had asked cheerily.

"Frozen fried chicken," Helen told him. "I was so rushed—"

"Oh," said Ken, cutting her off a little sulkily, for he now felt less central to her than ever, second not only to the baby, but to academia. "I think I'll go mix myself a drink."

This incident had prepared Ken to be less assertive than ever by the time the nightgown display took place. Earlier, he had felt that his sexual impact had been denied by the refused hug, and then that his impact for centricity had been denied by the frozen chicken.

Clearly, both are doing some mind reading, and also some mind ripping, as they behave as though they knew what the other wanted. Assumptions about each other's thoughts and feelings, intensified by their fears that their attempts at impact would fail, led both to crazymaking indirectness.

In the end, two people who love each other and are attracted to each other are separate. Ken is tapping his pencil at his desk, too distracted to work well and confused about why. Helen is in bed, trying to read a pornographic novel, but even the three-way-sex scene doesn't hold her interest. Both light cigarettes and look into space and think how simple and satisfying it all used to be and wonder why the simple things now drive them crazy.

The requirements of impact and the processes by which we are deprived of it are many and varied. But most of them are to be found in human relationships by late childhood. And for a simple reason: Impact is, in a sense, the way we demonstrate to ourselves what our power is. And children live in a world of unequal power.

For example, ten-year-old Eric is in his room, assembling a plastic model drag-racer.

"Eric," his father calls. "It's nine-fifteen. You have to be at Sunday School at ten."

There is no answer. Eric detests Sunday School. He makes great efforts to avoid it. So he turns a relatively deaf ear to what he reads as a rather low-level demand for impact.

"Eric, did you hear me?" There is rising irritation in his father's voice at this refusal of impact. This signals Eric that it is necessary to allow a little effect.

"OK," Eric says. But note that he does not really respond directly to the information about the time or to the question he is asked.

"Get moving!" Eric does hear this. And he speeds up his work with the model.

Ten minutes later, when his father appears in the doorway of his room, Eric is still gluing. "What are you doing?" his father asks. The question itself suggests that Father is also trying to avoid conflict. He can see what Eric is doing. He can certainly see that he is not ready for Sunday School.

"My model you gave me," says Eric, without looking

up. This in itself is a minor, and rather cunning, bit of impact crazymaking. For even as he gives an unacceptable answer indirectly, by saying that he is still at play, he signals appreciation for the model. A child's appreciation for a toy is an important way of letting adults have impact on him. If you doubt this, watch the adults' faces on Christmas morning. Watch Grandma's face as Eric opens the huge box with excited anticipation, finds it is a Mechano-Electric Atomic Power Station Set, shrugs, and turns to another package. Impact denied. Next case.

"Damn it," says Father to Eric. "Didn't you hear me? Why aren't you getting dressed? How can you be on time?"

"You didn't say to get dressed," retorts Eric, carefully selecting out one statement and ignoring the rest.

"For God's sake, how can you go to Sunday School if you're not dressed? Get dressed *now!*" says Father, whose voice is tensed for an explosion. "Put that thing down and get ready."

"Gee, I'm just finishing the windows, Dad. It's so neat. I don't want to wreck it. It'll just take a minute."

Father gets another impact concession for the model and bends a little. "All right. But just one minute. That's all. You have just ten minutes if you want to walk to church in time."

"OK."

Ten minutes more pass. Father reappears. "Damn it to hell!" he shouts in frustration. "You're not dressed yet!"

"Well, the windshield wouldn't go in right."

"I told you, you had just ten minutes."

"You said, if I wanted to walk. I thought maybe you could drive me."

Let us see how nicely Eric has worked his crazymaking gambit and what he has achieved by denying impact. At first he merely blocked. He was unresponsive. Then a sense of threat brought him to allow impact selectively.

His real wish was to deny the need to go to Sunday

School. So in selecting impact, he blocked connections between such facts as his father's words, the time, dressing, and his own general behavior. He held himself, as do so many youngsters when we are trying to direct them, "out of it."

When his father comes back to the room a second time, and is upset to find him still absorbed in the model, Eric turns to another form of impact denial. We call this *misinterpretation*.

The boy is not diabolical. He is simply not fully aware of the consequences of what he is doing. He tunes out the implications he doesn't like. And, especially, he misinterprets the statement about *walking* to church. For a reason. It not only allows him to see an alternative to getting ready at that moment, it accomplishes more.

There is a basic, important direct message that Eric would like to deliver but fears to express. It is:

"I don't want to go to Sunday School. It bores me. I go to school every day, and this is even worse. Anyway, if you really think religion is so important, how come *you* aren't going to church? And if you don't really think it's important, why should I?"

Eric has learned not to express this directly. He has learned that to do so is hazardous. He has tried saying it once. And it has brought him the full force of his father's authority—right to the seat of his trousers.

So though heartfelt, Eric's assertion about the matter is limited by fear. It must be made indirectly. He sends taciturn messages of agreement, vague, selective, misinterpreting. But he does not actually dress himself and go.

For Eric has a strong sense of the inconsistency inherent in his father's stressing of the importance of church, while he does not attend. This is crazymaking. For a child's sense of ethics, of matching idea to action, tends to be simple and uncompromising.

But Eric's only response must be crazymaking because of the enormous disparity of power between himself and his father. He will be overwhelmed if he sends any open message but one of compliance. He says yes, and acts no.

The delay thus becomes effective without being direct. He gets away with it. But he also gets something more. Eric forces Father into a confrontation with his own personal crazymaking. For the delay forces his father to drive Eric to Sunday School—after a frantic rush to shower, shave, and dress.

Thus, the father is not only discomfited. His split message to Eric about the importance of church is made open—and public. For he must go to quite a lot of trouble to get Eric to church. He must literally walk to the very door with him. But he does not enter.

While Eric's impact crazymaking involves some of the most important processes of maddening intimate behavior, it does not involve two of the most important. These we call *thinging* and *context switching*.

Thinging is, as its name implies, treating a person as a kind of thing rather than a whole person. The person becomes a facility—much in the manner of the service-station attendant or the elevator operator, who are often treated as nothing more than living extensions of machines. As we have suggested before, a certain amount of this is acceptable in our complex society. But when it occurs with intimates, it is crazymaking indeed.

We saw one example of a kind of thinging in Helen, who had begun to feel not like Helen but like "Mommy" and "Wife." For seeing people in terms of just a role rather than as human entireties has much the same effect as seeing them as depersonalized objects.

Public figures often feel their lack of impact as people for this very reason. Ian, the movie star, has met and spent a romantic evening with Karen, a young secretary in the office of his New York agent. He has been enchanted. He has felt young again. He asks her to his hotel suite and she comes. He takes her into the bedroom and she does not hesitate.

"Come close to me," he says, reaching for her zipper.

"Gee." She sighs. "You said that just the way you did in *Stranger in My Heart*. Remember? You and Lilian Lance had been caught in the storm after the murder, and—"

"Not now," says Ian, not wanting to realize what he

knows about this romance. "I just want to be me."

"But you are," says Karen. "So powerful—the way you swept her up and carried her up the stairs—"

"That was a stunt man; I have a bad back."

"Don't make fun of me." She laughs. "I know you. I've seen every movie since—"

Ian has been thinged. But what we find if we look more closely is that ultimately he has thinged himself. To dazzle Karen he has played movie star all evening. But somehow, underneath, he had hoped she would care about *him*.

On a more typical level, just as Ian presented an image rather than himself, so do most of us. We fear the assertion of what we are. What we are may not be acceptable. So we play Young Doctor, Carefree Girl, Macho Machinist, or any of a thousand roles. And then, ironically, it becomes crazymaking to find that our impact is in terms of this *image*, not of our whole and inner selves.

Sad to say, once a relationship has been established in terms of images rather than personal realities, it is doomed to be crazymaking for both people. The person who creates the image fears to break it. He must sustain it while by indirect means he seeks to satisfy the real person underneath. The messages go out:

"I am the image I have shown you."

"I am *not* the image I have shown you."

A common psychological term for retreating behind one's image and fearing to assert oneself is *role playing*. All of us do a certain amount of it in life, because a certain amount of it can be necessary.

For example, a child has fallen and has a bad cut on her face. The mother is at that moment, inwardly, a frightened twenty-three-year-old who may feel as helpless and scared as if she were fifteen. But she plays the role. The child needs the role. "It's going to be all right," the mother says. "Mother knows what to do."

And indeed, playing the role helps to steady the young mother. It helps her deal sensibly with the emergency.

Ken and Helen, who were seen earlier trying to have

impact on each other and ending in sad frustration, began to play roles when they married. They were still Ken and Helen. But they were now also Husband and Wife. And soon they became Father and Mother.

The roles have utility. But they can also become places to hide. In doubt of how acceptable one's message about oneself is going to be, one now can turn to a safer path, playing the family role. The catch is that then the real assertions of self are made indirectly, and crazymaking is the common result.

For example, Helen wants to have sexual impact. But this has become a little scary. It may be rejected. But showing her husband clothes she bought on sale is within the wifely role. The question becomes, should she or shouldn't she have bought the nightgown—not the more dangerous "Does my body still turn you on?"

Family roles, like all roles, are somewhat crazymaking in themselves because they project, even to the people who play them, a split, sometimes contradictory message about identity. The person *is* the role—but also *is* something else.

Remember, too, that even in the family, most of us have more than one role. Ken has his roles as breadwinner, Daddy, repairman, financial expert, protector, and so on. And if one role is a good place to hide from open assertions of self, several can be even better, safer.

Changing from one role to another as a means to avoid one's own aggression and parry the aggression of one's partner—with the ultimate aim of escaping from the more frightening kinds of conflicts—is a kind of context switching.

Context switching, in all its endless refinements, is perhaps the ultimate crazymaker. For within its tactics are incorporated layer upon layer of crazymaking effects. But the primary effect is to stop impact.

Let us go back to Ken and Helen. Each has thought their private thoughts, which swirl around the question of whether the impact of each still holds them central in the lives of the other. Each has suffered this day a number of little experiences which put the issue in doubt. Both, however, fear to express the question.

Unable to work, Ken goes to the bedroom. He does not know quite what he wants to say. Seeing Helen, he isn't really sure he wants to say anything. He notices the book.

"Any good?" he asks.

"Mostly kinky sex," she replies. "A threesome."

Keep in mind now the fact that sexual impact—and its symbolization of their deepest question, centralness of their places in each other's lives—is the matter that both want, and fear, to communicate about.

"Oh," says Ken after a long pause. "Sound interesting?" he asks with a little smile.

"I don't know. Maybe," says Helen. "But I'm so much a hausfrau now that I don't know if I could interest one person anymore, let alone two."

"Come on," retorts Ken a little irritably. "Any man who could have you would want you—"

"Well, I'm right here every night," she says with a tinge of bitterness. "Tell me something, if that had been that girl in your office, Doris, in your study a little while ago, with her pants off, would you have been looking at the lace so hard?"

"You asked me about the lace. If you want to know, I had a terrific urge to . . ." His voice trails off.

"Well, you didn't, did you?"

"Helen, it's just that I don't know where we stand with each other," he blurts out. But then, quickly, he turns himself from his real assertion to the indirect expression we call *blamesmanship*. "You've been changing. You're touchy. You're unhappy about things. What's going on with you?"

"What do you mean?" She is fencing.

"Well—you're so hard to approach."

"Approach? I just approached you half naked, and all you looked at was the needlework. You were angry, weren't you, because here you are working nights and I'm just spending your money. Isn't that right?"

"Money has nothing to do with it."

"No? Then why are you working nights?"

The context has just been switched from sex to money.

"I'm doing it for you," says Ken. "For my family. I love you, Helen."

"Well, you used to have a good way to show me how you loved me. I couldn't get you to leave me alone. Then, after the baby was born—"

"You may remember that some things changed after the baby was born. I mean, with your mother sleeping in the next room, I can understand why you didn't feel free—"

"Jesus, you're not going to blame your lack of interest in me on my mother now, are you?"

"I didn't say that. I was just trying to be understanding about why *you* weren't interested and—"

"If you're mad at me for buying the nightgown, why can't you just say so? I've asked you a dozen times, can't we have a budget? Then I'd know what I could buy and what I couldn't. Frankly, I think you like the power you get from being able to say yes and no about every penny."

"Hey, I never said a word about the money. I am trying to find out—"

"Well, tell me truly, do you think I need a new nightgown?"

"I guess not. But—"

"So you think it was wasteful of me."

"I didn't say wasteful—just not necessary."

"That's why I think I should get a job. There's a new day-care nursery opening up. I could leave Ginny there and then you wouldn't have to complain so much about money like this. You couldn't use it as an excuse—"

The context has now been firmly switched. The central question and its possibilities of rejection have been evaded. But what could have been meaningful communication has been choked off. Anger born of frustration does emerge. But the formless, disorderly expression of hostility does little to produce growth. It does not bring people toward intimacy.

What Ken and Helen wanted was to have impact on each other, and to know what impact they had. All that they learn by this fight, with its careful shifting away from the true center of concern, is that each feels frustration, and with the frustration anger, and with the anger a sad and empty distance apart.

Thus the crazymaking that blocks impact drives people apart. The sacrifice of the right to have impact, like the sacrifice of all other rights to sanity, gives only temporary safety from the threat of aggression. And at a sad price.

What is often the key area of communications becomes declared out of bounds, a place where neither may walk. There is a barrier of empty space, a neutral zone, a place of no impact attempted or allowed, a source of crazymaking.

There is a final irony here. It is that the right kind of space, staked out in another way, is not only psychologically sound, it is psychologically necessary. And the attempts to invade rightful space can be a primary means of crazymaking.

CHAPTER EIGHT

The Right to Space

In many ways the right to space—to a territory of one's own—is the most obvious of all rights. It is perhaps not only the most widely understood of rights, but also the most universally accepted and the most freely and confidently asserted.

Witness the myriad signs that say NO TRESPASSING, MEMBERS ONLY, NO ADMITTANCE, PRIVATE, KEEP OUT, PERMISSION TO PASS OVER MAY BE REVOKED AT ANY TIME. Witness the spiderweb of lines and walls and fences that crisscrosses the planet.

Moreover, this sense of territory is clearly related to some very deep and powerful—even violent—emotions. When our territorial rights are challenged, we tend to experience intense feelings.

Often our expectations that rights to space will be respected are so strong that for a moment we are shocked and confused when they seem to be denied. We are temporarily dumbfounded when someone takes our parking place, cuts into line ahead of us, or usurps our reserved seat on an airplane or at a football game. Or when a stranger walks onto our property or into the rest-room cubicle we occupy.

The moment of shock and uncertainty that follows is crazymaking, but only of a trivial kind. Because, while the feelings go deep, they do not tend to last long. They are quickly converted to simple, confident anger or indignation.

In fact, so clear is our obvious relationship to our space, that at first it is hard for many people to see how territorial violations can become genuinely crazy-making. But they can.

For, psychologically, the right to space can be the subtlest of matters. There are important kinds of space—from the hazy territory of time to the inner spaces of thoughts and feelings—of which the boundaries and the ownership are not so clear. There are territorial invasions so subtle that we are not even sure they are taking place. And in these uncertainties and subtleties, we may often be slow, reluctant, or even unable to defend our space.

Such common situations can be the wellsprings of the worst and most painful kinds of crazymaking.

Maureen has been occupied with her children's demands from the first light of the day. Finally, by nine o'clock, all three youngsters are in bed.

She goes into the living room and feels a curious sense of relief when she sees that her husband sits hypnotized by the television set. She settles into a comfortable chair, her special cozy chair, and simply lets her mind wander and smiles.

"Hey, you really ought to watch this," says Greg. "Do you want me to tell you what's happened so far?"

Maureen is annoyed. "No, that's OK. You know I can't get into these things unless I see the beginning."

"Well, it's a simple plot," says Greg. "The tall guy doesn't know it, but he's picked up the wrong briefcase, and now the foreign agents think he's the courier. Actually, he's just a mailman who used to be a pro football tight end and a martial arts teacher. Get the picture? His ordinary daily routine looks like—Oh, it's coming on again. But you get the idea."

"Yes I see it," says Maureen, not wanting to argue. The movie starts again, and for some reason her mind drifts back to the summer when she was nineteen, and she and Arthur would walk for hours in the woods.

"Hey, listen, Maureen," says Greg. "I can see you're not watching this." There is just a little hurt in his voice. "Since you're not doing anything, would you mind just getting me a cup of coffee? Instant is OK."

Maureen feels reluctant but dismisses the feeling. Why should she be annoyed? He doesn't want to miss any of his movie, and she is not watching. She gets up slowly, however. "And are there any chocolate chip cookies left?" he asks as she goes.

"Did you remember to put sugar in the coffee?" he wants to know a few minutes later as he takes a sip.

"I thought I did," his wife replies, getting up again. "I'll get you the sugar bowl. Oh, damn." She suddenly recalls something. "That's what happened. You see, Timmy broke the sugar bowl this afternoon trying to stand on a chair when he was watching me make the stew. It wasn't really his fault because it was the chair with the wobbly leg that you keep saying you're going to fix. You know, I don't see why I can't fix it myself, Greg. If you would just tell me where you keep that white glue that—"

"Honey, could we talk about it later? The movie—" he says in a somewhat strained voice.

"Oh, I'm sorry," Maureen tells him, and goes and gets the sugar bowl from the good company dishes. But for some reason she forgets to bring a spoon.

Inner territory has here been violated in a number of minor but irritating ways. Greg first wants to force his focus of attention on Maureen. His reasons are harmless. Most of us like to share a good movie or an exciting game with someone.

Maureen resists this sharing because after a day with the children she needs to restore her inner world, to have time to think and feel as she pleases. For if one is occupied solely with the thoughts and wishes of others, with their demands and the demands of practical necessity, one actually begins to lose one's own sense of identity—of existence even. The "trapped housewife" is at least in part trapped in the space of others. She feels stripped of space of her own.

One problem with inner space is that it is invisible. Greg cannot see that Maureen is occupied with hers. So it seems reasonable to use her apparent idleness.

Maureen is aware that this annoys her, but she cannot clearly see why. She sees no good reason to refuse. And being on shaky ground, she is less motivated to make an open assertion of her right to space. Her reluctance to trigger conflict over so small and vague an issue, however, leads to crazymaking.

Her open response to Greg is yes. But her forgetting of the sugar says no, in crazymaking code.

Her space is invaded again because of the missing sugar. Maureen wants to say, "Get it yourself." But again she is unsure of her rights; in fact she feels at fault.

So when she returns, she invades Greg's space, his TV watching, with the prolonged story about the sugar bowl. Observe that the point of the story—in addition to the interruption made by its telling—is that Greg may not have a clear right to his TV time. For the chair needs fixing.

Greg can reject this interruption openly—though inwardly he feels the pinch of the demand about the chair—because social convention defines certain space rights. (Openly interrupting another person is taboo.) He even feels free to point out the missing spoon.

She goes to get it and the telephone rings. Maureen answers it in the kitchen. It is her best friend Terry.

"Am I interrupting anything?" asks Terry, and Maureen wonders why this question annoys her so.

"No," she says after a moment. "I was just sitting. I just got the kids to bed."

"Well, I've got to talk to somebody. My sister called today and she wants to bring the kids out. She says she can't stand her marriage any longer. And you know how Charlie feels about my sister. Well, all hell is breaking loose, and I've just got to—"

Forty minutes later Terry has talked herself out. During this time Greg has come irritably into the kitchen and banged through three drawers to find the spoon he wants.

Maureen is now back in her chair, and back in that past, leisurely summer. In fact she is back in the double sleeping bag with Arthur when she is startled by a light touch on her arm. "Mom," says a small voice. "Why do elephants have such big ears?"

"Jesus Christ!" Maureen explodes.

Timmy's four-year-old face melts.

"For God's sake," says Greg. "Why did you yell at the kid like that? He was just asking a simple question. And can't I even see the last part of this in peace? It's no wonder Timmy still sucks his thumb if that's what he gets."

Maureen chokes down a number of responses. "I was just startled, that's all. You know I'm only human. There, there, Timmy. Mom didn't mean it. You just scared Mom. Let's go back to bed and Mom will read to you out of your elephant book."

Twenty minutes later, when Maureen comes back to the living room, she has her coat on. "Where are you going?" Greg wants to know.

"I—I just need a couple of minutes to myself," says Maureen. "I just want to walk around the block alone."

"OK," says Greg, and turns back to the TV. She is almost at the door when he tells her, "Hey, Maureen— as long as you're going for a walk anyway, you might as well take the dog with you—"

Maureen turns sharply, about to object with vigor. She wants to be *alone*. But she catches herself. Greg is only being sensible, after all. And how is a dog going to interfere with her walk? Yet she clenches her teeth as she gets the leash and slams the closet door shut.

"*Now* what's the matter?" asks her husband, looking up and seeing her tight face.

"Nothing. Nothing at all," she snaps. "I'm taking the dog, can't you see?"

"Hey, are you going to have your period or

something?'' Greg wants to know, trying to explain her reactions.

When the slam of the front door has stopped echoing, Timmy starts to cry. ''Jesus!'' snarls Greg. ''Can't a man have any peace in his own house?'' He does not realize how, with his simple, traditional question, he pre-empts the space of a whole family.

Why do our rights to space seem to carry so much emotional impact even when they appear to be very vaguely marked out? Why are we so sensitive about them?

In recent years there has been much discussion about personal territory. And two concepts of space have caught most of the popular attention.

One is mainly anthropological. Anthropologists observe that animals other than humans seem to be just as territory-sensitive as we are, or more so. They deduce that we all have some inborn need for personal space. And they see little difference between the dog that snarls when anyone encroaches on his sleeping corner and the human whose favorite chair is taken.

But as we have seen with Maureen and Greg and their border conflicts about very subtle inner spaces, territory is not a simple matter. Some inborn feeling about space may or may not be at work in all creatures—the case is not provable one way or the other—but this idea does not seem adequate to explain the subtle refinements we experience every day.

People are said to need personal space chiefly to insulate them from other people. This space is supposed to protect us from the stresses of involvement with the lives of others. For the more our lives are influenced by what others want of us, by what they think and feel, the less free we are to ''do our own thing.''

It is true that the more our existences concern only ourselves, the more independent we become. And it is true that the less we need others to give us love, to help us, to share with us, the less often we will suffer painful conflicts.

But it is also true that the more we are free, the

more we are alone. In this autonomous existence the borders of personal space become so many moats and trenches—firm barriers to shut others out. And as soon as there is stress in a relationship, the trenches are armed and the moats are flooded.

"You do your thing and I do mine" is the essential philosophy of this view. "If we get uncomfortable because our needs or goals conflict, then we simply back off."

There is some sense here, because *excessive* dependency on others can be dangerous. Everything we think and feel becomes subject to the relationship. And one can develop the belief that one's very survival requires that the relationship survive.

This leads to a terror of conflict. It begins to mean that any and every conflict threatens our very existence, so conflict must be avoided at all costs. Every assertion of self becomes an unacceptably severe risk. And then the pressure of fear dictates that crazymaking is the only remaining way to assert oneself.

Yet the idea of personal territory as an inviolable buffer against others leads us to the opposite extreme. It suggests isolation. And as we have pointed out in an earlier book of ours, *Pairing*, isolation itself can deprive us of sanity. For we need interaction with others to confirm our existence and to give meaning to our actions, to allow us to have impact.

Between these two extremes is a healthful center, well recognized by psychology. In this center is a balance point—between great dependency and great autonomy. For we can neither surrender all our personal space nor live behind impenetrable walls and remain sane.

So, we clearly need a concept of territory that helps to explain its emotional power, that shows how space functions in our emotional economy. Yet this concept must also allow some flexibility—in which our territory can sometimes provide shelter and sometimes be opened up to permit interaction, sharing, intimacy.

There is an essentially simple idea that fills this bill. It is a vision of our space as a means of identity.

In this view we must mark out our personal borders as a way of defining ourselves, as a way of saying, "This is where the rest of the world ends and I begin." Or perhaps, "This is where you and your influence end, and this is where I and my sphere of influence begin."

What is at stake is nothing less than one's very identity. So it is that since we are in part defined by our territory, we are so upset when that territory is not recognized and respected by others. An assault on our territory is a denial of our existence. At the least, a denial of our space implies that we are not of much consequence, that we do not matter.

With this perception it is not at all difficult to understand why we are so upset, so mind-blown, when someone invades space that is clearly ours. And with this same understanding, we can easily see what forceful emotions we must repress when subtler territory is taken from us by trickery or by force.

This vision of territorial rights makes possible much greater subtlety. For while our psychological borders are extremely important, they are not static. They change.

For example, at one moment it may be important to have one's private thoughts as it was for Maureen in our preceding story. And in the next moment we may enjoy sharing our thoughts and feelings with an intimate. Indeed, just as impact may be essential to prove that some action is real, that we are real, so we may need to have someone enter our space to help us confirm that our thoughts and feelings are meaningful. The need may be met as simply as someone can say, "I know how you feel. I have felt it too."

It is for such reasons that territory and its borders must not be rigidly maintained. We do not want to shut everyone out, all the time, but we do need confirmation that we control our territory, as surely as our front door is both a barrier which we may close to an unwanted salesman and also a welcoming gate which we swing open to a friend.

What matters most is that the opening or closing of

the door is up to us. This is true even in the crudest kind of spatial matters. At one moment we may be rushing to grab a seat on the bus, and in the next we may feel real pleasure in surrendering that territorial seat to an infirm old lady.

Crazymaking, however, can easily induce us to surrender these rights of control. It can do so even when the space involved has the clearest of boundaries.

For example, Amanda and her husband are vacationing in Rome. As Amanda walks down the Via Veneto, she feels a sudden brief squeeze of her left buttock.

Her shock changes to outright anger almost as quickly as she can turn around. There, a few paces away, she sees a little man wearing a maddening smile of self-satisfaction. He winks, and then with a courtly little bow of appreciation, he goes on his way.

There is no question that the buttock is Amanda's private property or that the squeezing hand is frank trespass.

She is furious. And though she is a little unsure about what she should do—for not only is she caught off guard but, typical of such situations, she is also a little frightened by the ease with which inviolate space has been violated—she spews nasty words almost until the offender is out of earshot.

She is confident about her indignation, however. And her outrage is quickly confirmed by the tight anger in her husband's face when she tells him of the incident. "The son of a bitch," he utters darkly. "I'd like to kill him. What a cheap, lousy thing to do, taking advantage of a helpless woman that way. Damn, but I'd like to get my hands on that bastard."

Nevertheless, even in such a seemingly obvious violation of space rights, we can see how easily such matters can become a little foggy. For the psychologist who hears the husband's reaction must ask a question: Is this man responding solely to the violation of Amanda's rights? Or is he in part indignant because there has been an infringement on *his* territory?

An answer is suggested later. For that night, after

they have drunk quite a little wine in a raucous place in the Trastevere quarter, the couple crawl into bed.

"My head is spinning," mumbles Amanda. "I keep having the feeling that the bed is spinning with it, Len."

Leonard is wound up too, but in a somewhat different way. "God, that was a wild place, wasn't it?" he asks her in the dark.

"My head is still wild." Amanda sighs. "It feels as if I can't get the mandolins out of it. And they are making me kind of sick to my stomach. Maybe if I can just fall asleep—"

"It made me feel really earthy," says Leonard, who is dwelling on his own feeling. (One's moods, we might note, are another kind of inner space.) "Boy, those are earthy people, the way they sing and dance. Hey, turn over, babe," he says, drawing her toward him. And, putting one hand under her nightgown, he gropes brusquely upward between her legs.

For a second Amanda feels a flash of anger. And then, for some reason, the earlier scene with the man in the street flits through her mind.

But she quickly represses these errant feelings, which might lead to trouble she doesn't want. This is Len, after all—her husband, her lover, the man who takes her to Europe and shows her a good time, isn't it? Didn't she long ago give him the right to put his hand there? And hasn't that same hand in that same place long given her comfort and pleasure?

So he's in an earthy mood just now and enjoying it. So it isn't her mood. So she has a touchy little feeling of offense. Is it really worth making a big thing about? Wouldn't it be a mean and picky business to make an issue of it?

So Amanda rolls over. In fact, because she is not really interested, she moves with unusual directness. She presses against him to help prepare herself quickly, reaches for him, hurries him into her. And the crazymaking begins.

First, note that we all regard our bodies as the clearest of our territories—and sexually significant areas of the body particularly so. This sense of space can never really be denied, not inwardly. We may grant access with more or less ease, but we still have the right. A prostitute can be outraged by rape.

But because Amanda is not intellectually certain what her rights are, she represses her awareness of them. She tries to bury the awareness. And in her let's-get-it-over quickness she not only yields, but sends Len the acceptable message that she shares his wish, that she welcomes his invasion.

Indeed, the coded second message—her rejection—is especially obscure. (This is often true in sexual crazymaking.) Ironically, her inner rejection is expressed by her outer vigor and aggressiveness. For when she sees that Len's orgasm is delayed by the alcohol, Amanda actually leaves her usual underlying position, mounts him, and pumps away at him energetically. Psychologically, we understand that each hard thrust is not only an attempt to speed Len up; it is also a blow struck with the pelvis.

The next morning they are dressing when Len proves again the principle that crazymaking begets crazymaking. The night before is fresh in his memory. He thinks especially of Amanda's unusual vigor. "Boy," he says, "Italy really agrees with you, doesn't it?"

"What do you mean?" asks Amanda defensively. "I know I have circles under my eyes and I'm hung over, but you don't have to—"

"No, no," Len protests. "I wasn't making a crack. I meant what I said. You were really great last night. I loved it." And as if to prove his earnestness, he winks at her and gives her rump a playful squeeze.

No gesture could have been less advisable. Serial images of the street incident, the blunt grope in bed, and the latest squeeze all link together. What is more, Len has sent the open message that he was especially pleased by the kind of sex they had. Amanda's reluctance to assert her space, together with the indirect aggression with which she responded, have backfired. In stating his pleasure, Len has posed the threat that he will seek to repeat the incident. Yet Amanda is still bound by fear of conflict. She cannot respond directly. So she quickly seizes upon an indirect way to protest.

"Damn it, Len," she bursts out as soon as he squeezes, "you've got shaving soap on my skirt. If I've told you once I've told you a thousand times. Polyester stains. You were the one who said we had to travel light. You were the one who would scarcely let me bring anything to wear. So for God's sake at least don't ruin the few clothes I have."

What Amanda has said indirectly, of course, is "Keep your hands off."

But because she has said it indirectly, it is not surprising that Len reacts to the openly stated objection. To him, the shaving soap on the skirt seems to be the problem, not the grab itself. He is a little shocked by the force of the outburst, which seems out of scale with the size of his offense as she states it. So, with a "What-did-I-do?" feeling, he tries to make amends. He reaches for a towel, wets it, and starts to rub at her derriere.

"Damn it, Len," snaps his wife, upset because she has produced still another invasion, "not with the only dry towel left! I don't see why we had to stay in this cheap place where they only give you two towels. But you must know I was going to use that towel to put around my shoulders while I finished making up, and—"

In one sense we are seeing that Amanda, typically, could not really choke down the resentment she felt about Len's violation of her sexual space. It was repressed only to emerge again as soon as she could find a more acceptable excuse for it.

On the other hand, Amanda, only semiaware, is using crazymaking in a different way. She is using it to defend her territory. Because by creating a vague, continuing hostility between them, she is putting space between her and Len. She is using crazymaking for the common purpose of *distancing*.

Thus, the bad feeling between them, which she cultivates all that day, makes it hard for Len to approach her. By evening she has created a situation in which he does not *want* to approach her.

When crazymaking is used for distancing, it can be destructive indeed. Almost invariably it is far more painful for both people than a simple, clear, and straightforward statement of a wish for greater space.

There is a whole language of such crazymaking, in which one says, "I want to be closer," but does not necessarily mean it. Thus we often hear "Let's get together real soon" without any specification of when or how.

Says the publisher: "That's a nice piece of writing, but it just doesn't happen to suit our needs just now."

The girl who has been asked for a date says, "Oh, I'd love to, but I'm busy. Another time."

But something more is involved as Amanda and Len troop grouchily through the Sistine Chapel in the afternoon, and as they silently munch their fettucini at Alfredo's that evening. Sniping in small ways, they hold each other at a distance. There is even a defense of space going on as Amanda calls Len's attention to the courtly manners of the white-haired gentleman in the restaurant, and as Len then calls Amanda's attention to the youth and nubile figure of the girl to whom the man is being so courtly.

The disturbing extra in their situation is that Len and Amanda are each dealing not just with one person, but with two. This is characteristic of most important relationships. For one relates both to the other person as he or she really is and to an *image* of that person.

It appears that clear information may be all that is needed to close the gap between image and reality where other people are concerned. But when one is afraid to assert one's realities, the other person tends to make assumptions about them and to react to images instead of what is real.

For Len and Amanda, this is the core of their problem at the moment. Amanda has used crazymaking to defend her space. She sees Len as coercive and is trying to stave off his coercion. But in reality Len has no desire to intimidate her into sexual yielding.

A little extra wine let him assert his sexual wish with unusual boldness, without asking permission. But Amanda has read something else into the move. She has read into it an unspoken, and unintended, "Or else."

Amanda has reacted to this image-husband. Had she given him a chance to deny the image he certainly would have done so. He would be horrified by the way Amanda now sees him.

Conversely, the evidence at hand supports an image in Len's mind of an Amanda who is turned on by being lusted after and forthrightly taken. So the next morning Len makes a more macho gesture of appreciation than is his usual style. The disparity of their images has the elements of tragedy.

Unhappy, Len drinks a bit too much again. As Amanda watches him becoming a little tight, she sees portents of new coercion to come. And she resents them. So he has married her. So he supports her. So she needs his protection in this strange place. He still doesn't own her body, she thinks defensively. She is not his whore.

And as they stand outside the restaurant, waiting for a taxi, Len looks at her and thinks that all this upsetting nit-picking between them is ridiculous, petty. But what can he do to wipe the nonsense away? What worked last night, he thinks, was to be masterful. She likes that.

"Listen, honey," he says to her as they wait. "It's ridiculous for us to ruin a whole day with this squabbling. Let's stop it." She looks up at him hopefully with a little smile. She expects that he is now going to become the usual gentle Len again.

He puts his arm around her and gives her an affectionate little hug. "Let's forget the whole thing. We'll go back to the hotel and straighten it all out. Probably all we both need is another good fuck."

It is only by the exercise of great control that Amanda keeps herself from screaming at him.

Much of the fear of aggression in crazymaking is of this kind. It is the fear of images of important others.

Pathetically often, the real person can accept an open assertion far more easily than can that person's image in one's mind.

Still more pathetically, the distance between the image and the reality can be narrowed by the simplest kind of assertions. Suppose that when Amanda had been approached brusquely by Len the night before she had merely said: "You know I like to make love with you. But right now I feel awful. I don't feel like a lover."

True, Len would have been disappointed and his mood of enthusiasm would have been dampened. But unlike the vague image in Amanda's head, it is most unlikely that he would have insisted, saying in effect, "You owe me what I want, and I don't care what you want."

Amanda would not then have had to try to bury her resentment about being coerced. For Len would have had a fair chance to show that he did not want to force her, that he was feeling his oats, but that he was not a wild, unstoppable, heedless male in rut.

Similarly, the other aspect of Amanda's buried resentment would not have smoldered, to burn out the next day in little indirect assaults. A little tact would certainly have been in order, and also a little delay. But the next day Amanda could have chosen a good time and then said, "There is something bothering me and I want to tell you about it because our lovemaking means a lot to me and I don't want anything to spoil it. I like to have the chance to say yes or no. Then I feel really free with you."

But Len was never given the opportunity to react. Amanda never checked out her image of him, never compared it to his reality.

We might note that when one is treated as an image, it has a special crazymaking effect of its own. The reason is simple and was explained earlier. It is that such behavior treats another person as a stereotype. It is another variety of "thinging."

This same phenomenon occurs in many ways. In the

preceding story, in which Maureen does not assert her space rights—in that instance, a little time for her own thoughts—she is responding to images of her husband, her child, and her friend. She treats them as though they would not accept her assertion of a right to some personal time, as though they would put their own demands on her space ahead of hers. Yet having failed to make her assertions, Maureen nevertheless acted as though her intimates knew what she wanted and denied it.

We might point out, however, that small children do not find such assertions of space by adults easy to deal with. One reason is that the conceptual abilities of very young children are limited. But perhaps a more important reason is that children have especially powerful images of their parents. They tend to see their parents as having a kind of monopoly on rights, and themselves as having almost none.

This perception of so great an imbalance of power is, of course, a key to why children can be so crazymaking. They are not given very much space to control. How often does the parent of a four-year-old accept the child's space rights—perhaps in terms of a closed door to his or her room or a drawer that is not to be opened? In fact, often the smallest assertion of such a right creates great suspicion in the parent. Why is Timmy so quiet? What is he doing behind the door he has closed?

It is no wonder that youngsters are so often driven to crazymaking to assert any right at all. We adults tend to reserve the right to enter their space when we choose. In this respect it is easy to give the child the same feelings about nonexistent space rights that convicts experience. With older children and adolescents, the denial of space rights can produce real crises and real rebellions. It helps to understand that part of a normal child's development must be the seizing and holding of some territory of his own.

The tendency to relate to images of one's intimates rather than to check out the realities is one that is often exploited by the unscrupulous. One sees this when mothers, rather than assert their demands, transfer the demands to the image of the father, and help to make that image a forbidding one.

For example, Katie wants to go on an overnight skiing trip with her high-school class. "I can understand why you want to go, dear," says her mother. "And I know we can trust you. But you know how your father is; if you even ask him he'll probably explode."

The truth is that Mother's vision is exactly what she says Father's is. In fact, Father may even be more liberal. But Mother does not want to be the bad guy. She does not want to assert her critical vision of what a sixteen-year-old ought to do or not do.

So she perhaps stifles the demand by using Father's image as the aggressor, denying her own aggression. She also blocks Katie from going to her father and in a sense usurps some of Katie's rights in paternal territory.

This is a common device for holding power. Many a secretary or receptionist uses this trick. They take on some of the power of the boss by getting control of some of his or her space or time. They control access to this power figure. And the more removed they can make the boss, the more they can use his or her image to wield some of his power.

The high-pressure salesperson is often a master of manipulating inner images. While he or she is often portrayed as simply being forceful and domineering, such intimidation does not usually make a star salesperson, who is a stranger and not important to us. As a result we are usually not so afraid of asserting refusal. We are not likely to be afraid of rejecting him; at least we do not have the same fears we have with intimates.

On the crudest level the salesperson may try to ingratiate, to take on the role of friend, so as to heighten our reluctance to reject, to keep him from invading the territory of our judgment—or that of our wealth. But this also has limited effectiveness.

The supersalesman or saleswoman codes more cleverly the possibly unacceptable demand to buy. The demand is made to appear to come from the image of your intimates. For the salesperson has shrewdly learned that then it is harder for you to reject.

Such tactics are most patent in the encyclopedia salesman, for example, who puts the demand to buy in the name of your children. But what he or she really confronts you with is not actual demands by the children. It is demands of their images that you are led to hear.

Such manipulations can be quite complex. Big Mike is a supersalesman of real estate because he is good at psyching out the images of others and using them. When he listens to the Warwicks' housing ideas, he makes the mental note that they could afford a much more expensive house than they ask for, with a bigger commission for him.

So when Big Mike shows them houses in the requested price range, he chooses those with flaws and then accentuates their problems. Meanwhile he has observed that the Warwicks are very loving and very accommodating and rather formal with each other.

Over the lunches he buys, Big Mike finds out why they are holding back on price. Each wants to travel.

How people choose to use their money is their own space. Mike wants to invade that space. So when he finally shows them a far more costly home, with everything they asked for and more, he then maneuvers to work on each separately.

"That room in the basement would be perfect for the darkroom Bill has always wanted, wouldn't it?" he asks Claire. "He's a fine man, isn't he? I can see he's the type who's always thought of himself last. And the pool would be great for him. I guess he knows it, too. Did you notice that remark of his about how if he had a pool like that he could get regular exercise, and how much a man needs that in his middle years?"

And he works on Bill in much the same way. To Claire, he has noted how a man likes to have some concrete way to demonstrate his success. To Bill he says, "Did you see Claire's eyes light up at that big dressing room with the sunken bath next door? Did you catch what she said about how grand a woman would feel coming down that stairway into the living room or greeting guests in the hall? You know, she told me she'd never had a full-size dining room.

"She's a real lady, isn't she? Not like those demanding women I see—buy me this and buy me that. I just know she's the kind of woman who would never put pressure on a man to get what she wanted. I'll bet she never asks for a thing. She'd fit right into a fine neighborhood like this, wouldn't she? I mean, that little house over on Pine Street is perfectly respectable, but I have to tell you the truth—the people aren't in her class."

Then, leaning a little harder through the day, Mike begins to work on the travel problem. "I see," he says to Claire, "that you keep comparing these other houses to the big one on Maple Street. I guess I shouldn't have showed you that, but it suited you two, especially Bill. He keeps seeing that darkroom, doesn't he? But he's told me how much the travel means to you. Of course, as a friend, I have to say that the house is an investment. You know, you travel for two weeks out of the year, but home is where you spend ninety-nine percent of your life—"

By the time Mike is through, Bill is hearing demands from Claire's image, and she from his. He leads each to feel that the other is making a sacrifice by giving up the big house.

The Warwicks do not communicate well. So when they make some effort to check each other out, they do it indirectly, gingerly, not wanting to assert their ideas clearly for fear the other will then accommodate.

(Underneath this kind of feeling is a sense that might be reduced to something like: "If I say what I want, then you will feel you have to give it to me. I am afraid that if you do accommodate this way, you will also pretend that you are not accommodating—but inwardly you will resent me. I do not want to be responsible for this decision, for it will stand there in brick and lumber as my assertion. And what if you don't like it?")

So a year later Bill is spending his vacation replanting the yard. Claire is worn out by all the carpets and windows to keep clean. Both dream of Tahitian sunsets and Paris cafés as they labor to keep the leaves out of the pool. And at the end of one day, as they sit tiredly over a drink on the deck, Bill looks up with a weary smile and says, "It's a fine house, isn't it?"

"A fine house," says Claire.

Two years later they will move into an apartment, without having given a single party, without even having bought an enlarger for the basement room.

All these stories of territorial crazymaking have one common theme: One does not accomplish very much by giving in to invasions of space.

In particular, one accomplishes little by fearfully believing in the images of one's close associates and yielding to the space concessions which they seem to demand.

In fact, even when we are genuinely coerced there are some reasonable limits to how much territory we can afford to surrender.

Gwen has been called into the presence of Mrs. Green, the office manager. She is afraid that she will be fired, for she has been making mistakes. And Mrs. Green, who is a territorial intimidator, does nothing to alleviate that fear, for she knows the power it gives her.

"Mr. Chambers has made some complaints," says Mrs. Green. "But of course I want to hear your side. He says you filed contracts instead of taking them in for signature. He's told me about some wrongly addressed letters. And then he says that on the big Florida job you sent the proposals out with some pages missing and some duplicated. Are these things true?"

The recital of her failures intensifies Gwen's fear and leaves her territory vulnerable indeed. "I—I really tried," she pleads. "I—just haven't been myself lately."

"Frankly," says Mrs. Green, turning the screw, "Mr. Chambers was upset. He suggested that perhaps we

ought to let you go. The mistakes have been embar-
rassing to him.''

Gwen drops her head and nods. "I suppose he's right.
I guess I can't even get a reference.''

"Now you know," says Mrs. Green, "that I'm not a
monster. We can understand human problems. But
you've been hard for me to get to know. You've
probably noticed that I like to know my girls, that I like
to care for them as if they were my family. But if I don't
know any of the problems they have, how can I help
them?''

"Do you—want to help me?" says Gwen, catching a
ray of hope. But she is also put off by Mrs. Green's
intimate manner. Mrs. Green does get pretty personal.
With a motherly demeanor, she counsels "her girls" on
everything from clothes to makeup to what to do about
"that time of the month.''

Gwen has always tried to nod and keep her distance.
Mrs. Green's closeness has made her feel restless and
smothered.

Above all, Gwen has shuddered when Mrs. Green has
wormed confidences about families and love affairs,
when she has offered a somehow irritating brand of
maternal comfort and advice.

"Now I don't mean to pry," says Mrs. Green, "but
I'd like to help you keep your job if I can. And I can't
do that unless we're frank with each other—dear.''

For some reason the "dear" sticks in Gwen's craw. It
feels like a presumption. Gwen bites her tongue.

"You're an intelligent worker," continues Mrs.
Green, "and for a year you were a good worker. But
something must have been upsetting you lately. I mean,
if there is something, then we could understand—''

"Well," Gwen says, feeling that it is foolish not to
yield a little space, "I have had a lot on my mind.''

"Do you want to talk about it?''

"No," says Gwen. And then she decides that she had
better soften this. "I mean, it's OK now.''

"Well, it must not have been OK Friday when you

put those proposals together and made such a mess."

"It's OK now," insists Gwen, almost pleadingly. For she does not want to share her secret with Mrs. Green.

"Are you sure, dear?" asks Mrs. Green, removing her glasses and leaning forward. There is silence. "Well, even if *you* can't be frank, *I* have to be. Do you know how many times you've been seen having lunch with Mr. Banning?"

Tears slowly well into Gwen's eyes.

"Joan," says Mrs. Green, "saw you with him at the museum last Saturday. I mean, some of us have seen what was going on all summer long—while Mrs. Banning was away at the country place with the children."

Gwen tries, but cannot speak.

"Have you ever met the children?" her boss asks. "Sweet little things. So young."

Gwen wants to shout Mrs. Green away, but she is afraid. She looks an appeal, but Mrs. Green does not stop.

"You might as well tell me. I'm not a prude. I know how a woman feels. But I also know how men can be. I've certainly seen Mr. Banning make enough plays for my girls in the last few years. How serious is it? I mean, I don't want to get personal, but have you been sleeping with him?"

Gwen does not feel that she can resist. And while part of her mind is appalled, she tells it all—in part because she does feel that Mr. Banning has exploited her. She has accommodated to him, too, and she really could use a little sympathy.

But all the time she is opening up, Gwen has a sense of being twisted inside with the shock and confusion of crazymaking.

Mrs. Green is sympathetic. She promptly sees Mr. Banning as the exploiter and Gwen as his victim. And she is quick to sympathize with Gwen's images. In truth, Gwen never made any demands on Mr. Banning. She made no assertions. She built her expectations of him upon her image of him, never talking about them, and now she has been disappointed. For Mr. Banning now treats her casually. The love affair has ended with Mrs. Banning's return from the country.

Mrs. Green does save Gwen's job. But then she treats her as an intimate, almost as her child, smothering her with advice on every issue. Gwen has become one of "her girls."

Gwen says nothing about Mrs. Green's incursions. She simply smiles and nods her head and does nothing about them. She doesn't lengthen her skirts. She doesn't take the recommended vitamins.

Gwen's lip-service concessions are crazymaking. And they lead Mrs. Green to redouble her invasions as she tries to have impact. Gwen feels maddened by every attempt. She cringes each time Mrs. Green puts a motherly arm about her shoulders or smilingly shakes a motherly finger as if to say, "Naughty girl!"

Gwen begins to dread going to the office. She feels strange there—as though she were supremely naked and vulnerable, small and demeaned. For, as we have noted, to be stripped of one's territory is to be stripped of one's existence, of one's identity. Three weeks later she resigns.

Yet the resignation does not end her upset feelings. She feels that something has changed, something fundamental, leaving her sad and pessimistic. Somehow, feeling that she must on demand recite what she has eaten for breakfast, whether she has had calls for dates, what she has done about them, how much she paid for a skirt, and more, has taken something from her.

On job interviews she is passive and sullen. She gives one-word answers to questions. She does not relate well to the interviewers. And some days it is hard for her even to decide what she will do when she has gotten out of bed.

Clinically, we would say that Gwen is in a state of depression. Her sense of self-worth is very low. Her manner is flaccid, beaten. These are the characteristics that therapists often find in women who have been raped. And indeed, rape is an appropriate symbol for those who have truly been coerced into giving up their territory. They lose identity. They regard themselves as nonpeople.

So overwhelming may be the abnegation of any of our rights to sanity. So does crazymaking, in the full sense of the word, deprive us of mental health.

In an important way the surrender of space typifies the surrender of any right to sanity. Perhaps it is the most graphic of all the denials of these rights.

Equally graphic, we should observe, is the other side of the coin of territory. For just as some people are uncertain about defending their space, so also are they unsure in their attempts to reach into the space of another.

For in the same way that we are fearful of denying others entry into our space, we may be equally reluctant to try to move into the space of others. For example, in the story of Amanda and Len, we saw that Amanda created a state of hostility during the day following their sexual crazymaking incident. In part, Amanda's indirect aggressions were the breaking out of her buried resentment. But they also served another purpose.

They were defenses of her territory. They were distancing—putting Len a long space away from her, and hence from her skirt. For when people fear to assert some important aspect of themselves directly, they must find an indirect method. Amanda defended her space with bad feeling.

So complex, so subtle does crazymaking become. We have merely hinted at some of the infinite variety of method and purpose and feeling. And as one subtlety begins to pile upon another, one can begin to despair of managing crazymaking.

But there is an answer. There is a simple way to stop the painful stress of crazymaking.

PART III

The Fight for Sanity

CHAPTER NINE

The Sane Response to Crazymaking

Once you have learned to recognize crazymaking—and once you understand why it takes place and how it can become so upsetting—you have already taken the first steps toward putting a stop to such painful experiences and preventing their recurrence.

For when you know what it is that makes communications maddening, you can readily understand some of the basic requirements of communications sanity.

You can see why sane communications (especially between intimates) demand that one's aggressions be faced and then expressed—not denied or concealed. You can see why the expressing of aggression must be open and direct—not veiled in the vague and confusing double messages of crazymaking. And you can see why sane communications require that each person respect the other's rights of sanity—not only the right to clear information, but also the rights to impact, to feeling, and to personal space.

But once crazymaking has begun, sane communications can become a tricky and treacherous matter. For inherent in crazymaking are certain factors that can make it difficult to respond in a way that restores sanity. Indeed, unless the options of responding to crazymaking, and their probable effects, are understood, the response is likely to add fuel to the fire.

For such is the nature of crazymaking that there is a tendency to respond to it—usually inadvertently, unaware—with *counter-crazymaking*.

Crazymaking tends to beget crazymaking. And the result is a vicious circle of escalating psychological warfare that we call the *crazymaking spiral*.

What is it about crazymaking that triggers this spiral? And what can be done to break it?

To understand the answers let us look at a typical example of an effort to respond to crazymaking in a sane way. Let us see what goes wrong—and why.

Phyllis has learned to recognize the signs of crazymaking experiences. And she has also learned much about what their underlying meanings are likely to be. So she is painfully aware that crazymaking has crept into her relationship with Ben.

Recently, Ben and Phyllis have become lovers and almost constant weekend companions. Their relationship is very rewarding for Phyllis in many ways. It seems to have a long future. And yet Phyllis worries about a problem that is increasingly crazymaking for her. The problem is that Ben is always late.

At first she tried to ignore her irritation. And she seemed to succeed. True, Ben's lateness made her uneasy. She disliked the suspense. Was he coming or wasn't he? Had something happened to him on the way? But these feelings disappeared as soon as Ben arrived. And his regret seemed so earnest, his explanations so reasonable, that Phyllis did not question his goodwill.

The closer the two became, however, and the more they expressed their growing affection for each other, the more disturbing each late episode became. Obviously, caring more about Ben, feeling that he was more important to her, made Phyllis worry more when he was late. But there was something else.

That something made Phyllis not only more anxious, but more angry, as she waited. And her irritability created a *buzz* of annoyance that began to persist into their time together. Phyllis recognized that buzz as one of the more common signs of the crazymaking experience.

Why was the lateness crazymaking? In general, Phyllis concluded after she had thought long and hard about it, because each episode of lateness felt to her like the coded portion of a double message.

On the one hand Ben set her many open messages that he cared for her and that she was becoming quite central in his life. He had even begun to talk about the possibility of their living together. He showed himself to be a thoughtful person, and in many ways he *was* particularly thoughtful of her—remembering her likes and dislikes in food, wine, and entertainment.

Yet on the other hand Ben seemed to be almost totally insensitive to the effects of being late. She had tried to tell him. At first she hinted. Then she tried making jokes about it. This of course is a common way of indirectly showing aggression. And finally she began to ask him earnestly to be on time just once. He expressed remorse. He soothed her. And then he continued to be late.

The effect of his behavior was one of rejecting her. If, as he said, he liked to be with her so much, why did he delay being with her? If he cared so much about her, why did he ignore what she said caused her pain? The tardiness began to make a kind of coded denial, not only of the caring Ben professed, but of the importance to him of the relationship.

"The whole thing makes me doubtful and angry," she confided to a friend. "By the time Ben shows up I'm bitchy and critical and hard to please for the rest of the night. I'm afraid I'm going to drive him away. I'm uptight even when we make love. Half the time I don't come anymore."

Phyllis' knowledge of crazymaking actually begins to make things worse. For she has become convinced that Ben's lateness represents an indirect way of expressing some aggression he fears to express openly. What can it be? If he doesn't tell her what is wrong, how can she change? Puzzled and frustrated, Phyllis finally determines, as she waits more than a long hour after the appointed time, to confront Ben—to demand the truth.

PHYLLIS: [*Opening the door*] It's after nine o'clock, Ben. You promised me that you'd be here by eight, that you'd be on time tonight. You said to go ahead and make a dinner reservation for eight-thirty.

BEN: God, I'm sorry, honey! But you don't know what I've been through. For one thing the train was late—

PHYLLIS: It was ten minutes late. I checked. The trouble was, it wasn't the train you said you would make. It was the next one. I told you how much it mattered to me.

BEN: Well, there's a reason why I missed the first train. I really tried, but then—

PHYLLIS: Don't, Ben. Don't even tell me. I don't think I can stand to listen to another reasonable explanation.

BEN: Really, honey, I didn't even go home to change. I stayed at the office and cleaned up some work, and then when I tried to get a cab—

PHYLLIS: Ben, *please.* I mean it. I can't stand to listen to any more excuses. They make it worse.

BEN: [*He bristles a little at the word* excuses.] But don't you want to know why I—

PHYLLIS: [*Losing patience*] Yes, I want to know why. But just once I want to know *really* why. Not a lot of crap about traffic jams and cab strikes. I want to know what you're trying to tell me by being late. I want to know the truth about your code.

BEN: [*He is both genuinely confused and genuinely annoyed.*] What do you mean, crap? I'm trying to get it through your head— [*He stops himself and determines to be reasonable.*] Honey, I don't know what you're talking about with all this stuff about codes and what I'm really trying to tell you. I'm sorry as hell that I was late. I really tried. What's with you? Have you got your period or something?

PHYLLIS: [*Now it is her turn to feel stung.*] I do *not* have my period or something! Yes, I'm mixed up and angry. You said you'd be prompt. You always say you'll be prompt. And then I sit and worry and—I just have to know. I need to know what kind of hidden message you're sending.

In this exchange we see the beginnings of the crazy-making spiral. Phyllis is right in deducing that she is getting a coded message. But she forgets something. She forgets that crazymaking is largely unconscious. She forgets that the coded portion of the message represents an aggression that has been denied. So Ben really believes what he is telling her. And when she labels his explanation as crap, when she says it is not real, she really begins an exercise in mind reading, mind raping, and mind ripping. In brief, she is indulging in crazymaking.

In Ben's mind, his attempts to tell the truth are being labeled as lies. His concern for her feelings—which has made him worry all the way from the city—is being denied. He *knows* he cares. And she says he does not. He *knows* he wanted to be on time, and she says he did not want to be. She implies that somehow he is late deliberately. He feels that what she is saying and doing is driving him crazy.

BEN: [*Trying to stifle his annoyance, he makes another effort.*] Honey, please try and listen. Please try to hold on while I tell you what happened—
PHYLLIS: [*Feeling a little desperate*] Will you try and hear me, Ben? I don't *care* what happened! All I care about is that you say you won't be late and then you *are* late. And I have to know what it really means.

And another crazymaking element is added. For each holds a personal vision of the truth of the situation. And each feels that the other will not even listen. Each has the feeling of being denied any impact. The frustration mounts.

* * *

PHYLLIS: Damn it, Ben, I have to know what's really wrong. I have to know what's happening, really happening.

BEN: But that's what I'm trying to tell you—I was right on time, and then I went out to get a cab and—

PHYLLIS: [*Her voice rising to a thin edge*] Jesus, Ben, will you please stop it before I go crazy? I've got to know the reason. I've got to know what you *mean*!

BEN: [*Driven to the brink of his patience and genuinely uncomprehending*] Damn it, there *is* no secret meaning! You are driving me right out of my skull. And I will not put up with any more of this goddamned— [*Suddenly he stops himself. He realizes that they are close to a breaking point. In a moment they will be shouting at each other. And he does not want to risk that explosion. Phyllis means too much to him. He does not want to say things that will make them split up. So he shifts gears. Gritting his teeth, he turns from an angry expression to a forced, ironic smile. Somehow, he is determined, he must make the conflict disappear.*] Are you really sure you want the truth?

PHYLLIS: [*She too feels an explosion is close at hand. And she too fears it. Besides, her demands are yielding nothing. In Ben's change to an ironic smile, she sees a way out, a way to retreat from the dangerous brink. So she too tries to smile. She nods.*] OK, tell me.

BEN: Well, a few weeks ago, I met this gorgeous lady train conductor. I've tried to fight it, but I'm helpless. Every time I'm headed for the train, to see you, I have to give in. I wind up screwing the lady conductor in this phone booth in Grand Central Station.

PHYLLIS: [*For a moment she is torn. If she continues to demand the underlying truth she seeks, she fears she will lose Ben in a blowup. And it looks as if she will learn nothing from him anyway. If she backs down and colludes with him in his weakly humorous evasion, she rationalizes, perhaps later the truth will just come out somehow or perhaps the lateness will stop. So she forces herself to smile.*] You see how useless it was to try to conceal it? I mean, a little thing like screwing a lady conductor—why didn't you just tell the truth in the first place? Let's go look for some dinner. I'm starved.

Having approached a hard confrontation, both Ben and Phyllis have become fearful that to continue will mean final separation. They see an impasse. And the only way out seems to be to back up.

What this really means is that both must choke down their aggressions in order to manage their separation fears. In colluding in this bit of forced humor, they come to an unspoken agreement to pretend that their urgent feelings are unimportant. In fact they begin to laugh uproariously over a joke which ordinarily both would consider only mildly amusing at best. They do so to confirm their mutual denial of aggression. They laugh until they put their arms around each other and then both feel unusually passionate. They make love there in the living room, almost violently. It is a kind of second layer of denial. And it is also a way to discharge some of their aggressive feelings.

For the first time, for example, Phyllis mounts him, aggressively. And he bites quite hard at her breasts.

Even when it is over, both are still quite fearful, still uneasy about how close they came to open conflict. Both try to add still more sugar-coating, with endearments, with pledges of love.

But if we look closely at what has happened, we can see a sequence that is the crazymaking spiral. And we can see just how insidious that spiral is.

In the beginning, Ben's continuing lateness was surely crazymaking for Phyllis. Although he was thoughtful in all other aspects of their relationship, his acts of lateness made a sharply conflicting double message.

In trying to break the code, Phyllis made demands for information she might have known would be unavailing. For Ben's lateness had to represent an aggression that was not conscious; it had to be an indirect expression of an aggression he had tried to bury and deny. And harsh demands are not likely to bring unconscious feelings into the open. On the contrary, threats merely confirm the fears that caused his aggressions to be denied in the first place. Phyllis' sharp challenge merely nails the lid of denial more tightly in place.

When Ben expresses his denial that he is sending a coded message, Phyllis reacts with crazymaking of her own. She begins to insist that he is not telling her the truth. She invades his sane rights by reading his mind—even though she does not pretend to know just what his lateness means—and by acting as though she knew what he felt and thought.

This crazymaking leads Ben to respond in turn with still another crazymaking double message. For while his anger is obvious, he denies it with his joke. Phyllis colludes with the joke. But now both have, fearfully, buried aggressive feelings.

These feelings emerge in a coded way in their silent and almost hostile lovemaking. Then the hostility is covered over with sugary words of caring. But what must eventually happen is obvious to us from our earlier observations. The aggressions which have been buried still lurk below the surface, waiting for some kind of expression. It comes almost as soon as they do.

PHYLLIS: Oh, Ben, I really do love you! I'm sorry I got so bitchy. It's just my worrying so when you're late, wondering if you've been hurt or got sick. How would I even know?

BEN: I'm sorry I started to lose my cool, honey. But it felt like you were calling me a liar, and I can't stand to have you think that. I can't stand to have you think anything except how much I care for you. I've never met a girl like you.

PHYLLIS: I've never met a man like you. You bring out so much feeling in me. You're such a good lover.

BEN: Boy, you were some kind of lover just now! I didn't know you were such a sexpot. [*Teasingly—and remember that teasing is a form of indirect aggression—he adds*]: I should get you mad more often. You were terrific.

PHYLLIS: [*She draws back.*] What do you mean? Don't you like the way we usually make love?

BEN: [*On guard*] Why, you know I think you're great, honey. But tonight you were really something else. I mean, this time you really made me feel you wanted it, wanted me.

PHYLLIS: [*A little testily*] You mean I don't show you that I want you?

BEN: Sure you do. [*Quickly*] It's just that—well, you let me do it and you do what I say. But this time you really went for me. I mean, I always knew you had it in you.

PHYLLIS: [*Sitting up and nervously lighting a cigarette*] Well, maybe that's because for once you didn't smother me with all that weight. I mean, it really makes it hard to move. It even makes it hard to breathe, to tell you the truth. You know, Ben, you really ought to try to lose some weight. You could have a really good body. I'll bet you looked terrific when you were younger.

Again, it is not hard for us to see what is happening. Already the buried aggressions are beginning to surface. Each has slipped little daggers into the sexual ego of the other, and they are becoming defensive. Once more they smooth it over. But then little bits of crazymaking begin to appear again during their late supper.

When Phyllis goes to the powder room she takes an unusually long time, for example. And Ben comments about waiting, which brings out more discussions about lateness and the pain of suspense. Ben smoothes this over by promising that from now on he will phone when he is going to be late.

And he keeps his word. He does phone—before almost every date, but often delaying until almost the appointed time. Phyllis no longer waits anxiously for his arrival—she waits anxiously for his phone calls instead. And they come later and later.

What is it that leads this crazymaking spiral to continue? One can describe what happens in many ways. For example, one can say that mutual fear of aggression assures that real feelings will be hidden, to emerge obliquely. But this does not answer the question fully. It does not explain why the person who feels like the victim of a crazymaking experience usually responds in a crazymaking style, to start the spiral going.

To get to the root of the problem and understand how to break the spiral—in fact to prevent it from beginning—we must understand an extremely important truth of crazymaking. It is that crazymaking carries a *sting.*

The sting of crazymaking develops as a natural consequence of repressing aggression. For when one cannot express aggression effectively, its character tends to change.

One can see this change most clearly when aggression is open and direct. Suppose, for example, the man sitting next to you—on an airplane, in a theater, or at a psychology lecture—falls asleep. His head tilts until it comes to rest on your shoulder.

You feel annoyed. Your space has been invaded. You nudge him a little, hoping he will wake and withdraw. He does not. "Sir," you whisper, nudging again a little harder. "SIR!" Nothing. He begins to snore and settles against you. You give his arm a shake. Still no response.

You are frustrated. You have expressed, mildly, your assertion of your space rights and nothing has happened. So you become annoyed. In fact you are angry.

Why? Because, fundamentally, aggression arises when you wish a change. When that change involves another person, a basic right of sanity enters the picture. *It is the right to have impact.*

For before the other person will cooperate with you to achieve the change, you must have impact. The assertion of your demand for a change must be received by the other. And that assertion must produce a reaction.

What if you fail to have impact? You can observe the result in your feelings and your behavior when the stranger who has fallen asleep on your shoulder does not move, does not even acknowledge your effort to communicate. You finally give him a good firm jab in the shoulder, perhaps with a loud word in his ear. And if you examine your feelings, you find that in the hard jab there is more than an attempt to get attention. There is hostility as well. You want to hit him.

For the fact is that when an aggressive assertion is blocked, when it is frustrated, one cannot help feeling hostile. Frustrated aggression leads to feelings of hostility as surely as a ball rolls down an inclined plane.

It is for these reasons that we envision aggression as having two phases, as occurring in two rather different modes. One we call *I-type*, or *impact-type*, aggression. This aggression seeks to have impact so that it can produce change. It is this type of aggression that may be as innocuous as asking someone to pass the potatoes or saying "Excuse me" as you step to the rear of the bus.

But I-type aggression can very easily shift into another mode. This happens when the attempt to have impact—and consequently to produce change—fails. The fundamental aggressive feeling continues. And its fundamental objective remains the same. But it now acquires an additional component. For the frustration has converted the I-type aggression to *H-type*, or hostile, aggression.

Contrary to what many people think, this conversion of aggression to the H-type is not limited to strangers. It includes intimates. In fact, because we are likely to be more dependent on intimates for the satisfaction of our wishes, the frustration of aggression with those close to us and the incorporation of hostility into our feelings may actually happen more easily.

This is not perverse. It is only common sense. For we believe that those people who are close to us are more interested in helping us to get what we want. We expect them to be sensitive to our wishes, to allow impact the more easily. And when that expectation is disappointed, especially when it leads to the level of crazymaking, we are all the more shocked, all the more frustrated, all the more hostile.

And there is an irony about the frustration of our aggressions by those close to us. The *possibility* of such frustration may lead us to choke down the aggression and then express it in devious ways. And then there is a powerful tendency both to deny the hostile component of frustrated aggression to ourselves and to conceal it from these important others.

For example, suppose that the person who invades our territory by falling asleep is not a stranger. Suppose instead that it is an intimate with whom we are sleeping. Suppose this more important person keeps us awake by rolling over onto us. Irrationally, but in a very human way, we cannot help but feel that this incursion is worse. For we are being injured by someone who is not supposed to injure us. So if we fail by gentle means to rouse the person and recover our territory, we tend to be extra frustrated. We tend more quickly to become hostile.

Now, when out of frustration we give a sharp and rather hostile poke, the intimate awakens and says blurrily, "Ouch—what the—" And then, immediately, there is a tendency not only to deny our hostility to ourselves but also to sugar-coat it. "Go to sleep, dear," we say affectionately, comfortingly. "It's nothing. Let me cover you up so that you'll be nice and warm."

Here are two factors that tend to evoke the crazymaking spiral, to make it more certain and to make it worse in close relationships. Let us see how they operate.

First of all we can see that crazymaking is always preceded by the blocking of the straightforward, I-type aggression. For it is this aggression that one fears to express. So one represses it, tries to deny it.

Ironically, in this phase of crazymaking it is really ourselves who frustrate the aggression. Yet in our feelings, it is the other person who is responsible for the frustration, because our fear begins with a fear of how this other will react, of the effect the aggression will have upon him or her. So in an important sense the other is blamed—without having had a chance to react. The effects upon him or her have been assumed. In this respect crazymaking is always a kind of mind-ripping, mind-raping exercise.

The net effect is that by the time the crazymaking occurs, it is always to some extent not only an indirect, concealed aggression. But that aggression has already been converted from one of the impact type to one of the hostile type.

So it is that crazymaking carries a sting. So it is that crazymaking always carries an element of hostility, of an intent not only to express an aggression one fears to express, and not only to express it in an indirect way, but also an intent, founded in frustration, to hurt.

Thus part of the pain of crazymaking goes beyond the confusion of the double message, beyond the shock of frustrated expectations of goodwill. In part it is the shock of having hurt inflicted by one from whom we expect only goodwill.

And the pain, the shock, and the surprise are further compounded. For there is usually the added confusion of a sugar-coating by which the crazymaking hides its hostile component.

Let us look again at the example of Ben and Phyllis. Whatever buried aggression is represented by Ben's lateness, it hurts Phyllis more, upsets her more, because the last thing she expects is to be hurt by someone who professes love for her.

This helps us to see why crazymaking tends to beget a crazymaking response, especially in situations with intimates. For there is a simple and universal human reaction to being hurt. It is to hurt back. But one cannot do this openly.

And this is why Phyllis' exasperated reaction to Ben's crazymaking lateness ends in her own crazymaking. She is not just hurt, she is also frustrated. The double message from Ben, in mystifying her, creates a powerful aggressive wish for change, at the very least a change that lets her understand why he behaves as he does.

So she does not merely demand an answer to the puzzle. As she makes the demand, her frustrated aggression makes her hostile. Unaware, she finds a certain satisfaction in saying, in effect, that he is lying to her, that he is not just explaining his lateness but is manipulating her with excuses.

For Ben's lateness, like all crazymaking, has the sting

of a mystifying and surprising hostility. And Phyllis responds not just to her puzzlement, but to the wound. So she does not just demand an explanation, she hurts back.

In this way, it is the sting of crazymaking that assures the beginnings of the crazymaking spiral. The awareness of injury perpetuates the spiral. For the response to the sting is likely to be one of two reactions, either of them quite destructive. It may be reprisal—in which case the angry response only confirms the fear that kept the original aggression hidden and denied in the first place, leading to further repression and further emergence in an indirect way. Or it may be withdrawal—a denial on the part of the injured person that someone close could do, would want to do, harm. But sadly, such a withdrawal reaction merely adds to the frustration of the original aggressive impulse. It becomes nothing more than another frustration. For it says that there is still no impact. And with no impact, there is no possibility of change. And this too leads to another indirect emergence of aggression, this time with an even more hurtful, though concealed, indirect aggression.

How can the cycle be broken? Fundamentally there is one essential requirement to stop crazymaking. *It is that the underlying aggressive impulse must be recognized and identified.* It must have impact. And it must be allowed to produce change.

But the problem is that this aggression is being hidden. It is being expressed in code. So the answer to crazymaking must be to find a way to allow the aggression to be expressed openly and clearly so that there can be a response, so that it can have impact.

To accomplish this two factors are essential. First of all one must not react to the sting as though it were the substance of the crazymaking. It is only an incidental. It is the element of hostility that has entered in through the frustration of the aggressive impulse.

In the example of Ben and Phyllis we can see what happens when this requirement is not met. The hurts are veiled. Phyllis does not tell Ben the simple truth—that she is becoming increasingly dependent upon his caring and that his repeated lateness threatens her with the idea that he does not really care. And Ben, concealing the real reasons for his lateness even from himself, cannot and does not tell Phyllis how deeply he is wounded by her assertions that he is not telling her the truth as he knows it, that she does not trust him.

So whatever the substance of their problems with each other, the clear facts of their respective feelings remain hidden. Instead, each responds to the other's injuries. They do it with an element of hostility as they make love. And they do it afterward. Ben implies that she has been a passive and unexciting sex partner. Phyllis implies that she has tolerated discomfort when they made love. Frustrated, she brings up Ben's overweight, implies that it makes him clumsy and that she has been uncomfortable in lovemaking.

What is important to the psychologist is that these stings and counter-stings are ways to divert interest from the truly essential concerns. And what is needed is a way to talk openly about, and resolve, the matters that most trouble us.

How can the sting of crazymaking be set aside? Mainly by recognizing its origins—by realizing that this hostility has its roots in a frustrated expression of aggression.

When one understands crazymaking, one can see that it may provide a curious kind of reassurance. For one does not repress aggressions unless one is concerned that they will not be acceptable. One does not deny such feelings, usually, unless one fears to lose a relationship which one values.

True, as we have observed, there are those pathological personalities who find satisfaction in crazymaking with intimates. But these people are few and far between. In the main, when crazymaking occurs between intimates, it is a kind of curious testimony that the relationship, and the other person's goodwill, are of great importance.

So a more realistic response to crazymaking than reacting to its hurtfulness is to try to obtain clear information about the aggression being expressed. And one way to do this is to understand the patterns of crazymaking.

For while the specific tactics of crazymaking are as various as crazymaking experiences themselves, in general they tend to follow a fairly limited number of patterns. If one is familiar with these patterns, it is much more productive to examine them and then take action according to what one finds than it is to respond just to the hostility of the sting.

Let us suppose that in Phyllis' case she understands these patterns. She can then ask herself some basic questions about the episodes of Ben's crazymaking. And she can begin to answer these questions as well—not by reading Ben's mind but by looking at the objective facts of the situation and by examining her own reactions.

The questions really fall into two groups. And Phyllis is quickly able to make some observations in her answers to the first:

What is the area of conflict?

Obviously it is to be found in the fact that Ben does not come on time. And in this fact, and its effects, must be a clue to the issue from which comes the crazymaking way in which Ben deals with their appointments. What does the lateness signify? What matters does it suggest must be translated from this code, brought out and discussed?

From her knowledge of the patterns, Phyllis realizes that the significance of lateness tends to lie in the delay of the meeting, that it represents a kind of withdrawal. Phyllis is able to match that withdrawal, that reluctance, to the crazymaking pattern called *hide-and-seek*.

This pattern, she knows, is a way of withholding oneself from a relationship. It is a way of creating some distance between oneself and another person.

Using the patterns in this way, Phyllis is also able to find some answers to a second question:

What kinds of effects are created by the crazy-making?

For these answers Phyllis looks to herself, thus avoiding the dangerous trap of mind reading. Moreover, remember that crazymaking is always designed to accomplish certain purposes in a concealed way. So the effects it produces are good indicators of what it seeks.

Phyllis is aware that she does not want withdrawal. In fact she hopes for greater closeness and commitment. And at once she can see one reason why Ben's lateness—if it does indeed represent withdrawal—is so upsetting.

She is aware that her dependency on Ben has grown. She feels committed to him. And so she needs signs that he is committed to her. The lateness makes her doubt that commitment, or its strength. It warns that her dependency may be insecurely placed. It says that instead of coming closer Ben is pushing her back.

Indeed, what Phyllis knows of the characteristics of the hide-and-seek pattern tells her that it tends to be a way to avoid another's dependency. It tends to be a way of sidestepping when another appears to lean too heavily.

Phyllis also realizes from this that the lateness signals, in its effects upon her, that she should not express her own aggressive feelings. For the most important of these, in regard to Ben, is to ask for more commitment.

If she could make her demand openly it would go something like this: "You have become very important to me. I welcome this importance. I welcome finding someone who can matter so much. But I need to know if I can depend on you, and in what ways. I need to know if you have reservations that remain unspoken. In essence I need to know how central I am in your life before I can allow you to keep becoming more and more central in mine. I need to know how much of myself I dare to invest."

And if she expressed her aggressive feelings about Ben's lateness, that expression would be: "When you are always late, I cannot help feeling you are saying to me that I cannot depend on you, that I must be cautious and restrained. Because the lateness gives me the feeling that I am not as important to you as you are to me. Your lateness says to me that I can't count on you. And that's why it drives me crazy. Because, at the same time, you tell me how close you feel and how close you want to be. And you never seem to reject my moves closer to you.''

With such awareness Phyllis can narrow the discussion with Ben to meaningful underlying issues rather than confining it to endless bickering about the time he arrives, which has been, and is likely to be, profitless. And when she does, the results provide some surprises. For Ben laughs when she talks about her wish for commitment.

"Don't misunderstand," he says. "It's not really funny. It's just ironic. That's the way I've been thinking about you. You may think you've been open about how you feel. I thought I was. But every time I've talked about living together, for example, you've backed away from me. You change the subject after three sentences. You never say yes, no, or maybe. It's been that way from the start. It drives me crazy, to tell you the truth."

What Phyllis and Ben learn is that they are much alike. Both tend, they feel, to become too easily dependent upon another's caring and closeness. So both, having been wounded in this way, are cautious, resistant when they feel the signals of growing dependency. They tend to hang back, waiting for strong signs of commitment from the other, and being extremely skeptical even when they get them. Their mutual fear of dependency has yet to be dealt with. But at least they have taken a first step.

Understanding the patterns of crazymaking can help people to see the broader outlines of their crazymaking experiences, help them to focus on the kinds of underlying aggressions being expressed in code and to bring their own reactions, the effects of the crazymaking, into clearer view. This delineation of the specific effects and the specific overt irritant in the crazymaking, we shall see, is important to its resolution.

CHAPTER TEN

The Purposeful Patterns of Crazymaking

To explain all the possible tactics of crazymaking would take a book with as many pages as there are people in this world. For it is virtually impossible for anyone to go through life without engaging in some crazymaking. And because the styles and circumstances of each life are unique, each of us invents and uses custom-tailored ploys of crazymaking that are uniquely suited to our own special surroundings and relationships.

Fortunately, however, in practical terms it is not necessary or even especially helpful to understand every detail of crazymaking. For just as in war and politics, while the tactics of each crazymaking situation are highly specific, the general strategies are relatively few in number. And remember, the objective in learning to recognize the patterns of crazymaking is *not* to psychoanalyze the other person. It is primarily to help us manage our own feelings so that we can respond in a sane way and avoid an unending crazymaking spiral.

Understanding and recognizing the patterns of crazymaking can help us do more than identify the area of conflict and obtain some idea of demand for change which the crazymaking represents. It can help to moderate some of the pain of the experience. For obvious reasons such understanding eases some of the confusion. But more than this it helps reduce some of the anxiety that is felt—for one can see more clearly that the crazymaking objective is not to destroy the relationship but to avoid open conflict, which might result from direct aggression. In these ways and others, recognizing the pattern helps to attenuate the sting of crazymaking. And so it lessens the temptation to reply with a countersting.

Thus the list of crazymaking patterns that follows is selected so that each represents a broad and common strategy. Each represents an important crazymaking theme. The reader's own life can furnish plenty of variations.

Once the patterns are clearly in mind, we can begin to see how to use them as guidance in choosing the options of sane response.

Your-wish-is-my-wish

Like virtually all the crazymaking patterns, this one develops out of ordinary and acceptable behaviors, so it tends to have the appearance of acceptability until the crazymaking distortion that underlies it is felt.

In this case the acceptable root of the pattern is *accommodation*. Accommodation is basically nothing more than adjusting one's own self-interest in order to take into account the interests of others.

One accommodates when one has two pieces of bubble gum and shares one with a friend, when one offers the better seat in a theater to one's companion, or even when one says, on coming to a doorway, "After you."

But *your-wish-is-my-wish* is a false kind of accommodation. The accommodator does not yield to another so much out of goodwill as out of fear of conflict. This forced yielding causes stress for the accommodator. The price is really higher than he wishes to pay. But he is afraid that if he says no, the stress will be still greater. Perhaps there will even be open combat if he does not make the offer.

So the accommodator goes along with whatever is asked of him. Often nothing has been asked. He is mind reading by trying to guess what the other person might *like* to ask. And this can add to the irritation that results. Crazymaking kinds of accommodation are common in sexual situations. For example:

HE: Gee, it feels good to be close to you. I know you've had a tough day, with the kids being sick and all. But wouldn't you like to roll over and come closer?

SHE: [*Exhausted but accommodating even though she feels little or no sexual interest*] You know I *always* like to be close to you. [*And she rolls over. But note that she does not answer his question about what she wants.*]

HE: [*Touching*] Does this feel good?

SHE: [*Again not really answering*] You know I always like it when you touch me.

HE: [*After some minutes of touching*] I want to be inside you. Do you want me inside you?

SHE: Have I ever said no, dear?

But there comes a time when the accommodator's partner realizes that *yes* did not really mean genuine and willing assent—only submission. When he tries to enter her, he finds that she is really not prepared for him to do so. So he tries to check again.

HE: I don't want to hurt you. Maybe I'd better—

SHE: You know you never really hurt me. It feels fine. I'm just a little tired, that's all. It makes me dry.

HE: Well—if you say so—

SHE: Ouch.

HE: See? I *did* hurt you.

SHE: No, it's fine now. It was just an awkward position.

HE: [*After another moment*] Honey, you're really sort of—well, dry—and you know, tight—

SHE: Don't worry. It doesn't matter. I love you. I never want to say no to you. I want to give you whatever you want. [*Then, after another minute*] What's wrong, dear? Why are you stopping?

HE: Well, I—it's just that I'm sure I must be hurting you. I'm sure it can't feel good and you're just—

SHE: [*Annoyance creeps into her voice, but restrained*] I said it was OK, didn't I? I said I wanted to give you what you wanted. But maybe you don't really want me. I mean [*Looking downward significantly*]— how can you really want me if you're like *that*?

In one way or another, usually indirectly, the person who has been accommodated in a nongenuine way is given the message of the truth, of the underlying resistance. In this case the true aggressive impulse for the lady has been to say no to her husband. She is afraid to say no. She buries the impulse. But her unconscious finds an indirect, crazymaking way of saying no for her.

In this way the person who has been accommodated is likely to be led to refuse the generous offer which is the accommodator's clear and open communication. Or, if he takes the offer, he is later made to feel guilt or obligation. And he has been warned by the crazymaking coded message that he must be very cautious in future about what he asks for and what he accepts.

Particularly when the accommodations of your-wish-is-my-wish are made to avoid rejecting another, the refusal is ultimately made anyway. And when it is made after the fact, when it is too late to withdraw the request, when the matter is really history, this is especially crazymaking.

For the accommodated person thought he had assent when he did not. So he developed false expectations. And when the genuine no is made clear, he is made to feel that somehow he forced the acquiescence of his partner, that he has been selfish or heedless.

There are endless variations of your-wish-is-my-wish. For example Jenny says, "It's a beautiful day for a drive in the convertible." And Jack agrees. But then, as darkness approaches, he says, "Thank God the sun is going down. The glare in this open car has been making my headache into a real killer." And of course he has never mentioned that he had a headache.

Nongenuine accommodation can also have many purposes. One of the most common is this: The accommodator says yes because he or she fears to say no. When a crazymaking no follows, the real message is "Don't make assertive demands on me. Because I can't reject them. So you must censor all your demands. You must try to read my mind and guess what I really want to agree to and what I don't want.''

It is easy to see how powerful this tactic can become, and how maddening. For it ends by depriving the other person of the right to express his or her wishes clearly and the right to have impact.

Often the tactic of your-wish-is-my-wish shades into a variant of false accommodation that we call *colluding*. We sometimes also refer to it as *me-too-if-you-say-so*.

Fundamentally, this form of false accommodation is a matter of going along with what one assumes the other wishes; in fact, usually pretending shared pleasure. When the rug is pulled out from under this deception, the effect can be extremely maddening.

The wife who let her husband understand, above, that she was a willing and interested sex partner when she was not was actually colluding in part. The revelation of colluding can be one of the most devastating of crazymaking ploys. For example, Mark's business has been in trouble. For weeks he has been worried, unable to sleep. ''I've tried everything,'' he finally says to Karen, ''but I can't make it. We're just going to have to sell our home and find something smaller.''

Karen soothes him. ''Well, that's all right. I've always hated this house anyway. But you wanted it so much.''

In what makes a very tangled crazymaking pattern, one can even collude with crazymaking. Suppose for example that Karen, in her dislike of her house, which she fears to express, has resorted to crazymaking to send this message indirectly. She accomplishes this by working hard at keeping house, yet usually managing to leave some obvious mess.

Mark arrives home from work when they are expecting guests. The living room is a jumble. Karen appears looking frazzled and worn. ''You'll have to help me,'' she complains. ''I've been working every minute straightening out the kitchen cabinets and cleaning up all the appliances we don't use very much. They get so greasy. And you know how it is when

Mildred comes over for dinner. She's always wanting to help. And what if she opens one of those awful cabinets and sees all that greasy stuff that hasn't been touched for months?''

"I see what you mean," replies Mark sympathetically. And he hurries about, picking up in the living room, vacuuming, washing up the guest bathroom, and cleaning household papers out of the dining room.

"There. Aren't the cabinets beautiful?" asks Karen.

"They really are," says Mark. "You work so hard. You really ought to have some help. I wish we could afford a maid.''

What Mark really wants to say, irritably, is something like: "Where is your sense of proportion? Sure, it's great to clean up the cabinets in the kitchen. But what about the basic things that had to be done? The hall closet is now full of all the junk I had to clear out. Somehow you're always setting me up so I have to do housework for you.''

Indeed, Karen is setting him up. But what Mark does not realize is that, by colluding in order to avoid conflict, he is deliberately ignoring Karen's endless indirect messages that she feels the house is too much for her to take care of alone. Mark's counter-crazymaking, which is part of his collusion, is constantly to promise that he will do some of the heavy work, but always to avoid doing it.

Thus the house becomes the instrument of an unceasing crazymaking spiral. Neither Mark nor Karen is comfortable in it. But they have entered into mutual collusion, which traps them in the situation. Mark does not want to see that the house is always a mess, no matter how Karen tries to leave messes under his nose. And on her part Karen is afraid to admit openly that she cannot manage the house alone, afraid to reject the house because Mark picked it out and she thinks he loves it, and afraid to ask for hired help because Mark might take it as a rejection of his ability as a provider.

One can easily see how extreme collusion can become as a crazymaking way of life. For this kind of non-genuine accommodation can end by building a whole set of false "shared" beliefs, dreams, and goals in a relationship.

Among the most common collusive patterns is often found at the beginning of love relationships. We sometimes call it *love-crazy*. And it might also be called *I'm-in-love-with-a-wonderful-fantasy*.

The false expectations in this crazymaking really begin with the culture, which gives us a fantasy view of love, and especially a vision of the Magic Lover who somehow will meet all our needs, happily grant all our wishes, and with whom we will live happily ever after. Sadly, such fantasies of perfection are not within human abilities to satisfy.

But somehow it seems as if each new pair of lovers tends to try to convince themselves that they are the exception to the fantasy rule. Indeed, the satisfaction of the love-crazy fantasy is often used as a criterion for whether or not love is real and the relationship has true potential for the long term.

Unhappily, the only way such criteria can be met is by denial and accommodation that are collusive. All differences in values, tastes, and preferences are smoothed over, swept under the emotional rug. New lovers often collude in avoiding any area in which conflict of any kind appears.

The love-crazy collusion can become especially evident when a relationship begins with what we call the *all-electric-meeting*, a kind of dynamic love-at-first-sight beginning. So overwhelming and fantasy-fulfilling can such meetings be that neither partner dares express any aggression that will rock the boat.

But this kind of collusion is exhausting. Every time they couple, the earth has to shake. Every time a wish is expressed or even hinted at, it has to be met with enthusiasm.

Cold reality is of course inevitable. And each reality—from the discovery that she really doesn't like chocolate all that much to the discovery that removing her bra will not inevitably produce an erection—becomes a kind of crazymaking experience. For the love-crazy collusion has simply built a false expectation of the other that cannot continue to be met. It is for this reason that so many torrid affairs end with a sudden, shattering feeling of having been deceived.

The many patterns of crazymaking accommodation are plainly among the most frequent and maddening of all the general strategies of crazymaking. The theme and pattern of your-wish-is-my-wish are readily discernible when the coded messages are received that deny the genuineness of the accommodation. But some of the pain of the crazymaking is relieved when we realize that the deception of accommodation is really not intended to cheat us. It is to hold us, to please us, to win favor. It comes about out of fear of conflict with us. With this understanding we can deal with the sting when an accommodative untruth is revealed. Perhaps above all, we can better avoid the temptation to deny that a coded, crazymaking message that contradicts an accommodation is real.

For as we have seen, both the clear and the coded parts of a double message have reality. Both need to be believed, at least to the extent that we can understand them. And even if the coded message is unclear, we can give some belief to the effect it has upon us. When a crazymaking experience makes us feel that an accommodation is being denied, we need to take steps to get an open expression of truth.

To-love-me-is-to-know-me

Sometimes known as *divining*, this crazymaking pattern has its roots in infancy. For the infant cannot say what he or she wants or needs, and depends instead upon the parents' ability to divine what is wished or required—whether he or she is hot or cold, wet or dry. The baby's only way to make an assertion is a nonspecific howl. It is up to Mommy and Daddy to figure out whether the howl is occasioned by an empty belly or an errant diaper pin.

To-love-me-is-to-know-me has a relationship to the general strategy of your-wish-is-my-wish. For if the pattern of nongenuine accommodation is acceded to, one is put in the position of having to divine what the other would like or accept. Remember that one of the aims of the pattern is to stop the other person from making demands that would have to be accommodated, like it or not. For the accommodator is unwilling to take the risk of saying no. Only hints—which can be mystifying indeed—are sometimes given. And of course there are the complaints and long faces afterward.

To-love-me-is-to-know-me contains a pattern that also relates to the expected perfection of the love-crazy expectations. For when one expects divining of the other, he is saying in effect that real concern or affection for him should automatically produce the ability to know what he wants or what he would have you do for him, without being told.

This is a hard and nerve-racking test to meet. And certain phrases are often good indicators that the test is being made. "You must have known" is one. "You should have known" or "Anyone would know" are others. And the failure to divine this person's wishes, to know what he or she thinks you are supposed to know, is interpreted as being a failure of love or loyalty.

SHE: Here's the extra shirt you asked me to buy, dear.
HE: [*Dismayed*] It's green!
SHE: Yes. I looked through your drawer so I wouldn't duplicate what you had, and you didn't have any green.
HE: Well, then, you must have realized that I don't like green shirts.

Despite the great popularity of the notion that those who love us and are suited to us are able to anticipate or divine our wishes, it simply is not true. And if one is persuaded to accept this false belief in a relationship, one can end by having a strong sense of inadequacy. For often one is going to be wrong. One has not failed, however, but has merely been persuaded to give up one's right to clear information.

The person who expects divining is likely to be continually disappointed in his or her partner. He or she commonly assigns little errands, little choices to be made, with the statement—which he or she believes—

"Oh, you *know* what I like." But these assignments turn out to be crazymaking traps. And yet such a person tends to cling to the belief that the other could always divine correctly if the attempt were made. Thus, any failure to divine, to please, is taken as a deliberate attack. It may well produce a look of sulking depression, of betrayal even. Watch the look on a baby's face when the spoonful Mother offers him turns out to be medicine.

HE: [*Returning from making a telephone call at a restaurant*] Well, what did you order for me?
SHE: A very dry martini, the prime rib medium-rare—and I also remembered how much you said you liked the rice pilaf here, so I—
HE: Jesus—
SHE: What's wrong?
HE: That's what I'd like to know. After a day like the one I've had today, a martini will give me stomach cramps. And it makes me feel really sabotaged when you order me a big piece of fatty meat like that. I told you I was going to try to lose some weight. At least, if I'm going to have to choke down all those calories, I wish I could have a potato. The rice was fine last time because I was eating lamb, and you know I always like rice with lamb. But rice with prime rib?

The tyranny exercised by the success of this kind of crazymaking is not unlike that with which an infant can hold sway in a family. And it tends to produce the same kind of anxiety in a household that a new baby brings.

Such anxiety is the result of feeling that one is always on trial, always being tested. And along with it there is bound to be resentment, a hostility one feels about being kept in such suspense.

Great power goes to the person who manages to convince another that divining is a realistic expectation. And the gaining of such power, putting the other person always in the role of trying to please, is one of the most important purposes of the divining pattern.

Perhaps it is not surprising to learn that the tactic is

often the resort of the person who does in fact feel a powerlessness akin to that of an infant. It is often the result of strong feelings of dependency, of a desperate need to be loved in order to survive. And partly because there is such great dependency, there is also great fear of being rejected or abandoned. This fear can lead to constant testing as a way of seeking continual reassurance.

I-know-what-you're-thinking

We have examined some aspects of this pattern under the psychological label of mind reading. And in a sense it is a kind of mirror image of *to-know-me-is-to-love-me*.

For this strategy can also be founded upon the belief that closeness or concern means one person has the ability to know what is going on in another's mind. In this case, of course, the belief is held by the mind reader. But careful experiments have shown that even people who have very intimate relationships, and who earnestly believe that they can read the mind of a partner, actually score very low when they try to demonstrate this ability.

As we have seen, attempts to mind read can violate any of the sane rights. However, when clear information is not available, it is easy to see why there is a tendency to try to guess. And there are many situations in which such guessing is really necessary. For example, one sees the need for attempts at mind reading in competitive situations, from bargaining to tennis or poker.

And of course there is generally nothing crazymaking about situations in which one is merely trying to express a goodwill interest by attempting to remember preferences expressed in the past or anticipating what will please. Few people are put off by an observation such as "You like your coffee black, don't you?"

But *I-know-what-you're-thinking* is quite different. It is usually experienced as an attempt to invade one's inner space. So that even if the mind reader proves to be right—which is generally unlikely—the gambit makes one feel uncomfortable. A common reaction is "Don't guess. Ask me and then I'll tell you—if I want to."

A further reason for the discomfort produced by mind reading is that the guess usually appears to be based on scanty information or none at all. In fact it commonly ignores things one has said or done. And this gives the person whose mind is read a feeling that his reality has had little impact on the mind reader, that he is not being seen as he is, but in terms of some private fantasy which the mind reader holds. In this way one can feel cheated of one's identity, of one's individuality.

Mind reading tends to figure in so many different kinds of crazymaking patterns for the simple reason that crazymaking so often results in the communication of little clear information. The fogginess of the coded message of crazymaking can easily prompt one to mind read.

Indeed, we shall see that there is a sort of legitimate use of a kind of mind reading, as a way of forming hypotheses about another. But we shall see that a crucial aspect of this use is first to gain another's permission. In this way, rights of inner space are not violated. The right to privacy of thought or feeling is recognized and respected. And with this, mind reading can be relieved of its crazymaking effects.

Now-here's-what-I-want-you-to-think

It is probably obvious from the name of this pattern how it violates sane rights, and also how it is related to mind reading. In fact this pattern commonly violates almost all of the sane rights at the same time. Its exercise can produce a feeling akin to that of being trapped in a psychological concentration camp.

Earlier, we have described this phenomenon as mind raping. It is commonly an assertion of a person who has great power over another, as in the case of its use by parents with their children. For example: "You don't want to talk to little Sally, dear. You know her mom was very mean to your mom. She didn't invite her to the big party the other night."

Because *Now-here's-what-I-want-you-to-think* is so

blatant a violator of one's sane rights, we can draw some conclusions about the person who permits it. Such a person must either be trapped in a situation in which he or she feels quite helpless and powerless—as a child is trapped in the family. Or the person must be very aggression-phobic.

We can also draw some conclusions about the person who uses the pattern. For mind raping is not only a reminder and a display of one's power in a relationship, its use also tends to foster extreme dependency. For it robs the victim of decision making and forces him or her to turn to the mind raper whenever choices are to be made.

On the other hand, one tactic of crazymaking is to collude with mind raping, to treat it not only as acceptable, but as necessary. In this way extreme dependency can then be used as a weapon, as an ironic way of gaining some power in an unbalanced relationship—"I hope you aren't going to be mad at me, dear. I know you're right in the middle of the annual board meeting, and I just hated to call you out. But you know the Smiths are coming over for dinner, and you're the one who really knows them, so I thought I'd better ask you what would be right to have for dinner. You know—I don't want to make a mistake that will embarrass you or anything. And I thought maybe you'd have some idea about the wine; you always know the right thing."

This crazymaking use of extreme dependency, which may also be seen as a defensive form of counter-crazymaking, we might call *take-care-of-my-little-brain*. It has some readily identifiable purposes. It may be used as a tactic for driving back the mind raper, for creating some greater distance. It appears to become necessary when the mind raper has too much power, apparently, to be rejected directly. And the heavy dependency of *take-care-of-my-little-brain* may succeed by making the mind raper retreat in order to avoid being interrupted and annoyed by constant requests for help.

An understanding of this pattern and the way it works

as a counter-crazymaking defense suggests one of the ways in which we can use the effects of crazymaking for insight. For we can see that if you find a partner drives you crazy by asking for your opinion and your guidance about almost everything, you can suspect that you are doing some mind raping without being consciously aware of it. And you may also guess that you may be in various ways creating the effects of a relationship in which you play an overpowering role. You might do well to check yourself to see if you are depriving your partner of rights that have to do with separateness and independence.

I'm-only-doing-what-you-want-me-to-do

This is a vexing and upsetting pattern that draws upon the strategies of both mind reading and mind raping, but that really stands by itself in an especially insidious way. We have seen it operate before, under the name mind ripping. And it consists of behaving as though the other had expressed a wish:

HE: I was really sort of sorry to leave the party. I wasn't really ready to go.

SHE: Well, I only started to say goodnight because I knew you must be tired, and I even saw you yawn when you were talking to Herb Fenway.

HE: [*Irritably*] But everybody yawns when they talk to Herb Fenway.

SHE: But then why didn't you just *say* that you didn't want to leave?

HE: How could I? You were going around saying goodnight to Helen and Bob and everyone. I had to say goodnight, too.

SHE: Well, you could have asked me.

HE: No, I couldn't. Because then you would have thought that I didn't want to go, so even if you wanted to go, you would have thought we had to stay.

SHE: [*Defensively*] That's not true. I might have asked you if you really wanted to stay.

HE: But then if you did ask me, and I said yes, you would have felt you had to be agreeable and stick around so as not to spoil things for me. And I wouldn't have known whether you were really happy about staying or whether you really wanted to say no, but you thought—

Such a dialogue could go on almost endlessly. And it suggests the relationship between mind ripping and the nongenuine accommodation pattern of crazymaking. For the origins of mind ripping often lie in people's inability to get straight, dependable answers from one another.

But one underlying aspect of mind ripping is also that under the guise of guessing what the other person wants and then behaving as if the guess were correct, the mind ripper can actually do just what he or she wishes to do. The blame or the responsibility for what is done can then be placed upon the other. Commonly, the habitual mind ripper becomes very good at accumulating evidence that he or she has acted upon cues supplied by the other person.

The dialogue above also suggests how easily, and commonly, mind ripping is turned back on the person who initiates it. This is a common form of counter-crazymaking.

In this counter-ploy the mind ripper is allowed to act, to go out on a limb. In fact, he or she may even be set up to do just that. Then the mind ripping actions can be criticized as a wrong interpretation.

By this means counter-mind ripping can serve as a variation of *to-love-me-is-to-know-me*. That is, it becomes a devious way in which a demand is made for divining. It can be used this way even if the mind ripper fails to act. For then the mind ripper's partner can always say, "You must have known I was dead tired, yet you kept sticking around. Didn't you see me yawning when I was talking to Herb Fenway? I could hardly keep my eyes open. Anyone could have seen how anxious I was to go. But no, you had to be the last one to leave."

Come-into-my-parlor

This pattern of crazymaking is a member of a broad category, a strategy we sometimes characterize as *the setup operation*.

In this strategy one is invited indirectly, or perhaps enticed, into actions sure to fail some sort of test—of sensitivity, of concern for the other, or of some other quality or ability. The crazymaker is sure the other person will fail because he or she is going to do everything possible to guarantee the failure.

The most important purpose of *come-into-my-parlor* is usually to discourage efforts toward independent thought or action. And thus it is not hard to see that it is the tactic of a person who is in a dominant role and needs to remain in such a role. It is calculated to keep the subordinate person aware of his subordination and to convince him that he is not really ready or able to act on his own. For this reason, come-into-my-parlor is commonly a tactic of business employers or superiors, intended to assert their control and the necessity for that control. But it is also not uncommon for those who need to feel clearly dominant in more personal relationships.

We can see a classic use of come-into-my-parlor in the brief exemplary dialogue below:

Boss: Chip, I've got to go down to City Hall and get a permit. How would you like to paint that west wall by yourself today? Can you handle it?

Chip: [*Eager but a little scared*] Gee, boss, do you really think I'm ready to handle it on my own?

Boss: Well, I don't know for sure. But you've been working for me a long time and you've been getting pretty good. Not as good as you think you are, but not bad. Anyway, from what I hear from Joe, you must think you're ready to work on your own. He tells me you said you were going to start getting some of your own painting jobs on weekends, setting up for yourself.

Chip: [*Quickly*] Just small stuff. Just to earn a little extra money. No jobs that you'd want.

Boss: Well, it must mean you think you know all the

answers now, that you don't need me anymore. So let's see if you really know what you're talking about.

It should come as no surprise that when the boss returns, he is extremely critical of Chip's work. He shakes his head and can hardly stop complaining. "So you think you're ready to be a painting contractor on your own," says the boss. And then he tells Chip that the work is so badly done the wall will have to be repainted the next day at great expense.

Chip feels humiliated, defeated. And he feels angry. Since he cannot see just why he should be angry, he assumes that he must be angry with himself for failing. And the boss has accomplished just what he wished.

In fact Chip's anger has probably been triggered by the boss' crazymaking double message. On the one hand he feels that the boss has given him a trust, and with that trust a test. On the other hand he senses that he was set up to founder.

And Chip is right. Although the boss' behavior may have been unconscious, spurred by the fear that a valued employee might be getting ready to leave him and go out on his own, it is no less nefarious. For whether consciously or unconsciously, the boss neglected to give Chip the instructions he wanted him to follow.

Come-into-my-parlor has a number of applications in the retention of power. It may be used to define territory, to maintain a distance—but essentially it is a means to keeping someone in a subordinate role.

The usual message is "Now you can see why it is that *I* make the decisions around here, and you need me." And with this goes the corollary message, "Now that you see how tough my role is, you won't want it."

A fundamental aim is to reinforce another's dependency, to say, "You need me."

There is one good clue that this pattern is being used. It is that a person who has cherished his or her role of power suddenly steps back and says "Take over" with a minimum of information about what is expected.

The strategy is not unlike that of the karate instructor when he says, ''Now I'm just going to stand here with my hands at my sides. Would someone like to try to knock me down—to hit me as hard as they like?'' Anyone who volunteers should be able to guess what is going to happen.

Come-into-my-parlor often generates a stratagem of counter-crazymaking called *only-you-Dick-Daring*. Another name for it is *baiting*.

Baiting is a way in which a more powerful person can be set up in such a way that he is forced to overextend himself and then fail. It is a defensive tactic for a person who is being kept in the role of the weaker and dominated partner.

You can see the tactic operate, for example, when a small boy has been bullied into subordination by a bigger one. ''Whaddya mean,'' says the smaller boy to a friend, ''nobody could climb all the way to the top of that tree? I'll bet Mike could,'' he says, referring to the bigger boy. ''*You* could do it, couldn't you, Mike?''

One basic purpose of only-you-Dick-Daring is to make the dominating crazymaker pay a price for his power. The hope is that this will cause him to restrain his dominance in the future. The tactic is a slice of humble pie in the case of the two boys. But it can also be the weight of extra responsibility, as:

''You remember how the last time I took the car in for service, dear, you were so mad because they fooled me about all those things I didn't understand? Well, it needs service again. And I'll bet if you took it in for me they'd have to watch their Ps and Qs. They can't fool around with you. You'd know just what really had to be done and just how much it ought to cost.''

The sky-is-falling

This is a crazymaking strategy for having impact when one feels ignored. It can also be classified as *crisismaking*.

A primary purpose of *the-sky-is-falling* is to achieve this desired impact without actually seeming responsible for it. When one accepts this gambit—which depends upon creating a tense, upsetting, confusing sense of emergency—one is led to believe that the crisis has arisen by itself, that the partner has nothing to do with it.

The-sky-is-falling serves another purpose as well. For the crisis state is demanding. It does not permit time or attention for the impact of others' personal wishes or assertions.

Politically, this has been an ancient strategy for foreclosing individual rights and thus holding power. It is a favorite gambit of tyrants, who commonly use war or the threat of war as an issue so demanding that individual concerns must be set aside. It is always promised that rights will be restored as soon as the emergency is over. But once a person has grasped crisis-making as a route to attention and power, somehow there is always a crisis.

An example of successful crisismaking can be seen in a young lawyer who becomes a corporate counsel. His title is important but the work is dull. He soon learns that all the interesting problems go to an outside legal firm, that he is being kept on hand for legal drudgery only, and is largely ignored except for checking minor contracts and making threatening noises about overdue accounts.

The young man is invited to staff meetings as a courtesy, but no one addresses any questions to him. He just sits. It drives him crazy. He has a prestigious job but with no sense of real importance.

Then one day, as he sits feeling bored and useless in such a meeting, he gets an idea. A new product is being discussed. "Excuse me," he pipes up, "but you know a product like this has a terrific chance of inviting liability suits, don't you—especially big class-action suits."

All eyes turn to him. Although the possibility is real, deep down he knows that it is remote. Nevertheless, as he gets attention he begins to expand on the risks. His impact is gratifying. And from that day he begins to specialize in manufacturing legal pitfalls, to begin to use his threats of crisis to invade everything from research to advertising. The corporate officers suspect he is dramatizing, but they don't want to take the risk of ignoring him, since there is never anything less than a million-dollar suit in the crises that he projects as possible. In no time at all the lawyer becomes a thorn in the corporate side, a kind of company crazymaker who has to be tolerated.

Crisismaking is often a strategy of the expert. For often no one else can tell much about how genuine a crisis in a specialized field may be. It's hard to ignore the doctor when he says mysteriously, "Hmmm. Have you ever had an electrocardiogram?" It's hard to ignore the plumber when he says, "Look at the rust on that vent pipe. Have any idea what will happen if that lets go?" Of course you have no idea. And it is hard to resist the attention demanded.

On the more homely side, a husband is helping his wife by vacuuming. "Look," he says, "this really doesn't take much time at all. Why do you say it takes so much time?"

"Well, of course," says his wife, "the way *you* do it. You know, when you move the machine fast like that it can't pick up the deep-down dirt. And sometimes the drive belt pops, and then try and find a new one."

In this exchange the threat of crisis serves a couple of purposes. It is used to protect territory and to establish the wife's importance as an expert in vacuuming. And it also adds anxiety, so that the territorial invasion becomes an uncomfortable experience unlikely to be repeated. Fathers often use this technique in giving long instructions, full of warnings, to the teenager who wants to borrow the car, creating an anxiety that may push the youngster back.

One of the signs you are caught in the tactic of *the-sky-is-falling* is that routine situations are repeatedly turned into experiences of tension, as in: "You're tending to ride the clutch, honey. Do you know what it costs to replace a clutch lining in a sports car like this? Try to keep the clutch in mind every time you shift." Another sign of the pattern is that the tension you feel is accompanied by a buzz of rising anger. This anger suggests you are somehow perceiving that although threats of crisis may seem legitimate, somehow the situation always makes you feel helpless and forces you to become dependent upon the knowledge or skills of another. For the crisis is being used to cheat you of your individual rights.

Let-me-help-you-or-else

This is another of the most common and broad of the crazymaking stratagems. Another term for it is *Red-Cross-nursing*. Its essence is to manufacture a need for help, which may be real or bogus, but which only you can meet.

In some respects *let-me-help-you-or-else* approaches the tactics of *the-sky-is-falling*. The two are differentiated primarily by their central effects. For *the-sky-is-falling* seems mainly to aim at enhancing the impact of the crazymaker and weakening the impact of his partner. *Let-me-help-you-or-else* is addressed more to creating dependency. When its code is translated, it generally reads: "I am very dependent on staying or becoming central in your life. I want to cripple you, to prove to you at every opportunity that you urgently need me."

The open side of the double message in this pattern is a great show of caring and protectiveness. But the indirect message is that the other is incompetent, so that disaster may follow if a dependent role is not accepted. "Here, let me do that, dear," says the husband, taking away the small nail and the hammer she holds. "These thin nails fold over really easily, and you can really mash a finger."

Much of the anger one hears in the women's movement is rooted in the common male use of Red-Cross-nursing. For beneath the protective surface is a hard statement of incompetence. It is not surprising that as so many women become aware of the tactic and its inner meaning, they have assertively begun to learn to change tires, shingle roofs, and mix cement. It is equally understandable that many such women have become very defensive in such circumstances, ready to bristle at the first sign of such nongenuine coddling. As one woman put it when a headwaiter struggled awkwardly to help her with her chair, "It's going to be a lot easier on both of us if we accept the fact that I can sit down all by myself."

Courtliness has its useful role. But both good manners and love are suspect when their exercise ends by depriving anyone of sane rights. And *Red-Cross-nursing* is, ironically, destructive to both partners. For exaggerated dependencies cost both partners their independence. The "patient" in accepting the tactic feels helpless and hopelessly bound to the "nurse." And the "nurse" feels heavily encumbered by the dependency thus created; it gradually forces him or her to become preoccupied with the possible needs of the "patient" and deprives the "nurse" of legitimate concerns with his or her own wishes and welfare.

The double bind of all crazymaking is especially troubling in *let-me-help-you-or-else*. If you accept the proffered help, you sacrifice your ability to think and do for yourself. If you resist the help, there is the or-else. In part this is the threat of what may go wrong, and in part it is the rejection of the other's caring gestures—which is likely to trigger hurt feelings, depression, and possibly a wounded anger.

A number of counter-crazymaking reactions to this pattern also emerge. Out of fear of the or-else, the "patient" accepts the nursing care on the surface, perhaps playing a role of *helpless-little-me*. This may be accompanied by an overloading of dependencies, similar to *take-care-of-my-little-brain*. Or another kind of coded message, aimed at creating distance, may be sent.

I-did-what-you-said-and-now-look is the name we give this defense against *Red-Cross-nursing*. In this tactic the surface submission is used to make the "nurse" responsible for everything that goes wrong, since he or she is calling all the shots. In fact, this tactic may be extended to include setups in which the helper is over his head when he tries to help—so that he becomes an unsuccessful amateur TV repairman, psychiatrist, financial adviser, or what-have-you.

These defenses against *let-me-help-you-or-else* often culminate in a tactic of *who's-going-to-pay-for-the-damage-now?* It is not hard to guess. And when *Red-Cross-nursing* goes far enough, the "nurse" can end by hopelessly trying to compensate the "patient" for all the mishaps and misfortunes of life.

I-will-explain-you-to-you

This pattern, also known as *analysis*, means, sadly, just what it says. One person sets himself up—on the basis of caring, knowing, and objectivity—to explain an intimate's feelings, actions, and motives. If the tactic succeeds, the analyst acquires great power.

HE: I feel very irritable tonight. I think I'd like to be by myself.

SHE: I suppose you talked to your mother today.

HE: Well—yes. But this has nothing to do with my mother. If you must know, I'm really bugged by the way you—

SHE: Well, you should know by now how you get after you've talked to your mother. You feel as if I bug you because she sends you into your macho bit, in which all women bug you. That's why you picked a fight with me just now, tricking me into saying things to make you angry.

HE: Look, I don't need you to tell me what I—

SHE: I'm just telling you what I see. I mean, I can see you objectively. How can you see yourself? And I'll bet what you're bugged about is that she got you to pay that hospital bill for her.

HE: Well, I did say I'd pay it. But it was my own idea.

SHE: You *think* it was your own idea. But she knows you—how giving and protective you are. It kills me to see how people take advantage of you. And all you ask is a little love.

HE: [*Melting a little and wanting to accept the flattery, so that he must also accept the analysis which yields it*] I guess I'm pretty easy. I guess you know how easy I am.

SHE: Yes, I know—better than anyone.

HE: [*His arms around her*] I love you.

SHE: See—and you thought you wanted to be alone.

The payoffs of submitting to *I-will-explain-you-to-you* are clear. In addition to avoiding the conflict that might arise out of resisting the analysis, it almost always ends in finding laudable values in the analyzed person. And it can be hard to resist getting strokes from those we value.

A closely related tactic is *attribution*. This is attributing motives to another, on little evidence. In its most innocent form it may evaluate another's qualities in the first flush of infatuation, as: "You're a fantastic lover. So considerate."

This is ego-building. But one must now work hard to live up to the attribution. One must keep the titles of Superlover and Superconsiderate. And one must also accept the analysis of one's motives along with these titles. For example:

"You don't want to marry me only because you're afraid—afraid that I'll treat you like your mother treated your father. You say I make you feel smothered. But you have no reason to say that, do you?"

In the end, *attribution* and *I-will-explain-you-to-you* become much the same thing, with the person who accepts the pattern becoming much what he is told he is, because this is how he begins to feel. Such tactics are often used with children. Tell a child he or she is "lovable but clumsy" and the child will tend to be just that.

These tactics often make a person feel nongenuine. For his inner feelings probably do not really quite match what he is told they are. And the reaction to this is likely to be a kind of inner retreat in which the person seeks out something that is his own and safe from the analyzing other. It may be a secret dream or a secret love affair, but it is a space he can call his own.

Two patterns that may be used to defend against such invasive crazymaking, and which can become crazymaking in themselves, are *ace-in-the-hole* and *secret alliance*. In fact, they may appear as responses to a variety of crazymaking tactics that are overpowering or controlling.

Ace-in-the-hole establishes a concealed base of psychological support. Tom uses it to help him maintain his marriage with Nina. He is very dependent on her. But she is very invasive and controlling. To endure his wife's crazymaking control over him, Tom uses a lady at his office named Donna.

When Tom assures Nina that she is the center of his life, he means it. Yet he needs the affair with Donna, on whom he is not so centrally dependent and with whom he can therefore risk expressing his aggression. For example, it is for this reason that most of the sex in his life, and the most satisfying sex, takes place with Donna, not in the marriage bed.

This still, however, leaves Tom with another psychological requirement—that of someone to share deep feelings with. For, of course, he cannot be fully open with either his wife or Donna. So Tom forms a secret alliance with his friend Ned. Only Ned knows how Tom really feels, among other things, about the two women.

How are these patterns crazymaking? Both Nina and Donna are led to believe that Tom's emotional center is with them. And yet both are aware that Tom withholds from them. Both press him to talk more about how he feels. And both are left with uneasy doubts about how important they really are to him.

Thinging

The effects of this endlessly variable crazymaking pattern, discussed in Chapter Seven, can be crushing. For it causes a person to feel like an object. And this depersonalization strips away all sane rights in a single harsh stroke.

A certain amount of thinging in casual relationships is inevitable and harmless. The telephone operator and the caller, the cashier and the customer, the driver and the traffic cop, may all see one another merely in terms of their function, much like machines.

On the other hand, at any moment any of these people may need to be recognized as a person. And in that moment of need they expect to be so recognized. If a passenger on a jumbo jet says to the stewardess, "Miss, I think I'm going to throw up," he cannot accept the bland, no-impact smile that goes with her seeing him merely as The Thing in Seat 22B, and the mechanical response: "Coffee, tea, or milk?"

In fact, one airline maintains that it proves to be the most favored among frequent travelers partly because it trains stewardesses that a personalized "passenger contact" must be made with each person aboard. By and large people require being seen as individuals and as whole.

It can be unbearably crazymaking to be thinged by someone who is supposed to see us as important. It can produce much anxiety if your doctor comes to see you before performing surgery and can't remember your name.

Kris, who works in an ad agency, has been given the chance by her boss to write an agency proposal. Proudly, she goes all out, even working on it weekends. On deadline day she delivers it.

Her boss flips through the proposal quickly and then says, "Nice job, honey. You know, I've been meaning to have a talk with you. You stand out from the other junior account girls."

Kris puffs up. "I do my best, Mr. Tennyson."

"I thought I told you to call me Alf." He smiles. "We're all just people in this office, you know."

"I'll remember that, Alf."

"Anyway, I've thought you and I might work well in a closer relationship. We seem to share some ideas—laugh at the same things. And there's something special about you. So how would you like a little closer teamwork—special title as my assistant, travel with me, meet people, learn the ropes?"

Kris is surprised and excited by the idea. "That sounds wonderful," she tells him.

"Good. We'll have some great times together, I know. I promise you." He rises to see her from his office and puts an arm around her. Then his hand slips to her buttock. "Yes, you're really special. Talented and the cutest, sexiest little girl we've had around here in years."

Suddenly Kris' expectations are dashed in confusion. The hand on her bottom and the "cutest little girl" remark disappoint her expectation that she is being recognized for her work, depriving her of pride. Badly hurt and angry, the next day she starts looking for another job.

No degree of intimacy is a guarantee against thinging, especially the aspect we call *stereotyping*. A common example, maddening for many women, is to be called "Mom" by their husbands. The single word can be a maddening double message. For while it openly seems to declare a loving attitude, it also stamps the woman in terms of her role. A woman who is "Mom" to a man is not very likely to feel like his lover.

A common variant of thinging is *segmentation*. While stereotyping encases a person in a role and sees him or her as that role, segmentation has much the same effect by viewing a person as one *aspect* of him or herself.

Gary, for example, is a good student. He also has a lively sense of comedy, to which he gives play. But when he calls on his major professor to talk about doing doctoral work, he receives a dismaying sort of reaction.

The professor lowers his glasses in surprise. "Well, I don't know, Gary." He clears his throat uncomfortably. "You know, psychology is pretty serious business, especially in the clinical practice. You're a capable young man of course, and you do your work, but—well, it strikes me that you like to get a lot of fun out of life."

"Sure, I enjoy a little humor."

"Exactly. So I wonder if you shouldn't consider a little aptitude testing. I'll bet you'd be a splendid salesman, for example, engaging, humorous. Or you'd probably do well in your own small business. But psychology? Our business is dealing with human pain, you know."

Gary bites his tongue, but the interview makes him furious. For he has been seen segmentally. His charm and humor have become *him* in the professor's mind.

And this has led to the unfounded assumption that he may lack sensitivity or empathy with sorrow. Meanwhile, he gathers from some of the teacher's remarks, those of his fellow students who look pale and earnest and unsmiling are assumed to have more feeling.

The crazymaking effects of any form of thinging are demoralizing in the extreme. One can ill afford to try to tolerate such effects for long without real ego damage.

Unreliable contact

This is a large family of crazymaking tactics, which derives from a basic requirement of all interpersonal relationships. That requirement is to set an *optimal psychological distance* between the partners.

By this distance we mean a degree of closeness that can be expressed in many ways. Each of us is different in the degrees of closeness we desire or can tolerate. A distance that one person sees as stiflingly close and intrusive may feel like remoteness to another, perhaps even like withdrawal and withholding.

For the very reason that an optimal distance in a relationship is so important to virtually everyone, there is often a great deal of fear involved in the aggressive impulse to move closer (which may threaten to appear to another as an invasion) or to move back (which may look like rejection). And so it is sadly common for people to express their wishes for nearer or further distance indirectly, by any number of crazymaking tactics. These tactics all profess to agree to the distance the other wants or is believed to want. But in fact, crazymaking patterns are being used to keep the other at the distance desired by the person using the tactics. Let us examine some ways in which this is done.

Hide-and-seek, already mentioned, is a tactic in which one acts by not acting. That is, one deals with the distancing problem by *not* dealing with it. One forces the other person to make all the assertions. In this way one remains a mystery, and a mystery who cannot be blamed or criticized for anything. This is a way of denying the rights of impact, however, and of clear information, and thus becomes crazymaking. This failure to act tends to push the other away. How it works can be seen quite clearly in one of its variations, *the-silent-treatment*.

So effective is silence in challenging another to try to have impact, and to take all the responsibility for the interactions, that it became one of the early methods of psychological therapy. Silence forces a person to resort to his own inner stimuli and thus reveal much of himself.

In crazymaking, *the-silent-treatment* avoids risk. It deals with fears of aggression by making the other person take all the risks of assertion or else make no open demands.

Yep-and-nope is a derivative of *the-silent-treatment*. And while it may make for lovable movie cowboys, it does not make for a lovable intimate. For the emotional context of one's reactions is not expressed. So a yep may mean "Yes, I want to," or it may really mean "If you insist, I'll go along."

All of these tactics force the other into a tension state of hunting for clues. A grunt or a noncommital "OK" are maddening answers to any number of questions, from "Was the lovemaking good for you?" to "Is your steak done all right?"

Now-you-see-me-now-you-don't is another important form of crazymaking by unreliable contact. A simple fact of relationships is that they are not really continuous, but consist of a long series of exits and entrances. People go in and out of one another's lives if only in such conventional ways as departures to and arrivals from work, shopping, and all the other ordinary business of living.

Part of the arrangement of optimal distances between people is expressed by these entrances and exits. For plainly, when a relationship is important, one factor that is relied upon is that the other, no matter what the nature of his or her departure, will return. In this context the renewal of contact must be reliable. The expectation of renewal must have some dependable parameters.

As it is whenever we find an important expectation in

relationships, we also find fertile ground for crazy-making. And indeed, many a confusing double message is sent concerning entries and exits. Keeping another in suspense with uncertain exits and entrances is a powerful way to madden.

The person who practices *now-you-see-me-now-you-don't* tactics is usually exercising a crazymaking way of getting the distance wanted from his or her partner. A casual "Didn't I say I was going to have to go to the office this Saturday?" or an "I'm sure I told you that I was going to have to spend a week in Cleveland" can be quite upsetting.

It is hard to rely upon someone as central in your life, or to feel that you are central in his or hers, when you are not obtaining clear information about future exits and entrances. And even minor kinds of arrivals and departures can be used for crazymaking tactics. For example, Penny has finally decided that she must confront John about his repeated *now-you-see-me-now-you-don't* behavior. And they have begun to talk about it—he quite evasively—when the phone rings.

For twenty minutes he chats casually with a friend about business, football, and a variety of things. When he finally returns, it is obvious Penny is angry because she has been put off. "Well, I couldn't just hang up on him, could I? I mean, I could see that he wanted to talk."

Penny stifles her resentment at this. Then, as soon as she resumes the touchy subject, John suddenly stands up. "Listen, I'm sorry. But you'll have to excuse me for a minute. I have to go to the bathroom." Penny bridles when he stops to pick up a copy of the *Reader's Digest* on the way.

When he returns some minutes later, they start again, but now John begins to yawn and look at his watch. "I'm sorry," he apologizes sweetly, "but it's been such a long day and I'm just bushed. Go ahead—what were you saying?"

Choking down great irritation, Penny suggests that perhaps she ought to make some coffee for them. John says this is a fine idea as she leaves for the kitchen.

When she comes back, he is fast asleep in his easy chair. For sleep, too, is another way to exit. And it too can feel like a crazymaking way to create distance, as anyone knows who has been made to feel livened and affectionate by a nice orgasm only to see his or her partner fade away into sleep.

In many ways the reliability of contact can be almost a measure of the intimacy of a relationship. And it can also be an important clue to a person's *style* of relating. For example, the moment of exit is often seen as a safer time to express a strong aggressive feeling which one has repressed. For one can either delay if such expression proves too safe or escape quickly if it looks to have been hazardous. This style is revealed in the person whose most meaningful conversation of the evening comes with a hand on the doorknob, or when he or she delivers meaningful information followed by a quick departure. A fearful and manipulative style of dealing with inter-personal distance may be revealed in the person who distracts us as he or she departs, leaving vague any arrangement for re-entry in the future. "Let's get together for lunch," or "See you," or "Next time we'll really talk this out" are perfectly acceptable con-ventions of casual relationships. But when one of the partners really depends upon the relationship, such vagueness, such unreliability of future contact, can be deeply disrupting. And upsetting, anxiety-making exits and entrances are often signs of crazymaking attempts to control without discussion the distance in a rela-tionship. Such one-sided control tends to indicate a crazymaking power-grab.

The feeling that such control conveys is often "He is never there when I need him." And if this is truly so, then one is probably dealing with a person who wishes quite a remote distance but is afraid to say so openly.

Perhaps the extreme of all distancing maneuvers is what we call *Houdini*, after the famed escape artist. And the Houdini practitioner is certainly good at escaping. In all probability he is so good because he wishes, indeed can tolerate, only the greatest of dis-tances, perhaps approaching a kind of emotional isolation. The *Houdini* act is typical of the pattern we call *autonomy worship*, the goal of which seems to be to enter into no relationship requiring a commitment that might control one's life in any way.

Often, this escape artist of crazymaking seems very quick to go along with implied or direct demands for closeness. He or she may rapidly become involved with another, in seeming depth, allowing the other to believe that the relationship is likely to be a long and important one. And then suddenly, with or without explanation, slip out of the bond. He or she may not only escape, but vanish.

For unlike most people the practitioners of the *Houdini* art feel little pain in quick exits. And they feel little guilt. These easy escapes are probably made possible by the fact that those who follow this pattern usually prefer to live in an autonomous way. So it becomes hard for them to identify with people who are upset by the sudden disappearance of another from their lives. If a behavior by someone else would not bother you very much, it is hard to understand why other people would be driven crazy by it.

In looking at crazymaking of the *unreliable contact* theme, it is important to make one fundamental distinction along these lines. It is important to try to determine whether the distancing effects you feel represent attempts to be autonomous or to keep a much greater distance in a relationship than is rewarding for you—or whether the effects are the result of attempts by a person who does want closeness but wants to be in control of the distance, so that it can be adjusted at pleasure. When the case is the latter, there is a much better basis for trying to work out optimal distancing through open assertions and clear negotiation. Moreover, in such a situation you may be able to learn much by looking honestly at your own distancing behaviors.

What, you may well ask yourself, has touched off an indirect and crazymaking style of distancing in your partner? Could it possibly relate to unconscious crazymaking behavior of your own—invading his or her space or perhaps trying to bring the distance closer or set it further apart according to your own wishes of the moment? For like almost all crazymaking patterns, those involving distancing are likely to trigger counter-crazymaking, usually in the same arena of avoided conflict.

Carrot-dangling

In this pattern a promise is held out, a future expectation is created. But there is a requisite, a requirement that must be satisfied before the promise is fulfilled, before the carrot is handed over. Just what the requirement represents is usually kept somewhat vague. But somehow it is never met. The carrot dangles but stays out of reach.

Such tantalizing also usually includes allowing the other person to have an occasional nibble, a now-and-then taste of the promised reward, to preserve interest. For animal experiments show clearly, and human psychology confirms, that the best way to guarantee a behavior is to give occasional small rewards but to deny the reward most of the time. It is probably this psychological truth, more than any other, that keeps the Las Vegas casinos and the pari-mutuel windows so well supplied with cash. It is much of the allure of habitual gambling.

Carrot-dangling builds crazymaking dreams. The employee is led to believe that if he holds on just a little longer he will win a bigger job. The occasional sleeping partner is led to believe that in time this may lead to a stable, long-term relationship.

Often a component of carrot-dangling is the tactic *if-only-I-didn't-have-to*. This clause can be filled in with an infinity of chronic problems, from the need to take care of Mother before marrying to the need to get the children into college before divorcing; from the need to work overtime that keeps Daddy away from his children to the need to reach any number of intermediate goals before the carrot can be delivered. There is always a light at the end of the tunnel, yet the end is never quite reached.

Those who tolerate *carrot-dangling* must, in a sense, enter into collusion with the crazymaking. For the hope is held out and then withdrawn too often to be realistic.

After a certain time, the tolerators of *carrot-dangling* have a right to demand some clear and finite information, to take the hope out of the territory of the never-never. In some instances we must conclude that a special kind of counter-crazymaking has become rewarding for the tolerator. It is, perhaps, a route to power, a power that he or she earns by putting up with the unending disappointments and delays. For the person who dangles the carrot can see what is happening and can easily be made to feel guilt and obligation. The double message of this crazymaking is the collusive impression that the tolerator really continues to believe that one day the carrot can be collected, whereas the true realization, sometimes unconscious, is that it will never be.

Derailing

We have seen derailing in action before, in Chapter Six, and so we can see that it serves as a means to avoid another's aggressions.

The essence of derailing technique is to keep the other from arriving at his or her conversational objective— much as a small object correctly placed can cause a train to go off its track. This is commonly a technique of a person who feels that he or she may be overpowered by the other's force or cleverness.

When one has something one urgently wishes to communicate, even a yawn or a cough can be enough to derail. Or one may have built a careful chain of logic toward a point, only to hear at the final crucial moment, "Did you remember to fill the dog's water dish?"

In crazymaking terms, probably the essential effect, other than simple frustration, is the denial of impact. Derailing can occur at all levels of communication. It happens when someone laughs before you tell the punch line of a joke. It happens when someone says a seemingly well-meant "Good luck" just as you draw back for a golf swing. It happens when you have reached a pitch of sexual excitement and your partner asks, "Did you hear something downstairs?"

Overloading

Overloading is another tactic we have seen in operation. It is also capable of many variations. In essence it is a matter of supplying more information than can be used or dealt with at the time it is given. For example, it can produce the reaction, usually unexpressed, "Will you please stop arguing? I keep telling you that you've won." And in a somewhat different context it can make one want to say, "You're giving me so many directions that I don't know what to do!" Or perhaps it is bad timing that produces the overload. Linda is hurrying frantically about the kitchen in the last phases of preparing Thanksgiving dinner. She is checking the pie crust for doneness, basting the turkey a last time, trying to get the cranberry jelly out of the mold, and more. Her husband, Luke, enters. "What do you think?" he asks. "Norman tells me that he can help us get a second mortgage on the house for half a percentage point less than we were going to pay. Now the problem is that there'll be bigger monthly payments, but no balloon payment at the end, and the loan fee is only half a point, and—"

It is not hard to see why such overload crazymaking is maddening, simply because one can deal with only so much to think about. What is more obscure is the purpose.

One may be to cause someone to fail at a task, as when a teacher gives so many instructions about details that the central point is lost and the student cannot perform the basic task being taught. Ifs, ands, or buts can become so numerous that one merely becomes confused and paralyzed.

Overloading with trivia may have another purpose. In many cases it is intended to force another person out of desperation to try to point out what is the central issue for us or perhaps to take responsibility for a decision that really ought to be our own. "A drink with lunch?" asks Hal. "Gee, I'd like one. But this early in the day? I guess a lot of those expense-account guys do that. Except I've got Mrs. Anderson coming into the office, and you know how she is about drinking. Of course, if it was vodka, she wouldn't be able to tell, would she? And then, too, I guess you could say this is sort of a special day, isn't it? And—''

This goes on until Hal's companion finally says, ''Just have the drink, Hal. It's all right.''

Of course this leaves a later crazymaking opening. For Hal can say, ''I wish you hadn't insisted on my having that drink at lunch. I mean, I felt I had to go along, and—''

Conversely, other examples of what look like inadvertent *overloading*, perhaps through bad timing—as in consulting Linda about the loan when she is swamped with the details of her Thanksgiving dinner—can be used to get the response ''For heaven's sake, *you* decide! Whatever you want to do. Just let me get the dinner on.''

Again, this provides a later out. ''Well, I explained the whole thing to you,'' Linda's husband can say. ''If you didn't like it, you could have said so. But you didn't want any part of it. You told me to go ahead and decide.''

Underloading and the transference-trap

If *overloading* is one way of being able to do what one wants to do, and especially without having to take full responsibility for it, *underloading* is another. The art of underloading is simply the giving of too little information to enable the other person to make clear choices or perhaps to carry out a responsibility.

Underloading can involve a number of other crazymaking patterns. *Divining* is a kind of *underloading* tactic. The set-up-operation can also use underloading to help produce failure. *Underloading* is often carried out under a cloak of being easygoing, as in ''Go on and take the boat out by yourself. You've seen how I start the engine.'' But the casualness disappears when on his return the amateur boat operator botches the untutored difficulties of docking.

We have also seen another kind of *underloading* in such distancing and withdrawing tactics as *the-silent-treatment* and *yep-and-nope*. But these techniques of withholding reaction may have insidious kinds of crazymaking effects, quite different from those we have seen.

An example is the *transference-trap*. This is often used without the person who uses it realizing why it is rewarding for him. For undercommunication can have some subtle results. Early in modern psychological experimentation, Freud found that if he revealed little of himself and minimized his reactions to what his patients said, they began to treat him as a kind of blank symbol. They would fill in that blank with important images from their own minds.

More specifically, he learned that his patients projected onto his silent image their own mental images of others important in their lives, particularly their parents. Today we know that anyone's continued silence can elicit such feelings. And they can become extremely difficult and troublesome for both partners. In other words, in such crazymaking, problems may develop that neither partner really wants or can handle.

"When he goes into his silent routine," one woman says, "after a while I feel as if I'm in the presence of my mother. It makes me anxious and really uncomfortable. Then a lot of the time, he wants to make love. And seeing the image of my mother in him, I feel as if I just can't. Or if I give in and do it, it's really awful. It feels as if my mother is watching—you know, with those disapproving eyes of hers. I just have to try and grit my teeth and not think until he gets it over with."

If we can learn something from these unhappy, inadvertent results of crazymaking, it is that the human mind and heart are delicate instruments. Manipulating them with crazymaking can be as hazardous as trying to do home experiments with viruses.

Context-switching

This pattern can be seen as a sort of relative of derailing. We have seen it before, in its primary role as a crazymaking way of depriving another of impact.

Context-switching is accomplished by shifting a discussion out of its original format, its original milieu, and transferring it to some other subject. It is commonly used to change an argument into a less toxic arena. For example, Alicia's husband is furious because he has discovered she has been having an affair with their next-door neighbor. Alicia is aware that she cannot defend the affair itself, so as her husband tries to talk about the matter, she continually shifts the context. She asks defensively, "Well, what do you expect when you're out of town half the time? I didn't think I was marrying a half-time husband. You keep saying you're going to travel less. You've been saying it for years. But just you look at our tax records. Every year you travel more. And do you realize all the extra money you spend when you're traveling—money you can't charge off on your expense account? I mean, do you realize when the last time was that I bought a dress that wasn't on sale?"

And so on. In many ways, *context-switching* provides a means by which one can move from a conversational territory in which one is vulnerable to a context in which one's partner is vulnerable. And often its crazymaking effect stems from the disappointment of an expectation that one will be undeniably right. Often its defensive value is that it shifts the roles of good guy and bad guy. And this is most convenient. For in almost any relationship, each partner is both wronging and wronged.

Gaslighting

The pattern takes its name from a film in which one star deliberately sought crazymaking effects by trying to convince the other star that what she *thought* she perceived (a mysterious dimming and brightening of the gaslights) was purely illusory on her part, that her perceptions were not valid. The essential purpose is usually to convince partners not to object to certain behaviors, since the partner may not be perceiving these behaviors correctly.

SHE: [*Greeting him at the door*] You got a bill today. From the Starlight Motel. In Springfield, Illinois. It's a bill for a *double* room.
HE: So?
SHE: Damn it, who were you fucking in Springfield?
HE: Well, I was sharing the room with Jeff, from our

Chicago office. But I didn't fuck him because he has this really ticklish mustache. Maybe you should call him and ask him if I did.

SHE: You know perfectly well I can't call your Chicago salesman.

HE: You could if you really had to. Maybe it would teach you to stop jumping to conclusions. Of course, it would make a fool out of me in the company. Maybe that's what you really want—to get me thrown out of my job. [*Then, quietly, he smiles a little as he recalls what a little tigress Beth really was in Springfield.*]

Gunnysacking

The fear of aggression leads almost inevitably to the storing up of the expression of grievances one has feared to express in direct ways. We have repeatedly seen that strong repressed feelings must eventually be expressed. Eventually the small wounds collected in the gunnysack must finally burst out.

Just as the proverbial straw breaks the camel's back, it is hard to predict when one irritation too many will cause someone's gunnysack to burst, to result in a tirade that may seem utterly inappropriate to the present circumstances.

The result is a kind of crazymaking shock, as when a husband explodes and his wife replies, "For God's sake—all I said was, would you mind picking Tommy up at school on your way home from work! He's rehearsing for the senior play. And suddenly I get all this stuff about how you do your job and I'm always expecting you to do my job, too. What's going on?"

The gunnysack may also serve as kind of museum of past injuries, one that can serve in such crazymaking patterns as *context-switching*. As an example, it can be hard to make a point about the size of a charge account when the opening gunnysack recalls a forgotten birthday three years ago, the time when a trip to the beach had to be canceled, and an obscene gesture one made to a truck driver on the freeway last month.

Sexual crazymaking

This is really not so much a pattern for crazymaking as it is a sensitive field in which various tactics can often be played out most easily. The inherent difficulties of sorting out crazymaking tactics as they are displayed in sexuality are really the results of the fact that sex is actually only another means of interaction between people.

Sex is so susceptible to the crazymaking style, however, largely because it incorporates so many split feelings, so many divisions between impulses and taboos. Thus the sexual playing out of the crazymaking style may be deceptively concealed in sexual behaviors. We are used to conflicting emotions in this arena. We seek at once to be close through sexuality and to be free, to be both gently kind and assertively blunt, to feel that we belong, yet not to be possessed. Above all, we fear as the most poignant of total rejections the rejection of openly expressed sexual impulses.

Thus, the expression of sexual wishes, hamstrung by convention and taboo, is cautious, often coded, often tentative. Virtually every question about fantasies and desires may be booby-trapped with implications. It is fair game for any interpretation that the other might care to make.

What is practically certain is that when the crazymaking style exists in a relationship, it will be exhibited in sex, either through a behavior that spells reluctance or rejection, or through an interpretation that can make normal sexual curiosity, normal sexual exploration, into pathology.

Teasing

Much like sexuality, playful teasing is likely to be a part of any relationship. But there is a fundamental question about teasing, for it is the product of double messages. The question is, are these conflicting messages sent in playfulness or as an acceptable substitute for openly hostile aggression?

The answer lies in the inner motives of the teaser, which cannot and should not be guessed at. And the judgment must be made in terms of the feelings of the teased. If teasing feels like an indirect way of stating an objectionable truth, then it may be so. If when a husband says, "Laurie thinks that if you charge things you're not really spending money," and if this feels like an accusation, then it quite well may be true. For the very impression of truth is likely to be perceived, not from another's vision, but from one's own.

On the other hand, while in this way, one may be receiving critical feedback of a genuine kind, one may be certain that it is not truly justified. What may be missing is clear information for the other, a clear message about why and how one uses charge accounts. Honest consultation with one's own feelings is necessary before one responds honestly.

If teasing has its realities in another's feelings, it may really be a question rather than an accusation. And in this case what is required is not defensiveness but honest response about what you really feel. A teasing request for valid information is still a real request. Meeting it with reality accomplishes far more than meeting it with angry self-defense, and is likely to help stop the crazymaking of teasing.

The tyranny of trivia

When we look closely at crazymaking, it is hard to avoid concluding at some point that we live in a crazymaking world. And certainly not all the crazymaking experiences of our lives are personal ones. It can be useful, and even important, to recognize that a certain amount of crazymaking simply derives from living in a complex and imperfect society.

Consider how many trivial crazymaking experiences we are exposed to in an ordinary day. The morning newspaper that describes the world and what is happening in it is full of crazymaking—wasteful spending of our money by those who are supposed to be our governmental caretakers, pointless killings by terrorists, needless suffering and disease.

We phone Information to obtain a number that is not in the phone book and are forced first to listen to a recording asking if we have tried looking it up there. On the more personal level, too, there is a constant barrage of trivial crazymaking incidents that seem to be just part of life. Someone has used the hammer but has not put it back where it belongs. Someone has driven the car and mislaid the keys. Someone has left the oven on overnight. And what is sometimes very crazymaking, the someone may turn out to be us.

We go into a supermarket, as nonsmokers, and end up in a long checkout line with a chain-smoker who ignores the "Please Don't Smoke" sign. Or, as smokers, we are caught in a meeting in a school building in which smoking is not permitted. We walk down the street and step on a lump of gum dropped right next to a trash container. The new no-iron shirt comes out of the wash a hopeless mass of wrinkles. And so on and on.

What should we do about these things? Should we try to change the institutions, the people involved? Or should we try to grit our teeth, smile, and forget it?

What can we do with the aggressive, even hostile, feelings that such trivial crazymaking evokes? If we respond to them all, we will have little time or energy left for anything else in life.

The essential answer is that each crazymaking experience presents us with a set of options. And the most basic of these options is to determine how much of ourselves it is reasonable to spend in trying to bring sanity out of the madness. To decide, we need only apply some simple criteria. We must ask ourselves how effective can we really hope to be. How difficult is it likely to be to break through the crazymaking to sanity? And how rewarding will a sane relationship with this person, this institution, this lump of gum be?

Perhaps the most important truth to know about the trivial patterns of crazymaking is that these maddening episodes are indeed trivial. Clearly, the importance of understanding the patterns of crazymaking rests with the hope of making sane the relationships that mean most to us. It is in these relationships that sanity is worth fighting for.

CHAPTER ELEVEN

The Fight for Sanity

While the patterns and tactics of crazymaking vary endlessly—with each tactic being unique to the person who uses it, to the relationship in which it is used, and to the immediate situation within the relationship—they are also always the same. And in that sameness we find the last of the keys we need to break the bewildering crazymaking code.

This key lies in the fundamental purpose behind every tactic of crazymaking. It answers the question, what does crazymaking really seek to accomplish?

If we look back at any of the crazymaking maneuvers we have examined, we find that hidden within it is an attempt to reach the same essential goal.

That goal is change.

Seen in the light of its purpose, almost every crazymaking behavior is really a devious way to demand a change. And as we shall see, once we can understand what change is wanted, we have a way to stop the maddening effect.

For in itself, of course, there is nothing maddening about the wish for change. All of life is a continual process of change. And being able to adapt to changes —both within us and in our relationships to the people and environments around us—is the way we survive.

But while in general we all accept the need for

change—whether it is occasioned by a sudden drop in temperature, a dead battery in the car, or the arrival of a new baby—there is a human tendency to resist it, even to deny it. People tend to try to maintain a comfortable status quo.

This is especially true of the prospect of change in important relationships. There is a common fear that any change may be for the worse, and that a demand for change may mean displeasure with the whole relationship.

Typically, the reaction to a statement such as "I'd like a change in our relationship" is anxiety. It tends to produce a degree of alarm. The first reaction is likely to be "What have I done wrong?" or "What's wrong with you?" or "Is our relationship in danger?"

The closer the relationship, and the more we depend upon it in any way, the more intense such reactions are likely to be. And the vaguer, the less clear is our information about what kind of change is wanted and why, the more upsetting is the demand.

This is an important reason why expressing a demand for change in the puzzling, conflicting double message of crazymaking is so disturbing. For in crazymaking, a change is never asked for openly.

In fact, crazymaking is specifically designed, albeit unconsciously, to bring about change without admitting that one even wants it. Indeed, most crazymaking is so arranged that it actually *denies* there is a wish for change, even as it manipulates or forces that change.

Put very simply, one way to envision the typical double message of crazymaking in terms of its purpose of change is to set it in the following form:

Coded Message: I am uncomfortable. And to become comfortable I need to make a change. But I need to have you change to make this possible.

Open Message: I am perfectly comfortable with our relationship as it is. So I want to stay just as I am. And I need to have you stay just as you are to make this possible.

In the conflict of these two simultaneous, implied messages, we have a poignant essence of how crazymaking produces some of its most maddening effects. For how can one realistically hope to satisfy such a double demand? How can one both change and stay the same?

The maddening quality increases with the importance of the relationship. The double bind grows worse the more we genuinely care about the other and the more we want the other to care about us. In very close relationships, the feeling of damned-if-I-do and damned-if-I-don't can become overwhelming.

On the other hand it is not hard to see that as soon as the demand is brought into the open, admitted and made clear, the double bind is broken. So clearly, our objective in dealing with crazymaking is to find ways to bring out the demand, to make it as specific as possible, and to strip away the denial of it.

To accomplish this takes some special knowledge, some special technique. But actually we will find that we already have much of the needed knowledge, from our earlier explorations of how crazymaking begins, how it achieves its effects, and what its tactics mean. We will find, too, that we already know a good deal about the resistances we are likely to encounter as we seek to make the messages clear and understandable.

We need know only a little more, and to recast what we have learned in terms of crazymaking's objective of change and our own objective of finding out exactly what the required change is all about. So let us for a moment review what we know and see what more we need to know, beginning by looking at a common variety of crazymaking incident in a slightly different light.

Almost all her married life Marian Burns has been quite housebound and tightly bound to her children, who now number four, the youngest still in diapers. And Clay, her husband, likes things that way. For while he plays a rather dominant role in their marriage, he is actually very dependent on Marian and is more comfortable when she is somewhat isolated and dependent on him. He has been the one who pressed for more children. It was he who wanted a large house that would keep Marian busy.

Clay also engages in a fair amount of Red-Cross-nursing. A bright young banker, he takes the position that only he in the family understands the ways of the world, especially where money is concerned.

True, money is his business. But he uses his superior knowledge of it to control, and to foster Marian's dependency. So he steps in wherever money is spent. Whatever Marian's choice of a vacuum cleaner or a washing machine, he second-guesses it. He goes with her to the appliance store, even to buy dishes or a toaster, to cast his financially trained eye over every deal and keep Marian from being fooled or cheated. Somehow there is always something wrong with her choices from an economic point of view. If she so much as sends in a magazine coupon for a mail order, he tends to sniff a bit and often to deliver a lecture on the high charges for handling or mail-order ripoffs.

As with all "patients" in *Red-Cross-nursing*, Marian cannot help resenting this crazymaking, but she does not say so. She tends to be afraid to assert her wish for greater independence. But pride leads her to keep trying, for example, to look for bargains that will win Clay's approval.

We have seen similar situations before. But let us consider this one in terms of wishes for change. On the surface, as is often the case, Clay's forced help looks like an effort to keep things the same, that is, to keep Marian dependent and weaken her sense of competence.

Yet actually, each incident of this money-oriented crazymaking is a demand for change. For each time Marian tries to make financial judgments of her own, Clay uses crazymaking to drive her back and deny her independence. The change he wishes in each case is that Marian give up her effort to decide without his help. In each instance, Clay's wish for change applies to Marian's small thrust for independent action.

Recently, with all but one child in school, Marian has for the first time found some meaningful involvement outside her home and marriage. Mainly because of Clay's position as one of the small town's bankers, she was invited to join the fund-raising committee of the local hospital, especially to help with the annual dinner-dance.

Marian plunged into the job with zest. At first she was insecure about whether she could perform. But she found that she had actually learned quite a lot about money from all of Clay's home lectures. And her joy at feeling competent in her own right at something besides cooking, cleaning, and mothering was great.

Clay becomes annoyed, however, when every evening he comes home to find Marian busily phoning, selling tickets, and getting donations. He does not like waiting for supper while she finishes her business, and then getting a very simple meal. He does not really like the compliments he hears on the good job she is doing.

He begins to offer help, but Marian smiles and says everything is fine. He mutters warnings about her legal liabilities in handling others' money, but she does not worry. But finally, when he offers to go along to one of the committee meetings with her, she is unable to refuse. Once there, he takes center stage, pushing Marian into the background. All listen to him because he is a money professional. And when the chairman says how much he appreciates all the help Clay must be giving to Marian, he does not correct him.

The standard crazymaking pattern has been invoked again. But this time Marian does not feel just vague resentment. She smolders. For this time she has seen clearly that she is capable. Clay's manipulations do not convince her that she requires his nursing care. And she has some perception that by his accompanying her to the committee, by his dominance in the meeting, and by his failure to correct the impression that Marian's success was really due to him, he is injuring her in a serious way.

Marian's perceptions are right. For this time Clay is dimly aware that his crazymaking demand for change is not effective. His demand that she change and go back to her old role of isolation and incompetence does not have impact on her. And his failure to have impact leads to a much more hostile aggression, a more blatant depriving of others' confirmation of her worth and ability.

Psychologically, what is especially important is that Clay cannot either clearly admit his demand for change to himself or express it directly to his wife. For his real feeling is "I don't like it when you succeed at anything without needing me. I don't like it when you find others to confirm that you can do well on your own. I am losing control over you, and that makes me anxious."

On her part, Marian also fears to assert openly a change she would like from Clay. What she wants to express is "I want you to leave me alone for once while I do something on my own that makes me feel like a worthwhile individual. Why don't you tend to your banking and let me have this one thing for myself?"

Instead, for a few days Marian tries to push Clay back with crazymaking demands for distance. In this, she falls back on a counter-crazymaking such as we have seen before, a tactic along the lines of *take-care-of-little-me*. She calls Clay repeatedly at his office, asking what she ought to do about the problems that come up. When he comes home, she tells him in dreary detail every fund-raising step she has taken. And she begins to make maddening little mistakes in her account-keeping and then asks Clay's help in straightening them out.

The double message of her tactic goes like this:

Open Message: Since you're so interested, and since you're so good at these things, I want your help, just as you've always given it. I want you to continue to behave as you always have about money matters.

Coded Message: If you continue to interfere with my one individual thing, you're going to have to pay for it with constant nuisances. I want you to leave me alone this time, to change the old pattern.

But Marian's counter-crazymaking is insufficient to stop Clay. He begins to talk about some new plans he'd like to suggest to the committee. And it becomes harder and harder for Marian to choke down her resentment. She presents more and more problems to Clay, and he offers more and more helpful little criticisms to her, as the two enter into a rapidly mounting crazymaking spiral.

The mutual crazymaking begins to reach a peak late one afternoon, when Marian calls Clay at the office.

MARIAN: I just wanted to know if there's any reason why you might be staying late at the office tonight.

CLAY: Not a thing going on. I wouldn't let it go on. It's football night on TV, remember? You know that's one thing I never miss.

MARIAN: Oh, dear. I guess I forgot that, too.

CLAY: [*Suspiciously. He picks up on the possibility that his weekly football ritual may be threatened*.] Too? What do you mean? What's wrong?

MARIAN: Well, I don't know how I did it, but I completely forgot there's a meeting of the fund committee tonight, a dinner meeting at Charlie's Inn. Now I can't get a babysitter. So I'm afraid you'll have to go without me.

CLAY: But why should *I* go? [*He is flustered*.] It's your committee, not mine, after all. And you know how I hate to miss the football. Damn it—

MARIAN: I'm really sorry. It's all my fault. I made a mess of everything as usual. I know you keep telling me to write everything down on a calendar. But I have so little to write down that I usually remember.

CLAY: Well— [*He stifles his annoyance*.] There's no way to change it now. But I don't see why you think I should go.

MARIAN: You know perfectly well that you just took charge last time, and everyone listened to you, and they all liked what you said. I certainly can't talk about tax writeoffs for donations and things like that. And you did say you'd help.

CLAY: Oh, hell. And just when it's the Cowboys and the Steelers, too. [*He pauses*.] Look, you really should be the one to go. This is your thing. I'm an extra.

MARIAN: But besides my not knowing what you know about money, there's the problem of the kids. You know how you hate to be bothered when you're watching the game. Ginny will probably need to be changed right in the middle of a touchdown or something and start to cry. And Craig and Jimmy will probably start to fight or keep asking questions.

CLAY: [*Irritably*] I know, but I guess I'd rather see the game that way than not at all. And anyway, the main thing is that the hospital business is really yours, not mine.

Let us review what is happening here, with an eye to the motivating wish for change. As in all crazymaking, the episode begins with a feared aggression. The aggression here is Marian's wish to make Clay give up going to her meeting and let her go alone. This is a wish she has had ever since the previous meeting. But she has been afraid to express it in an open way.

There are two important observations to be made about our identification of the feared aggression in this way. The first is a principle. And the principle is that the aggression that leads to crazymaking is almost always a wish for change. What is almost always feared is to express this wish, to make a direct demand for change.

The second observation is an important factor to remember in trying to deal with crazymaking. It concerns the identifying of the wish that triggers the incident.

A thoughtful reader may wonder if there are not some deeper wishes behind Marian's crazymaking. And certainly there are. For example, Clay's ten years of *Red-Cross-nursing* certainly fuel Marian's wish. And in the recent present there is the whole subtle and complicated array of Clay's large and small interferences with Marian's hospital project. There is the more general issue of Clay's sabotage of Marian's newfound realization of herself through her work as a volunteer.

But trying to open up such whole museums of frustration and irritation is sure to result in a hopeless tangle. There is simply too much diversity to deal with effectively. And much of this concerns past offenses about which nothing can be done. Our experience with thousands of relationships has proven that to produce meaningful change one must start by selecting out one clear, specific demand. This much can be dealt with. And if it is, eventually the deeper issues will also tend to emerge, but in a manageable way, not as the dumping of a long-accumulated gunnysack of resentment.

This is particularly important in the easily confused world of crazymaking. The demand for change that we wish to bring out is the immediate, specific change sought by the crazymaking behavior—in this case, that Clay stay home and that Marian attend the meeting.

As always, this demand, having been at first stifled and denied, emerges as a double message. The emergence has been accomplished by Marian's unconsciously determined "forgetting." She herself can hardly believe that she forgot. She remembers, shortly after the date was set, meaning to tell Clay and to arrange for a babysitter. But somehow it all slipped her mind. What makes Marian feel even more uneasy is that the chairman had asked her to choose the date when Clay could return. And she had selected the football night "without thinking." She had simply chosen one of the nights when his calendar was open, she thought.

This "forgetting" has a double effect. First it makes possible the setting up of a situation in which the following crazymaking message is constructed:

Open Message: I want you to go to the meeting even if I have to stay home. You know so much more about these matters. I expect that you will take over and tell me and others what to do. I endorse our status quo.

Coded Message: Whatever I have to do, I am going to block you from going to the meeting. This business is mine and I want you stay out of it. I want you to change your way of interfering with this project and taking away my confidence and the strokes I am getting from these other people.

The open message, we should note, contains a good deal of sugar-coating. For having made the mistake, Marian says she will stay home because Clay is more valuable. In other words she is unconsciously careful not to tamper with Clay's image, either of her or of their relationship.

The second effect of Marian's "forgetting" encodes

another purpose. For the choice of football night has made her gambit effective. It has made it safe for her to offer to stay home with little fear that the offer will be accepted. But more than this, it also incorporates a sting.

The sting is not only a reaction to the frustration she experiences when she cannot openly mark out the hospital as her territory. It is also a response to Clay's invasion of that territory, together with its sting—the belittling and undermining of her capability. The sting she administers is in the form of the four youngsters, who will be in the den with Clay along with the Cowboys and the Steelers.

Other factors, other manipulations, become involved in this crazymaking incident. For example Clay is even manipulated into saying outright what Marian wants to hear, that the hospital project is her thing, not his, that she is needed at the meeting more than he. And of course Clay's rights of sanity are invaded. He is not given a choice, but is trapped into staying out of the meeting and trapped into opening his football-watching territory to the children.

In fact, so effective is Marian's crazymaking that an hour later he calls her. Unconscious of why he does it, and really feeling fearful of telling Marian what has happened, he suddenly remembers a batch of loan applications he has left undecided for a week. He suddenly feels most remiss in having neglected them, especially when he looks at his calendar and finds that the next few days are quite crowded.

Feeling that this is very poor service to his customers, he calls his assistant, a young bachelor loan officer. "Hank, I've just realized how I've delayed on your loan applications. I guess these should really be cleaned up, shouldn't they?"

Hank agrees. What else can he say to the boss?

"Listen, Hank, I hate to do this to you, but do you have any plans for this evening? Just the ball game? Well, if you wouldn't mind too much, I think we owe it to these people to give them answers right away. I'll bet that if we got on this right now we could get it all out of the way in time to get down to the Blue Boot by the second quarter and watch it there. They've just got one of those giant projection TVs, and I'll pop for dinner.''

And when Clay tells Marian, a new crazymaking spiral has begun.

On the surface, this exchange between Marian and Clay may seem to bode ill for the future. They may seem locked into a crazymaking style. Yet the fact is that all their manipulations and counter-manipulations, even their hostilities, can just as easily be put to work to give them growth and sanity. We need only identify the barriers that block them from asking for change in an open way, and learn how these communications barriers leading to crazymaking can be broken—giving access to sane assertions and responses.

The rejection barrier

Perhaps the most puzzling and pathetic question about Clay and Marian—in fact, about all intimate crazymaking—is, why can't these people simply tell each other what they want? Why can't they tell each other directly rather than in code; openly rather than in devious behaviors?

In the simplest possible terms, when they are afraid of aggression, when they are afraid to assert the changes of which they feel the need, what is it they fear?

It is important to know the answer. For if the solution to crazymaking is basically to bring the demands for change into the open, then we must know what has prevented people from doing so in the first place.

If we ask people directly what they are afraid of in such situations, we do not receive especially illuminating answers. Suppose, for example, we ask Marian—

"I don't know just why I couldn't say these things straight out to Clay. But I guess I feel very strongly that I can't, that he wouldn't like it."

And what would Clay do if he didn't like it?

"Well—I suppose that he might get angry."

Is Clay's anger especially fierce? Is he likely to lose control of himself, to strike out, to throw things? Might he storm out of the house and demand a divorce?

"You mean," says Marian, "just because I said I wanted to go to the meeting alone and have him stay away? Well, that would be ridiculous. That would be way out of all proportion to the situation. And as for having a violent temper, that's not Clay. He's a sane, sensible man."

Then what, specifically, frightens Marian so much that she cannot express wishes that mean so much to her?

"Maybe," she puzzles, "it's that I don't want to hurt his feelings." She pauses. "But that's not really the problem. When I think about it, when I try to understand my feelings, I have to say that it's not a fear for him that stops me; it's a fear for me."

The vague but very powerful feelings operating here, thwarting aggression and forcing it to be denied, to be expressed only in the indirect language of crazymaking, take root very early indeed. They are the universal human fears of rejection.

These fears are born in early infancy. For not many days of life pass before the infant perceives that he is totally dependent upon the mother figure. Her nurture and protection are all that stand between him and annihilation. Soon that nurture and protection are represented by her love.

Later, the father figure begins to be seen in a somewhat similar light. And while it will not help here to go into all the complex dynamics of the child-parent relationship, it is plain enough how parental love and acceptance become equated with survival. And the threat of rejection becomes tantamount to a threat to survival.

It is hard to imagine greater psychological power than this. The extent and form of an individual's feelings about rejection can vary infinitely. They are shaped by many kinds of experiences as the infant, and then the child, develops. How they are shaped derives largely from the ways and conditions under which the parents give love or hold it back—the ways in which they use rejection or acceptance as punishment or reward. In general these experiences determine how much rejection an individual can tolerate or risk. Certainly, some people are much more rejection-sensitive and rejection-fearful than others. And certainly those even who are most insensitive to rejection are still vulnerable and tend to have some extremely tender spots.

Whatever the degree and character of one's rejection fears, no psychologically normal person is so callous or so autonomous that he does not experience these fears to some considerable extent when dealing with important others in his life. When these fears arise, it feels perilous indeed to chance direct aggression. The fears still carry some of the blind power of infant feelings. It becomes much safer-feeling to repress the aggression, to choke back the wish for change, rather than chance expressing them.

It is worth noting here that parents can unwittingly become tyrants in children's rejection fears. By using rejection fears, parents can gain almost unlimited power in their relationships with children. For the parent can invade any of the child's rights to sanity with impunity. In order not to be rejected, the child must submit.

In a somewhat similar way, a parent who is rejection-sensitive can teach a child to be afraid of rejecting others, to be afraid to say no. For such a child learns that if he rejects, he is in turn rejected.

For example, Billy says openly, "No, I don't want to go to Grandma's with you. There's nothing to do there, and you yell at me if I do anything wrong. I'd rather stay home and play spaceship with Larry." Many a parent feels rejected by such direct statements and withdraws.

Withdrawal is one of two prime psychological refuges for children (and for the adults they become) if they are much manipulated by rejection games. And the other, more common refuge is crazymaking, in which the child learns how to appear to submit to the parents while manipulating them to get what he or she wants.

What we see developing in the child at this point is his or her first skill in accommodation and collusion. These skills, like crazymaking itself, are virtually universal. And they lead us into a trap that becomes a second important barrier to the open expression of wishes for change.

The imaging trap

Rejection sensitivity is especially acute during the early stages of relationships. So in order to give new relationships a chance to develop, there is a strong tendency to show oneself in the most favorable light. One is likely to try to guess what another wants—of a friend, a lover, an employee, even a brush salesman—and then to try to accommodate to fulfill that image.

The trouble is, this image becomes a source of strong expectations for the other person. One becomes trapped, locked into the accommodations one has made in order to avoid rejection. Such imaging varies in its importance, but at any level it can later make it impossible to express one's wishes openly if they conflict with the image that one has created.

Priscilla goes to a job interview. As a receptionist, she dresses in conservative taste, buttons buttoned and makeup modest, for the employer is a law firm.

During the interview her nose itches. But she grits her teeth and keeps her hands in her lap. As she stepped off the bus, she snagged her stocking. So she keeps that leg turned away from the interviewer.

"By the way," the interviewer says as Priscilla is about to leave, sure she has the job, "you do take a little dictation don't you—in case we need you to fill in?"

She does not. On the other hand he practically said that little dictation would be needed. Perhaps she can fake it, if necessary, with abbreviations and fast writing. "I took shorthand," she says finally, but without mentioning that she dropped the course after three weeks.

The interviewer is about to pursue the subject, but he notices Priscilla's hesitation. He likes everything else about her, so he colludes. "Well, you can always brush up if you have to," he says. They smooth the subject over.

But the result is what we might call a split image. Priscilla's idea of what has been said is that she is not really expected to take dictation. The interviewer's idea is that she can be counted on in a pinch. And the seeds of some office crazymaking have been sown.

Now Priscilla goes to lunch with her boyfriend. She does not think of her stocking run. She takes off her jacket, opens two buttons of her blouse, and vigorously rubs her nose. She talks much less primly, using a few four-letter words.

What is the difference? It rests with the image she has set with each of these men, for one thing. And for another, the interview situation, being a new relationship, held what we call *a low threshold of rejection*. That is, since there was virtually no background to the relationship, no bond of any kind, rejection would have been easy and could have taken place for rather superficial reasons.

The relationship with Dennis holds more important things as binding elements. Priscilla and Dennis have spent much time together, slept together a lot. The rejection threshold is quite high. No small matter is likely to cause rejection. Dennis, after all, has seen Priscilla scratch more than her nose.

As they eat, Dennis says, "Mom loved meeting you when they were in town. In fact she's asked us to come and spend a long weekend with them over Christmas."

Priscilla is not pleased. She did not like the way Mom took possession of Dennis and treated Priscilla as an outsider. But clearly Dennis is attached to his mother, and lately he has spoken of marriage when they have been in bed. Priscilla stifles her wish to ask for a change. "How nice," she says. "It would be fun."

The strong tendency to produce accommodating personal images for others yields a later impediment to aggression. For the image creates an expectation. For example, one of the problems in our story of Marian and Clay, early in this chapter, is that Marian, realizing Clay favored very traditional husband-wife roles, created an image of submission. The difficulty is that a person who creates an image that is not quite valid, that is distorted in some way, is aware that he has done so. Thus he may well feel that he has been accepted on a somewhat false basis. If he reveals his real feelings, his real preferences, he can fear he might be rejected.

Marian still does not mind letting Clay lead in many ways. But she no longer wants to be submissive. And since she—like everyone else who feels locked into an image that is not real in its entirety, like everyone else who used imaging in new relationships to forestall feared rejection—does want some independence, she has only one way to assert the wish. She can support her old image on the surface and use crazymaking to assert what she really feels.

Partial versus total rejection

A third barrier to the open assertion of the wish for change really derives from the other two, particularly from exaggerated rejection fears. But even though it is derivative, it is helpful to understand it as a separate entity.

This phenomenon stems from the child's difficulty in distinguishing between partial and total rejection. For example, Baby, nursing, bites Mother's breast. "Ouch!" she says in shock and surprise, receiving a bit of crazymaking as her expectations of a passive, harmless infant are broken by the unexpected bite. And she pushes the baby away, saying, "No! No!" The angry, startled reaction shocks the baby. He begins to howl desolately, disconsolately.

What the baby is not able to understand is that it is his particular behavior that has been rejected. He has not been rejected wholly.

We may tend to feel very superior to such a naive and pathetic reaction, to such a simple vision of rejection and acceptance. But many an adult has trouble making similar discriminations.

A simple awareness of the problem can help deal with this difficulty and free open assertions. The important point is, in a relationship that is well established, that has strong bonds basically, even if a wish for change proves to be unacceptable, one is not likely to destroy one's image or be rejected.

The simple fact is, as we are about to see, that either to be able to assert one's own wishes for change in an open way, or to be able to elicit another's, one must be willing to take some risks of rejection. But if the directions given here are followed, and if the relationship has any real solidity, any kind of a base at all, there is little danger the rejection will be anything but a partial one.

Remember, partial rejection is the rejection of only one idea, one assertion, one wish for change. It does not imply a total rejection of the person.

Similarly, one must realize the same thing about one's own sometime need to reject the wishes or aggressions of another. If only acceptance is considered possible as a response, continued crazymaking is inevitable. For what this really means is that neither partner will be able to receive clear information from the other; neither will know when they have real impact; neither will know where they stand or what the other person feels; neither will know when they are trespassing on the other's territory.

The unwillingness either to risk being rejected or to take the risk of rejecting, means that the rights of sanity are certain to be invaded. Aggression is forced underground and sane communications become impossible.

Breaking the rejection barrier

With our understanding of the nature of the rejection barrier, we can understand how to break through it. We can see how to bring crazymaking's concealed wishes for change into the open.

To break the barrier is not usually difficult. But to do so one must not only understand the dynamics we have explored, the keys to sanity we have found. One must also understand how they relate to one another.

For as with every aspect of crazymaking, one is confronted by the mask of bewilderment and complexity that hides each simple inner element. We have looked at these simple elements mainly in a kind of stark relief; we have attempted to isolate them so as to display them more clearly. But in day-to-day human exchanges they are not usually so clearly arranged. Rather, they tend to be interwoven. And especially when one is emotionally involved in a crazymaking experience, it can be hard to unravel the knot without some guidance.

For this reason we have developed a sequence of steps with which to penetrate the crazymaking camouflage. This system and its sequence are not, however, intended to be rigid. Once one has mastered the technique of unmasking crazymaking interactions, one can deal with them flexibly. But at the beginning it is really best to pursue these steps as systematically as one would follow the instructions for assembling a Christmas toy.

Because forgetting any of the principles and cautions involved here can cause trouble. Remember always that one has an unconscious temptation in any crazymaking situation. That temptation is to distort any response at all into a tactic of counter-crazymaking. It is a temptation to give back sting for sting, confusion for confusion. One must stay keenly aware that there are no villains and no victims here, especially when crazymaking has become part of the style of a relationship. In such relationships, we must be realistic enough to accept, the creation of a style of crazymaking for expressing aggression has been a joint effort.

In the fight for sanity, the hope for victory is not a hope for triumph over another person. It is certainly not retribution for the past crazymaking wounds one has suffered. For the chances are overwhelmingly good that, aware or not, one has inflicted as many such wounds as have been received. The enemy is the crazymaking itself—not the person who is close to you.

Without such a realistic insight and approach, one is doomed to failure. For people are incredibly sensitive to hostility. And when crazymaking has long held sway, both partners have become even more sensitized to its stings. If the effort toward sane communications is really only a veiled demand for the *other* to change and communicate openly, while you continue to express your wishes indirectly, by manipulations and double messages, the maneuver is bound to make itself felt.

As we have seen, the rule that repression and denial of aggressive feelings must lead to an unconscious emergence of them cannot be avoided. Emerging as a double message, they have a reliably crazymaking effect. One cannot be clever enough to prevent that effect; it is part of the substance of the phenomenon; it is a standard technique by which the unconscious reveals itself.

To break the rejection barrier and put a stop to another's crazymaking, one must be alert to one's own crazymaking. Sane communications cannot be a one-way street. Any sign of crazymaking will tend to reinforce the rejection barrier of the other person. For the double message is bound to be felt as a sting, evoking only defensive, indirect expressions of the other's wish for change—together with more of the hostility that launches the crazymaking spiral.

With these cautions in mind, let us now try to apply the keys of sanity to a crazymaking episode. Let us start with the incident that began this chapter.

Remember that, at the heart of the episode, Clay, the banker, and his wife, Marian, are struggling over Marian's wish for greater independence. Marian has tried to assert that independence in indirect ways. In the simplest view, she is fighting for her sane rights to space. At the same time Clay uses crazymaking to fight for his wish to narrow her space, to keep her dependent upon him. His *Red-Cross-nursing* demands, in order to be successful, that he make her feel incompetent in certain ways. It requires that she need his intervention, his repeated rescues. So, primarily, what we have watched is a form of fighting for optimal distance.

Marian has her idea of an ideal distance. Clay has his. Both fear to assert these ideas openly. They are afraid that to do so is to risk rejection. And since their ideas do not match, they have engaged in a seesaw crazymaking battle—each with the aim of imposing his or her wishes without asking for agreement or even admitting what is wanted.

Common sense tells us that what is needed here is negotiation. But how can one negotiate when neither partner will say what is wanted?

On the evening when we observed the situation, both tried to force compliance with crazymaking tactics. Clay won, it seemed. Marian had tried to go to her volunteer meeting and keep Clay at home. But Clay, pleading the demands of business, blocked Marian's effort.

Both had resorted to techniques of crisismaking. Marian, by "forgetting" the meeting to which they were to go, tried to create a situation in which Clay would stay home. Clay responded with a crisis of his own making, which made it seem necessary to stay at the office.

As we have seen, the aim of such tactics is to deny responsibility. The theme is that some outside force compels a certain choice. The demands of work, of economic survival, are among the most common and powerful of such outside forces. But there are many others. Marian tried to use the demands of charity, of community responsibility. But one can as easily use the demands of duty, honor, country, compassion.

The stock lines of such crazymaking are familiar to us all. And, maddeningly, they are often valid. "I can't let Mother down." "The team is counting on me." "But little Gerry has been dreaming about the circus for two weeks." "If you say we can't go, all right—but this could be Grandfather's last Christmas, you know."

The real message of such statements, when they are used for crazymaking, is "The only thing we can possibly do is exactly what I want to do."

So while, as we have shown, to understand the tactics of crazymaking can give us insight into the problem areas, into the immediate aims suggested by each, they must not be used for exercises in amateur psychotherapy. To try to break through the rejection barrier by such analysis, and by the resulting ploys of mind reading, mind raping, attributing, and the like, all end in crazymaking. They yield double messages. They deprive of sane rights. And each carries its tendency to sting the other into reprisal in the same terms, to launch a crazymaking spiral.

What then? How do we use our keys of sanity to turn the lock of crazymaking? Having looked at some fundamental dangers, let us now see how we can safely arrive at sanity, how we can break the rejection barrier to free ourselves of the pain and confusion.

1. Stop, look, listen, and feel

Plainly, the defense against crazymaking begins the moment we feel its characteristic sting. We have described the sudden mixture of confusion and disbelief, of conflicting feelings, of split motivation, that accompanies the crazymaking experience. And the appearance of such feelings must be taken as an alarm signal.

But it is not a call to battle stations. It is not a signal to load the guns. It is, first of all, a signal to think, not react.

For if one responds without thinking, one will merely tend to return the sting. And the substance of the wish for change will only be buried more deeply.

How does one suffer the sting in order to relieve it?

First, by understanding that crazymaking is at work—by facing the fact that the dimly perceived code of the hidden message is real, that it has meaning, even if one cannot decode it.

Second, using what we have learned, one must realize that decoding attempts within one's own mind are not only futile. They are also the roots of counter-crazymaking. One must understand that only one person can know the real meaning of the crazymaking double message—the person who sends it.

Why not strike back? Because one should now recognize the most fundamental meanings of the injury.

One is that it almost surely represents, not a real wish to hurt, but a wish for change that the other fears to express openly. Why? Because most probably it is feared that an open expression of the wish may bring about rejection—your rejection. And why would the other person be fearful of rejection? Because he or she is anxious that it will end the relationship.

In other words one of the first perceptions one can make on recognizing crazymaking is that it is really an attempt to secure change without driving you away. In this way the crazymaking behaviors of those close to you are affirmations of caring, statements of their fear of losing your love or friendship.

Ironically, the truth is that crazymaking is generally resorted to as a way to preserve the bond between people. It is only when one fears to lose a relationship that one cares enough to veil one's demands.

Such understanding helps us tolerate the first shocks of crazymaking. It helps us to ask, not how can I strike back, but what is wanted of me? It helps us focus our interest and our response on opening up the wish for change.

It is for this reason that one must begin, not by trying to divine the other's feelings and intent, but by pausing to identify one's own feelings. For one's own feelings, as we have suggested, are not just important ways to zero in on the area of the crazymaking. They are also indicators that the *conditions of crazymaking* exist. It is these conditions that trigger a renewal of Clay and Marian's crazymaking exchange.

2. Be aware of the crazymaking conditions

These conditions are really more subjective than objective. And while this fact may seem to confuse the situation, actually it makes them simpler to discern. For again, one has no need to guess and make assumptions about the other's feelings. One has only to examine one's own feelings.

Clay and Marian provide a good example of these conditions on the morning after their crazymaking exchange, which ended in Clay's working late at the bank and Marian's failure to get to her hospital meeting. We see why at once, when we look at the crazymaking precursors:

First, *crazymaking becomes likely when people are denied an open expression of their wishes for change.*

Certainly, Marian has not been able to say she wants to feel more potent, better identified as an individual, apart from Clay and the children. And certainly Clay has been unable to say he does not like Marian to find an identity outside her roles as wife and mother.

The result is that both are in a tension state. Both are

aware that they have not expressed their real wishes, but have instead tried to force compliance to those wishes. Whether these manipulations have been successful or unsuccessful is not as important as one might think. For in any case, they have sought only a relief of the moment; they have not clearly expressed what they wanted.

Second, *crazymaking tends to be fomented when people feel a sense of powerlessness*.

This feeling is ironically likely when one feels unable to assert real demands, whether one is objectively the more powerful or the less powerful person. The important point is that a sense of powerlessness tends to accompany the inability to make demands in an open way.

Marian feels overwhelmed by Clay's power, by her dependency upon him as breadwinner and family head. But Clay, while he holds these powers, also feels powerless because he cannot directly tell Marian to stay home and depend on him.

Third, *crazymaking is potentiated when people feel that open demands for change may result in total rejection*.

Again, we have the irony that Clay (who appears to be the more powerful person in the relationship) is really as fearful of rejection as Marian. And the inner meaning of this is that actual power may have little relevance when crazymaking takes place. Company presidents may be as inclined to crazymaking tactics to assert power as the youngest mailroom clerk. This is further evidence that rejection-sensitivity is more a function of inner feeling than of outer power and influence. So it is that the powerful may use crazymaking to affirm their status rather than asserting it openly, just as much as those who feel powerless may resort to crazymaking to assert that while they have little overt power they have meaning and personal identity; that they too are important.

Clay cannot say "Knuckle under or else" any more than Marian can say "Don't interfere with me while I confirm my worth as a separate person."

A fourth condition of crazymaking is that *one does not want to be identified as the agent of change*. This is really a corollary of the feeling that one does not want to assert demands for change as one's own—but feels safer in creating changes without taking responsibility for wanting them.

Essentially this means that, without regard for who holds power or exercises it, one does not wish to be held responsible for the results of the change. Again, because if the change takes place, and it does not go well, there is a fear that one will be rejected as the initiator.

While there are other possible conditions for crazymaking, these four are most prominent, along with one more factor that must not be overlooked.

For a fifth crazymaking condition is what we call the *crazymaking continuum*. That is, when crazymaking has become part of the style of the relationship, the incidents cannot be isolated. Each one sets up another.

The links between crazymaking episodes are of several kinds. As we have seen, the failure to express wishes for change openly means that the underlying issues are never really resolved. And a resentment simmers beneath the surface of expression.

Moreover, being aware of the natural laws of crazymaking, we can easily recognize that the continuing lack of resolution and the failure to have full, clear impact add to the sense of aggressive frustration. It may appear that one is able to tolerate this repeated repression and denial. But in fact, a gunnysack of resentment is continually building. When the gunnysack is full enough, it spills over into another crazymaking episode.

And finally, the crazymaking continuum is kept alive by another basic law of such interaction. For as we know, each crazymaking episode carries its stings. And each sting tends to provoke a counter-sting.

The frustrations, the failure to get resolution or be recognized by the other, the scars of the stings, all add up to an irritable, defensive state. And the mutual perception of this state in each other tends to heighten the partners' fears of rejection.

All these conditions of crazymaking leave Clay and

Marian well primed for further crazymaking after their manipulations involving the meeting. In fact they are ready to dump their gunnysacks of resentment and frustration.

We might now try to apply our first two rules for dealing with crazymaking. It is the morning after the night of the controversial meeting. The children, except for two-year-old Ginny, are off to school. Clay is about to leave for work. He and Marian are having coffee and reading the newspaper.

What follows might seem trivial to someone who did not understand the ways of crazymaking. But as we know, the most earnest aggressions of crazymaking are often disguised as minor annoyances, as little accidents of speech or action.

CLAY: Look at the time. I've got a heavy day ahead. I'd better get started for the office. I'll just have another half cup and then run. [*Clay watches Marian for a second to see if she will offer to get it for him, as she often does. He is testing. He knows perfectly well that she is bound to have some resentment about the night before, even though she does not express it.*]

MARIAN: [*Does not look up from her paper*] All right, dear.

CLAY: [*He gets his own coffee and goes back to his paper. He is uneasy about where he stands with Marian. But he is also fearful of opening up the matter again. So he merely reads in silence.*]

MARIAN: Well, what do you know—

CLAY: [*He looks up quickly because he is in a mild state of tension, inwardly waiting for a reaction to his maneuver of working late the previous evening. But Marian says nothing.*] What is it?

MARIAN: [*Abstractedly*] What did you say, dear?

CLAY: [*Restraining some irritation*] I said, what is it?

MARIAN: [*Innocently*] What do you mean, what is it?

CLAY: [*Irritably*] You said, what do you know?

MARIAN: Oh, that—it was nothing. I was just sort of thinking out loud. [*She goes back to her paper.*]

*   *   *

What is happening is that the crazymaking spiral is being renewed. And using our keys and the rules for employing them, we can see that we have already passed at least three points at which the spiral could have been broken.

Point one. Clay could have been aware of his own feelings and recognized the buzz of irritability and tension that is so often the forerunner of crazymaking, that is a warning sign of an existing crazymaking condition.

What could he have done about this? He could have simply said what he felt rather than trying to repress it. But instead he hopes Marian will say something first. His announcement that he must leave for the office is a kind of bait, a mild way to try to elicit an open reaction from her.

Point two. Marian's situation is the same. She is resentful. She feels stung and wants to sting back. But she does not want to appear responsible for any hostility. And she still does not want to make an open demand for change in the matter of independence.

So Marian, mainly in an unconscious way, embarks upon a crazymaking tactic rather than trying to communicate directly. The failure to respond to their feelings of frustration, their refusal to openly acknowledge that each tensely feels the need for change, is what launches the spiral anew.

Such feelings call for careful looking and listening. If we, as observers, look and listen carefully as the situation develops, we can recognize the seeds of what is to happen. We can see that Marian has been made to feel powerless, dominated by the incident of the night before. So she is likely to want to try to restore a balance of power, to assert her importance in some covert way.

In her calling for Clay's attention and then frustrating him, we see an early sign of her intent. And if we note that this happens right after Clay says he is about to go to work, we might even guess that Marian is about to use crazymaking to keep him from doing so. For remember, Clay manipulated her by exerting his power as the breadwinner, by using his work as a controlling outside force for which he did not have to take responsibility. It is consistent with the logic of crazymaking if Marian now asserts in code that she is more important than Clay's bank.

Point three is the moment when Marian teasingly calls for Clay's attention and then denies that she wanted it. Again, given the feelings he has, feelings that indicate a potential crazymaking situation, and given the information he has that the conflict of the previous evening was not really resolved, he could have avoided falling into a crazymaking trap.

Let us see how easily such opening gambits can be escaped. For in the process, we will find some other rules for dealing with crazymaking. We can first watch as the exchange goes forward in an uncontrolled way, returning to the conversation as Marian denies wanting Clay's attention.

CLAY: Well, what were you going to say?

MARIAN: I just reacted to something, that's all. I spoke before I thought, and then I decided not to bother talking about it.

CLAY: [*Persisting, somewhat tensely*] Look, honey. You know perfectly well you were going to tell me something.

MARIAN: I was, but I decided not to. I didn't want to get into some big thing just when you were going to leave.

CLAY: [*As usual finding it impossible to resist invading Marian's inner territory and also aroused by the hint that Marian thinks it is important*] What do you mean, get into a big thing? If it's that important, you really should tell me about it.

MARIAN: It's not important. Not really. I wasn't even going to consider buying it. But if I talked about it, you'd probably make it into a big thing. Can't we drop it?

CLAY: *Buy what?*

MARIAN: You see, I knew if it was anything about money, especially anything so foolish—I mean, look how you're starting to bite my head off. I just didn't want to start the day with a lecture about wasting money, when I wasn't even going to spend any. I really try hard not to waste your money.

CLAY: It's your money, too. It's *our* money. God, Marian, haven't I always tried to give you everything you wanted—everything we could afford?

MARIAN: Yes, but you're the one who decides what we can afford. After all, you know all about money and you make the decisions. And that's all right, but I hate the way you think I'm foolish about wasting money. I just know what you would have said about the blouse.

CLAY: What blouse?

MARIAN: The one in the ad that I was going to tell you about.

CLAY: Is that all we're fighting about? A crummy blouse? [*He sees an opportunity to escape from the threat of further conflict and from the crazymaking he is experiencing.*] Look, just buy the blouse. I've got to get to the bank, OK?

MARIAN: I wasn't going to buy it. Even on sale it's too expensive. It's true, I saw it before and fell in love with it. But anyway, it's too dressy. Where would I get a chance to wear it—to the market or the PTA or to Monday night football? Why should I buy it?

CLAY: [*Trying to ignore these extra stings and smooth the situation over, he puts an arm around her.*] Just because you're my girl and I want you to have something nice, that's all.

MARIAN: That's very nice. But I don't want to buy it. I never did.

CLAY: Come on, honey. I just want to show you that I love you.

MARIAN: Oh?

CLAY: What do you mean, oh?

MARIAN: Well, if you still love me so much, then how come you haven't touched me for two weeks?

And they are off into a bitter sex fight, a shrill open battle. How is this possible if both are so fearful of rejection, so unwilling to aggress openly? The answer is simple and important. It is that sex, for them, is a safe area. Both feel well accepted sexually.

True, they have lately tended to keep each other at some physical distance because of the abrasions that have attended Marian's assertions of independence. But they can be relatively open about sexual matters because these are not a matter of contention.

What we have seen is the steady escalation of the crazymaking spiral, in which the discussion gradually shifts from a trivial conversational ploy into the subject of money, which has been their symbol of the core problem of independence. Money has been Clay's primary means of control.

But when the money talk gets too close to the real business of the authority to make decisions, again the fear of rejection produces a shift of context. Clay's attempt to smooth the situation over leads them to let out the emotion they feel, but in terms that are not dangerous. Indeed, ten minutes later, they are making love, having discharged some of their tensions—not only by fighting openly about a safe subject, in which rejection did not threaten, but also through the sexual release.

The trouble is that though the battle is over, the war will go on. In crazymaking ways the central problem will emerge again and again, for it is unresolved.

This exchange could not only have been broken up and the partners spared the discomforts of crazymaking; it could also have been used to yield growth and improvement in the relationship, as is the case with nearly all important crazymaking episodes.

At the simplest level, the incident could have been stopped with Marian's original, seemingly trivial bit of crazymaking conversation, when she called for Clay's attention and then denied she wanted it. Clay would only have had to follow a third anti-crazymaking rule.

3. Do not react blindly to the sting

Clay felt mildly stung when Marian refused to tell him what she had found in the paper to exclaim about. He reacted by demanding she tell him and by insisting the matter was important when she said it was not.

If Clay had recognized the ploy as crazymaking and

understood what is behind such gambits, he would have been alerted to the fact that Marian was beginning to express a wish for change. He could then have taken steps to bring the wish into the open.

Instead, Clay violates another basic rule for dealing with crazymaking.

4. Respect others' rights to sanity

Perhaps more than any other, this rule is the best guardian of one's own rights to sanity and the best relief from these maddening experiences. Clay violates the rule by reacting with some crazymaking of his own. When Marian says she has decided not to talk about the matter that had caught her attention, Clay does not respect her decision.

Instead, he mind reads. He says, "You know perfectly well you want to tell me something."

The combination of his persistence in invading Marian's inner space, and the sting involved in his mind reading, soon lead Marian into telling *him* what *he* thinks.

If Clay had respected Marian's sane rights, the early part of the exchange would have gone something like this:

MARIAN: Oh, that—it was nothing. I was just sort of thinking out loud. [*She goes back to her paper.*]
CLAY: Whatever you say. [*He goes back to his paper.*]

Although this example is a very simple one, the principle extends into virtually any crazymaking circumstance. By not responding to the sting itself, and by not invading Marian's rights, Clay creates a situation in which crazymaking communications are not encouraged. He makes clear he will respond only to open communications.

Moreover, something else happens when Clay responds only to what Marian says openly and does not violate her sane rights by trying to mind read. For such a response constitutes acceptance of the other person. It does so by permitting impact. And the result is to lower fears of rejection.

In a slightly different perspective, by accepting Marian's cutoff of the subject, Clay also shows that he can accept a *conflicting* wish. And this is another important element in encouraging the open expression of aggression.

What is at work here is a kind of psychological balance. The urgency of an aggressive feeling is balanced against the fear of expressing it directly. What we seek to do is to tip that balance so that the aggression can come through. To do so, we must lessen the fear.

The alert reader may notice what looks like a basic flaw in Clay's instant stop of the crazymaking, however. For while it prevents the crazymaking spiral from taking hold, it does not bring out the real substance of Marian's wish for change.

This is true in one respect. But we can also expect that it is only Marian's small crazymaking tactic that has been blocked. Her deeper aggressions are bound to try to emerge again. But our hope is that they will eventually appear in clearer form so they can be dealt with.

On the other hand, if Clay is in touch with his feelings and his awareness of the situation, he realizes that the crazymaking conditions still exist. He still feels tense. And Marian's stop-start communication has made him more tense. If he tries to deny these feelings, as we have seen, they will tend to break out as more counter-crazymaking.

If Clay consults with himself, he realizes that what leaves him uncomfortable is that he doesn't know whether Marian really wants to dismiss the subject or if she is merely baiting him. The next rule for achieving sane communications offers a very simple solution.

5. When in doubt, ask for the clear information that you want

Let us see how this can work for Clay. Having stopped the first gambit, he is still bothered by it. He also notes that when he looks up at her she seems also to be watching him out of the corner of her eye. So he asks:

CLAY: Marian, I want to ask you something.
MARIAN: [*Somewhat warily*] What is it?
CLAY: I don't want to crowd you. But a while ago you started to say something and then pulled back. Now, if you really don't want to talk about it, that's fine. But if you do, and you're hesitating for some reason, then I want to listen. I'm curious.
MARIAN: [*This open approach suggests acceptance. But Marian still feels reluctant to get into the subject. She is still afraid he will criticize her.*] Don't worry about it; it was nothing at all.

In some circumstances this response would have been enough to clear up the tension. But given the crazymaking condition that has been set up, Clay continues to feel disturbed. And he is limited in the information he can ask for and hope to get.

For Marian has denied that there is any significance. If Clay says, "I want to know what you are really thinking," or asks, "What's at the bottom of this?" he will be invading her sane rights again. The limits of such information requests are suggested by a sixth rule.

6. In asking for clear information, confine yourself to matters that are open and immediate

Again Clay consults with himself. And he finds that he has already explored the only clear information Marian has given in the immediate present. Is this all he knows clearly about the situation? No. For he also knows his own reactions.

Would it be wise to say how he feels? Indeed it would.

7. To obtain clear information about another's feelings, share your own

Remember that the fear of rejection is enhanced by not knowing where one stands with another person, by not knowing the other's state of mind and emotions.

When we take the risk of revealing ourselves, we lessen the threat of such revelation for the other. In a sense, in revealing feelings we make ourselves vulnerable. And a vulnerable person does not tend to seem so threatening.

In fact the revelation of feelings will do well to include the open expression of any fears of rejection. Suppose Clay now asks for information in this way:

CLAY: Honey, I've got to leave for work. And the truth is I'm still bothered about whatever it is you started to tell me about. I don't want to bug you, but are you sure there isn't something you want to say?

MARIAN: Really, I'd rather leave it alone. Why does it worry you?

CLAY: Well, I guess I'm still feeling bad about last night. I know that meeting was important to you. I'm afraid you're upset about missing it and upset with me. I wonder if that's what was on your mind.

MARIAN: I guess I did get upset about the meeting. But it was my own fault. I could have remembered and told you about it earlier and got a babysitter. Then it wouldn't have mattered if you had to work.

But anyway, that wasn't what I was going to say. I was just struck by an ad I saw for a blouse on sale.

Observe that the sharing of real feelings on Clay's part allows him to get into the subject matter which really concerns him. He can now let go of the conversational gambit. He can either ask for more information about the ad or let it go. It is not longer burdened with such powerful emotional coloring.

Also, by volunteering some feelings, and something about his own rejection fears, he makes it possible for Marian to make some expression of her reactions to the previous evening. This helps tip the balance of the crazymaking scale in a desirable way. For Marian now knows that he is concerned about her feelings, and also that he accepts a certain amount of distress, even resentment, that she may feel about the incident. It suggests, further, that he would like to help repair the situation. And this in turn opens the possibility of talking about how similar incidents might be avoided in future. Briefly, here are the elements of willingness to change, elements of the kind of change that is Marian's deep wish.

There is one more basic step that can help elicit wishes for change that another fears to express. It is encompassed in our eighth rule:

8. One cannot avoid having some assumptions about how another thinks or feels. So check these assumptions out—but with permission. Do not behave as if they were true.

We sometimes refer to this approach as *mind reading with permission*. And one of its values is that in the process of expressing one's feelings about another's seeming thoughts or feelings, one indicates one is willing to think, is indeed thinking, about ideas the other may fear are unthinkable. Another value is that in this way one is able to check out concerns about where one stands with the other. For in the usual case one is likely to have many needless fears and doubts, especially about what the other would like to demand and what one could grant.

Mind reading with permission can for these reasons often uncover real feelings, real wishes that would otherwise remain concealed, to foster crazymaking. Let us see how it works.

Although Clay and Marian have had some exchange of feelings, they have so far avoided the dependence-independence struggle at the heart of their maneuvering. Then, about a week later, they are in bed, watching the late news, when Marian opens the subject again.

MARIAN: Oh, I'd better not forget to tell you. The next hospital meeting is set for the evening of the nineteenth. Is that OK for you?

CLAY: The nineteenth— [*He thinks.*] But that's another Monday, isn't it? A football night?

MARIAN: Oh, no. I forgot again. And it's too late to change.

CLAY: Damn it— [*He starts to respond to the sting,*

the maneuver of the double bind, and the threat to deprive him of his sports ritual. But then he catches himself.] Look, Marian. I'd really like to help with that meeting. I mean, I think everyone expects me to. Like, they've got to straighten out their tax status.

MARIAN: I know. Of course, Joan Porter said her husband was willing to help. He's an accountant—

CLAY: [*He tries to share his feelings again.*] Listen, I don't want to let you down, and I know it seems pretty unimportant compared to the hospital, but I really get a lot out of those games. I really look forward to them. And this whole situation is beginning to give me some very uncomfortable feelings.

MARIAN: [*Apprehensively*] What kind of feelings?

CLAY: Well, do you mind if I tell you? I mean, I can't help having some hunches about what's going on in your mind, and I'd like to check them out with you.

MARIAN: Well—go ahead.

CLAY: I have a hunch that something's gone wrong between us. I can't quite put my finger on it, but I have the feeling that you're put off about something, that you're angry with me, and you're trying to find ways to keep your distance from me.

MARIAN: No, I really don't feel angry.

CLAY: Well, it seems as if you must. This hospital thing feels like it's a way to avoid me—you know, being busy with the phone calls and the records every night while I sit alone. Then it feels like you set up these Monday night meetings I have to go to so that I lose the football. And for more than a month you seem to avoid me when I start to touch you.

MARIAN: I don't say no.

CLAY: But it feels as if there's a wall. I don't know. I just don't feel wanted—in any way. So you seem as if you must be angry with me. Is that true?

MARIAN: No, it's really different, Clay. The truth is I feel as if *you're* angry with *me*. I mean, it's felt as if you've been bugged ever since I took on this hospital thing, as if you want to stop me from doing it.

At this point the effort toward sane communications

threatens to bog down. Too many ideas and complaints are being introduced. Let us suppose that Clay recognizes this, that he recalls the rule of focusing on a specific and immediate issue, one single point about which to express feelings and to seek information.

CLAY: Suppose we narrow it down just to this new meeting. If I can read your mind again [*Marian nods.*], it feels as if you've set things up so that I'll want to stay home. Is that true?

MARIAN: [*She is tempted simply to deny this out of fear of making Clay feel rejected. But by his leveling with her he has made clear that he already feels rejected in a total way. The crazymaking balance tips. It becomes safer to set the record straight—to risk a small rejection of him rather than have him feel wholly rejected. So she takes a deep breath.*] Clay, I'm not angry with you. And I didn't intentionally set up to spoil your football or anything. But I do think I'd rather go to the meeting alone.

CLAY: Then you *are* angry with me? What about? What's gone wrong?

MARIAN: No, it's not a matter of anger. It's just that I'm kind of excited about the hospital fund. It's giving me something that feels like my own. It makes me feel—important. People listen to me and trust me, and I really like it. But you're so much stronger than I am, and you know so much more about money things. So when you get involved, it feels as if you're trying to take it away from me.

CLAY: [*Protests*] But I'm just trying to help. I mean, you ask me for help.

MARIAN: Sure I do. But sometimes it seems as if that's just because you expect me to—as if it's just a habit or something. And then—it's hard to express, but you help too much. It makes me feel as if I can't do anything on my own.

CLAY: [*Testily. For remember that for years he has followed a practice of Red-Cross-nursing. The style of a relationship does not change so easily or quickly.*] Well, if you don't want my help, then why the hell are you always asking for it?

MARIAN: [*At his small show of anger, she backs away at first.*] I suppose because I feel you expect me to ask. And of course there are plenty of times when I need it. [*Marian, now starting to feel fearful as she tries to express her wish for a general change in their relationship, wisely returns to a focus on a single issue, a specific demand. She recognizes that this is safer ground. For one thing Clay has shown he is willing to talk about her wish to go without him to the meetings, that he can deal with it. For another, she sees that broadening the issue too much and too fast provokes resistance. And she realizes, too, that she herself does not yet know clearly what kind of broad change she would like in their relationship. So she goes back to the matter of the meeting.*] Honey, let's not make this too earth-shaking. It's this one thing that I want to get straight. I don't want you to think that I'm angry. I don't want you to think that I love you any less. But I just want to do this hospital thing as mine.

CLAY: Then you're not mad about anything?

MARIAN: No, honestly.

CLAY: Then why have you been backing away from me?

MARIAN: I guess because I was afraid to tell you. I was afraid that you'd be angry or feel hurt. But it isn't that I don't want you. It's that I want this for myself.

CLAY: [*His fears of rejection are now much lower.*] I guess I understand—as long as things are all right between us.

MARIAN: [*With a flush of genuine warmth*] Come over here and I'll show you. [*She impulsively slides her hand down his body. She has never been the aggressor in sex.*]

CLAY: [*He reacts with a start, but with excitement.*] Hey—you never did that before—

MARIAN: [*Quick to doubt her newfound confidence*] Is it all right—?

CLAY: [*Grinning*] It's all right. It's fine—

MARIAN: [*Still hesitant*] I've always wanted to do that. But I was afraid you would think it wasn't—right for a woman. Is it?

CLAY: First thing in the morning I'm going to call all the hospitals and see if they need a volunteer.

Clay and Marian have made a beginning, a beginning of sane communication. The stresses and discomforts of crazymaking had reached a point at which they began to be greater than their fears of rejection. Particularly, Marian's sense of her independence, of her competence apart from Clay, had made the old style of their relationship obsolete.

At first Marian tried to meet her needs, in her newly discovered individuality, through the old methods of indirect aggression. But as her feelings of aggression, her wishes for change, became stronger, the crazymaking began to increase in its intensity. The old accommodations and collusions, stretched to serve the newer needs for change, had to go too far. She and Clay both became too uncomfortable.

This new discomfort made it possible for both to try new ways of open expression. And their understanding of the ways to deal with crazymaking manipulations made it possible for both to overcome some of their fears of change, their fears that open aggression, open demand for change, might destroy what they had; that it was too dangerous to take the risk.

Clay and Marian still have a long way to go before they reach a sane style of communication. But they can begin to see its value. One by one they are likely to deal with crazymaking incidents in a sane way.

By following the rules of sane communication, they will discover the worth of honoring each other's sane rights. They will see that what is won with clear and open communications—which permits real choice and avoids coercion—is more valuable than what they can win with the painful and cryptic communications of crazymaking. They will learn that the only risk is partial rejection—the rejecting of one feeling or behavior—not total rejection by the other.

So let us recap and amplify these keys to sanity.

1. Stop, look, listen, and feel.

Whether in response to crazymaking or to one's own wish for change, which one fears will lead to rejection, pause. Understand that manipulating some change will not produce true impact, that with it one merely gains submission, and that the price is that the confusion and resentment will tend to trigger the crazymaking spiral.

2. Be aware of the crazymaking conditions.

They are warning signs that either oneself or one's partner may resort to an indirect expression of aggression because the fears of rejection have been heightened.

3. Do not react blindly to the sting.

Remember that the object is to bring into the open the demand for change that has been frustrated, that any sign of hostility is not likely to be a wish to injure as much as it is the result of an inability to have, or risk, impact.

4. Respect others' rights to sanity.

And of course respect your own rights. Each person has the rights to clear information, to his or her own feelings and the freedom to express them, to have and to register impact, and to reserve to him or herself a reasonable space, both outwardly and inwardly. One can negotiate these rights when they come into conflict with the rights of another. But to force concessions is deadly.

5. When in doubt, ask for the clear information that you want.

Efforts to read minds, attempts to tell another what his or her thoughts and feelings are, or to behave as if one had guessed correctly are gross invasions of sane rights. They are sure to lead to resentments, hostility, and the feeling that the assertion of aggression risks rejection. They are blatant crazymakers, sure to draw crazymaking responses.

6. In asking for information, confine yourself to matters that are open and immediate.

As we have seen, it is necessary to focus on single issues in the here and now. Expeditions into broad generalities, into history, and into the far reaches of the future tend to elicit vague and evasive responses. Useful information must make a request for change—whether it is your own request or another's—highly specific. "I want you to spend more time with me" is an invitation to crazymaking. How much time? How spent? When? What is "more"? A specific demand would be "I want us to go out together on Friday nights."

It is pointless to make demands about either the past or the dim future. The future may always be just around the corner. The past cannot be changed. Sane interactions deal with the present—as the only possible rectification of the past and the only realistic determinant of the future.

7. To obtain clear information about another's feelings, share your own.

Since the open expression of feelings is the core of sane communication, and since that open expression entails a risk, to relieve a crazymaking communications style it is important to take the risk oneself. A cat-and-mouse game of who-opens-up-first? is crazymaking in itself. Don't expect to receive confidences without giving them.

As a realistic note, if your true feelings about another person or relationship do prove to be totally unacceptable, perhaps you must face the fact that the relationship is supported only by illusions. You cannot know unless you take the risk of expressing your feelings. And if you do not know, you can never be sure that you are accepted for yourself rather than for the image you have conveyed. Imaging merely creates false expectations which you may be unable or unwilling to fulfill.

8. One cannot avoid having some assumptions about how another thinks or feels. So check these assumptions out—but with permission. Do not behave as if they were true.

Remember, such "mind reading with permission" is really a way of exposing your own feelings. As such, it is a way of taking the first risk. It can often help to reduce the fear of rejection, since the other person has only to correct your hypotheses, not volunteer to bring out the feared wishes for change by themselves.

Within all these rules, there is room for endless options. There must be. For as we have pointed out, no two crazymaking experiences are the same. No two sets of crazymaking circumstances are entirely alike.

But beyond these options, we shall now see, there are some others that ought to be considered before we take any action against crazymaking at all.

CHAPTER TWELVE

The Options of Sanity

Not all crazymaking can be managed by the rules we have explored in the previous chapter. For these rules are specifically designed to deal with the most important kinds of crazymaking—those in which intimacy is at stake and in which unlimited growth is desirable.

But crazymaking occurs in relationships of every kind. And while some of the rules of sane communication have value and meaning in all crazymaking, we may not wish to become intimate with the lady who pushes into line ahead of us at the supermarket. We may have little wish or hope for growth with the man who writes the instructions on the income-tax form.

Yet these people, and endless others—from the big boss at the office to the teenager who drops his bubble gum on the sidewalk—can drive us crazy. To preserve our sanity, in small ways and large, we need to understand how to deal with all the forms of crazymaking in our lives. We need to know how to respond to all forms of crazymaking in a sane way.

Ideally, of course, we have seen that we would like to be able to understand the coded messages of crazy-making. For if generally these are demands upon us to change, sanity demands that we recognize what change is being asked for. And we would then like to have the freedom to choose whether or not we want to grant the change, or perhaps to negotiate, to compromise between our own wishes and those of others.

Sadly, such information is not always open to us. And even more sadly, although we may be able to obtain information about the change that is wished, we may not be able to get the opportunity to choose. Moreover, even in some situations in which it would be possible to get clear information and then to choose, it may be unrealistic to try to do either. It may even be wiser to let the masked aggressions behind the crazymaking remain concealed—both ours and those of the other person.

Let us now look at the broad classes of sane response, and at the ways we can evaluate our crazymaking experiences so that we can recognize what we might want to do and what it is reasonable to try to do.

In many ways the simplest forms of crazymaking to deal with, those in which the options are clearest, are the matters of what we might call *casual crazymaking*. These are incidents that occur with complete strangers, with certain institutions, and with people with whom we may be familiar, but who mainly serve functional purposes in our lives. When these people or institutions have a crazymaking effect, we have some simple options.

1. Total rejection

Often, casual crazymaking is no more complex than the failure of a person or institution to meet the expectation we have been given. For example, you are mildly interested in having the local weekly newspaper delivered. But often the delivery boy skips your house. And when he does deliver, it is with a toss into a mudpuddle or some thorny shrubbery.

Or the dry cleaner makes a crisis of every item you give him, perhaps as a way of establishing his importance. "I don't know what you paid for this dress, but look at these skimpy seams. I'll do my best, but I'm not sure they won't pull out. And this fabric"—he looks at the label—"I'm surprised that store is selling this kind of stuff. Once you get a grease spot on it—''

Total rejection is the easy solution to these crazy-making problems. You simply cancel the newspaper or switch to some other cleaner.

One principle here is that of repetition. A single incident with the cleaner, a single missed delivery or hunt through the shrubbery for the newspaper, can be dismissed. But repeated incidents suggest that a crazymaking style can be expected in the relationship.

Another criterion for choosing a response is whether the crazymaking is personal or impersonal. For this suggests what you may have to do to put a stop to the behavior. For example, you can tell the newspaper boy or his circulation department that unless the delivery is made in a reasonable way, you will cancel. Your demand for change can be made without becoming engaged in a crazymaking spiral. The situation is cut and dried. Either you get the newspaper as you want it or you will stop it.

But the crisismaking of the dry cleaner is another matter. To put a stop to his remarks, you would have to use the techniques of a more intimate relationship. You would have to assert your demands for change by sharing your feelings. Unless his services are somehow unique, you are not likely to want to spend the emotional energy it will take to secure the change you want. Indeed, to suffer all the struggles of a close relationship when the actual relationship is only a functional one would be a form of self-crazymaking.

Ironically, we must recognize, there are people who use crazymaking as a bonding technique. It can be a curiously useful technique of establishing an emotional relationship where none needs to be. And particularly, as in the case of the cleaner, it can be a way in which a person tries to convince you that you are dependent on him. But it cannot work unless you are willing to collude.

2. Tolerance

As we observed in looking at trivial crazymaking, in some cases tolerance may be the only way of dealing with maddening factors in our lives. For example, in the instance of the newspaper delivery boy, suppose he brings the only good morning newspaper.

You could threaten to cancel your subscription, but are you really willing to do so? If not, threatening may only lead to an unending crazymaking game. You like to have the morning newspaper with your wake-up coffee. So you don't want to drive downtown to buy one. Of course you can reasonably demand a change either from the boy or from his employer. And if this is not effective, toleration is the only alternative.

But don't waste your time and energy muttering and being vexed every time you have to fish the newspaper out from under a car. If you fail to have impact when you have made demands for change, only two realistic options remain. You can stop the delivery or you can philosophically put up with it. Again, if you really cannot tolerate the situation without being continually upset by it, you have only yourself to blame for the repeated crazymaking effect if you allow it to go on.

Developing some crazymaking tolerance is necessary for all of us. We can learn to watch the ads for Maggie's Mixes, ads that promise us instant cakes that taste like Mother's, and know that the claim is untrue. We can even buy Freddie's Frozen Dinners and read on the package "Old-Time Home Cooking From Your Freezer," knowing that what we are going to eat is a tasteless TV dinner. We may shake our heads, but the experience need not be crazymaking.

What is the secret of such tolerance in trivial or casual crazymaking? Essentially, it is that crazymaking does not occur when we do not allow false expectations to hold sway. Perhaps the first time we buy one of Freddie's Frozen Dinners we really do hope for something more, looking at the picture of nice old "Mrs. Freddie" on the package, stirring away on a wood-burning stove. But one look, one bite, tells us that the expectation is not real. If we buy the dinner again it is by choice, and there is no good reason why the false expectation should have recurred.

The situation is much the same in many common crazymaking settings. If we are realistic, we know we are going to have crazymaking experiences from time to time while driving a car, when making an airline reservation, when waiting for the telephone installer or the plumber to come. We know that in a complex world there is bound to be a good deal of trivial or casual crazymaking. For in modern civilization we are endlessly dependent upon others who provide the products and services we need or who merely share a crowded society with us.

This of course does not mean that we should tolerate all casual or trivial crazymaking, every breach of rules, truth, good manners, or good sense. But it means we need to distinguish between what we can and what we cannot change or have a part in changing. The rest we must be able to tolerate, either as part of human comedy or of human tragedy.

To put to work our knowledge of the dynamics of crazymaking, let us keep in mind that aggression, to succeed, must have impact. If we repeatedly aim our aggressions where we can see that impact is unlikely or impossible, we are the agents of our own crazymaking.

Tolerance can become more difficult when dependency is greater, however. For example, suppose you have been buying your gasoline at the same station for years. As you leave your home you notice that one tire seems to be soft. You pull into the familiar station and there is a new attendant.

"I seem to have a soft tire," you say. "Would you mind checking the pressure?"

"Do you want gas?"

"I just filled my tank here a couple of hours ago. I always fill my tank here, have for years."

"Look, this is a service lane—for customers. I got better things to do than check everybody's tires."

The situation is crazymaking, but again you must reasonably assess what change you can hope for. You can ask. You can demand. You can even threaten. But beyond this there are rational limits. Effectiveness is again the criterion. Certainly you may want the attendant to behave as you have come to expect attendants in this station to behave. But the essential change is not to have your expectations fulfilled; it is to take care of the tire. Again, the situation calls for tolerating the crazymaking in order to serve your own best interest. Is it better to ask again, politely, perhaps holding out a dollar, or to express one's frustration vehemently and then limp down the road?

3. Limited tolerance

Between absolute rejection and absolute tolerance there rests an infinity of possible combinations. These involve limited tolerance of crazymaking.

For example, even in an important relationship there may well be crazymaking elements that are intractable yet not disturbing enough to lead to true rejection. He snores and tosses restlessly in bed, but awake he is a good friend and gentle lover. She cannot seem, no matter how hard she tries, to avoid last-minute problems—from a forgotten stain on the dress she planned to wear to forgetting to put gas in her car.

There are myriad such maddening factors that are not necessarily purposeful but are genuinely crazymaking. In such circumstances one need not, so to speak, throw the partner out with the crazymaking. For the crazymaking may be the result, not of frustrated aggressions in the relationship, but of essential personality or character difficulties that are inner matters, not indirect aggressions.

And there are even situations in which the repeated crazymaking is not an integral factor in the personality, but represents an indirect aggression. Yet tolerance is nevertheless a reasonable choice. For example one may have an excellent job, working for a boss who is essentially fair, yet who is insecure in his or her own power, who fears to assert that power in direct ways, and instead periodically asserts it in the form of crazymaking.

In essence, if an aspect of an important other's

behavior is crazymaking, one ought not to make assumptions about motives. To do so, as we know, is to initiate a crazymaking of one's own. Rather, one can ask for clear information. One can give clear information. One can share feelings. But if these efforts have no effect, then one must conclude either that the crazymaking is tolerable or that it is so damaging that one must reject the relationship.

For example, Janet is entirely happy working for Harvey, with one exception. He cannot resist indulging in little sex games that are vexing to her.

She knows that Harvey does not keep her on merely because he finds her attractive. He is a crackerjack sales manager and he tolerates nothing but first-rate work. In a business way, he treats her simply as a capable executive assistant. But from time to time, in certain circumstances, especially when they are alone, he cannot seem to avoid flirtatious or seductive remarks.

Janet finally finds the courage to tell him that these upset her, that they make her wonder if she holds her job because of her ability. Harvey quickly reassures her. But when they are out of town again, he makes small overtures once more. And if they work after hours together, he cannot seem to avoid little gestures of affection, little side comments about how attractive she is, about how nice she must be to hold, about how she understands him as no other woman ever has.

What should Janet do when Harvey persists? She has really done all she can when she tells him that sex is not what she wants of their relationship. Above all she has tested the situation when she has, in a number of ways, dared to reject him.

Having been open is Janet's insurance policy against this mildly crazymaking behavior. For she has tested and found that he does not reject her if she rejects him sexually. His continuance of the game that they really have a kind of sexual alliance has proven not to be a real threat. Why? Because it has not insisted upon a real change in their relationship. As always, the reality of the crazymaking lies in the reality of the implied demand for change.

What Janet has learned by risking the giving of clear information is that to reject is not necessarily to be rejected. And while Harvey's overtures and asides are maddening in a way, Janet's open assertions have assured her that there is no real double bind—that sexual concession is not necessary to avoid total rejection.

So it is that limited tolerance becomes possible without the sacrifice of sane rights if one can only test the situation with open demands for change. These demands need not necessarily be met. They need only fail to result in real rejection. For it is only when one is really afraid of total rejection, when the choice seems to be either to submit or to be set aside, that crazymaking has real power.

4. Segmental distancing

There are many relationships in everyone's life that are neither truly intimate, nor capable of becoming intimate, yet are far from casual. When crazymaking tarnishes these relationships, a painful question may arise.

Because the relationship is close, because one may value it and even depend upon it in some ways, the crazymaking is disturbing, too disturbing to tolerate. Yet to terminate it may in some circumstances be impossible.

Such semi-intimate crazymaking may take place with a valued friend. Or it may occur with an in-law, a colleague, an important client. In these cases segmental distancing may provide an answer.

The term derives from the concept of segmental relationships. These are alliances that are important, necessary, or valued—but acquire their worth and meaning through some special attribute or group of attributes. That is, the relationship is rewarding, but only in certain limited aspects.

A good client or colleague may be a splendid working partner but not a person one really wants as a friend. A good lover may have no potential as a spouse. A friend one enjoys as a dinner companion is not someone one wants as a lover. And so on.

As an example, Kelly and Beth have become good friends as well as neighbors. And at first they confide in each other. They visit back and forth over morning coffee. They shop together and share each other's tastes. But as their closeness grows, Kelly becomes aware of a crazymaking component.

It is not at all clear when it begins. But at times Beth leaves Kelly feeling confused and upset, betrayed even. For instance, at first Beth treats Kelly's six-year-old, Richard, as her own. Then suddenly, one day when Richard is overtired and continually interrupts the two women's conversations with crying and whining demands, Beth says, "You know, I understand there's a new family-counseling clinic in town that's awfully good with disturbed children. I mean, Richard is such a bright child. It would be a shame if his behavior problems spoiled things for him."

Kelly is wounded. And she is confused. She trusts Beth as a friend. She is not aware that Richard has "behavior problems." Is it because she is not objective? If Beth sees them, do others see them too, but feel reluctant to say anything? Kelly assumes that Beth speaks out because she is such a good friend, and that she speaks the truth because she has Kelly's welfare at heart.

But a week later, when Kelly finds some bargains in clothing and hurries to show them to Beth, the reaction is painful. "I can see why you couldn't resist at that price," says Beth. "And if you just lose a few pounds, they'll fit you perfectly."

And so it goes. After several such stings, Kelly begins to wonder. (Remember, repetition is a key sign of important crazymaking.) She sees that her expectations that Beth will react as a friend are dashed when Beth's reactions are so often those that feel hurtful, betraying.

Kelly sees a trend toward a tactic we sometimes call *undermining.*

Undermining is related to other patterns we have seen that repeatedly take the edge off all small triumphs, that nitpick while complimenting and thus undermine one's sense of accomplishment. We have usually observed related tactics in the hands of a more powerful person who seeks to keep control. But Kelly does not see Beth as anything but an equal.

Troubled because she does not want to lose such a good new friend, but periodically made to suffer for the friendship, Kelly tries to analyze further but cannot. So she decides to try to get information about what kind of change Beth wants, on the deduction that demands for change must lie behind Beth's crazymaking.

They are in Kelly's kitchen one morning, and Kelly is telling Beth about a party the night before, showing her how she wore her hair. "Nice," says Beth. "But it might be better if you didn't brush it so far out to the side. Your face would look thinner."

Stung, Kelly asks Beth why she said this. She shares her feelings about it, too. "It makes me feel as if I must have looked like a hulk all night."

Beth reassures her, saying she is only trying to act like a friend, and that Kelly should not be so sensitive. Kelly is frustrated by her try at sane communications.

Then she notices something. Just as crazymaking falls into tactical patterns, so also can it have patterns of timing, which can also be clues to the inner demand for change.

Kelly notices that the stings seem to follow any reference to activities with, or concerns for, another friend, or even a relative. She watches and finds the pattern holds. It happens when she tells Beth about a shopping day with Nina, about going on a business weekend with her husband, about a dinner at the Monahans'. Kelly also observes that Beth has very few friends who are at all close.

Kelly now determines to try her hypothesis. She asks

Beth for permission to read her mind, gets it, and says, "I keep being upset by the put-downs, and I wonder if you realize what's happening. I can't help feeling that it happens when you resent my other friendships."

Beth immediately denies this. She expresses regret about Kelly's bad feelings. She says she will try to be more careful since Kelly is so sensitive. "But I can't help wondering—if you really trusted me as a friend, maybe you wouldn't take it so badly when I tell you the truth. You really shouldn't take everything as rejection."

Somehow this response clinches it for Kelly. She realizes that if she is to continue her friendship with Beth, it cannot be an entirely open relationship, that it must be a *segmental* one. In other words she has identified an area of conversation that dependably elicits crazymaking. Total tolerance would be self-destructive. Total rejection would lose Beth's company, which in most ways she enjoys. Limited tolerance would be foolish when Kelly is certain that she knows what will bring on the crazymaking.

Kelly tries her theory and finds that it works. She avoids mentioning activities with others. She avoids asking Beth to join in any kind of a group. And the stings are gone.

Segmental distancing is an effective instrument in certain specific instances, especially when one is bound into contact with another and is able to identify a well-defined area of trouble. It can be a useful resort in dealing with the crazymaking of an in-law, for example.

But it cannot really make for a very close or meaningful relationship. A defensive sense of avoidance pervades. It can be a grim failure in marriage or for any relationship in which contact cannot be controlled and tends to range over the whole of life. The closed areas of communication cut off growth when one tries to use segmental distancing in what normally should be an intimate relationship. For one thing its use in such situations tends to evoke a crazymaking style of distancing to maintain the segmentation.

5. Conflict

For many people, perhaps for most, the very word has a repugnant, even somewhat frightening overtone. It has a ring of harshness, of hostility, of wounding mutual assault.

Yet these are connotations that have been added—perhaps through the universal fear of aggressions—to what is otherwise a simple and straightforward word, one that merely describes the meeting of opposing forces.

Why do we make so much of the word and its implications? The answer is plain if we look back through this book.

We have found that crazymaking is essentially nothing more than a concealed way in which necessary aggressions, necessary assertions of oneself and one's needs, can be expressed. We have seen that these aggressions can be viewed as nothing more than wishes for change.

We have observed that fear—usually a fear that openly stating the wish for change will end in some form of rejection—blocks the aggression. And we have learned that the only effective way to deal with the painful and destructive crazymaking forms of asserting these wishes is to bring the wishes into the open.

But then what? Each of us experiences wishes for change, wishes of great or small importance, almost constantly. And if nothing intervenes, we merely respond by setting out to do whatever must be done in order to accomplish the change—whether it involves something as simple as scratching an itch or as complex as finding someone to hold close.

But things do intervene, things both within us and outside us. And thus at the root of all psychology we find the continuing requirement for change, the attempts to achieve it, and the fears and frustrations that accompany the attempts.

Essentially, it is the wish for change to which the psychologist looks when his client is troubled. And he tries to help the client identify the wishes, to understand the inner and outer barriers, to manage the feelings that surround the wishes, and ultimately to seek out constructive changes—openly, hopefully, and fruitfully.

These wishes for change, which are the core of human behavior, are simpler to deal with when we are alone. But isolation, as we have explained, is an unhealthful state. We need others with whom to share life. And the problem is that they have wishes too.

Inevitably, continually, partners' wishes become contrary to one another. And in many ways caring permits them to accommodate to one another in a healthful manner. They can share food, money, a bed. But not in all. So the wishes come into conflict.

Obviously, what then becomes required is another kind of sharing—negotiation, a granting and asking for adjustments, concessions, taking turns. This is not to imply that healthful accommodation is without discomfort, even without pain.

But easy or painful as the solution may be, one simply cannot deny the conflict. From time to time, everyone tries to deny it for fear that conflict may lead to rejection. And one of the results is crazymaking.

Yet in the long run, we have seen, crazymaking is sure to produce far more real rejection, far more pain, far more likelihood of separation. The conflict is merely concealed; it is not avoided. The adjustments are merely forced; they are not negotiated or freely given. And always the price is the chipping and tearing away at what ought to be the inalienable rights of sanity—wounds too deep, too crippling to ignore.

The simple truth is that when we are able to put a stop to crazymaking, it is only by letting the wishes for change into the open. And ultimately, this will make some conflict more visible.

But the conflict is not new. It has been there as long as the wishes for change were there, at work in subterfuge. Now, however, the conflict is visible.

To the psychologist, this visibility, this emergence, does not signal the common fear that the cold and hidden battle will flare into open, ruthless warfare. It is instead full of hope.

For it is now possible to deal with the conflict in controlled, realistic ways. Concealed, the conflict is a fight to win over the other, to wound, to take power. In the open, reasonable caring and sharing can come into play. When each knows what the other wishes, it is possible for the two to work out their mutual interests, each to satisfy the other while satisfying him- or herself, to let the other grow.

An end to crazymaking means the beginning of open conflict, in intimate or close relationships. But it also means the beginning of real understanding, and of sharing without smothering or being smothered, without overpowering or submitting, with genuine choice and change freely made.

One cannot totally banish crazymaking from one's life—or even from one's own behavior. We have seen that now and then a little crazymaking must be tolerated. And that tolerance must extend occasionally even to those who are close to us, and even to ourselves. For remember that crazymaking is a gambit of the unconscious. And the unconscious plays tricks of which we are not aware.

But by and large, by being able to recognize the experience, by understanding how it has its effects, by realizing that it represents a wish for change, and by having some tools with which the wish can be revealed, we need not let crazymaking deprive us of our sane rights. We need not suffer its miseries or its limitations in important aspects of our lives.

We cannot be free of crazymaking. But we can know how to move toward sanity.

APPENDIX I

Crazymaking: Some Theoretical and Clinical Notes

The term crazymaking (CM) is used to encompass a wide variety of pathogenic communications that may be characterized as passive-aggressive demands for change; these generally incorporate simultaneous conflicting messages (although often only by implication). Their pathogenicity appears to lie not only in the operational double-bind that presents itself to the recipient, but also in the actual conflicted motivations of the communicator.

Our clinical experience at the Bach Institute in Los Angeles (formerly the Institute of Group Psychotherapy) has been that insight into the CM patterns provides us with a valuable theoretical and therapeutic instrument. For elements of CM seem to be virtually intrinsic to intimate communications, fundamental devices for the avoidance of the aggressive interaction that is inevitable in intimate relationships. And a primary focus of our creative-aggression approach to relational problems is the therapeutic management of such avoidance.[1]

Observations of CM communications are classic in the world's literature. But the systematic study of CM processes is recent, a part of the emergence of communications and field-systems theories.

Some early scientific observations of CM processes

were made in the 1920s, under the tutelage of Kurt Lewin, at the University of Berlin. In one early experiment, Lewin's student Tamara Dembo set problems involving two sets of "barriers" for her subjects—with increasing difficulty of choice proceeding to impossibility. Trusting in the fairness of the test, the subjects tended to persist in a stressful situation of failure, not unlike partners in a failing, but persisting, marriage. Unable to win, escape or fight, subjects displayed irrational, regressive and hostile behaviors.

In other experiments, Lewin and his colleagues (among them George Bach) studied subjects in conflict situations "between opposing forces in the cognitive field"—noting increased tensions as barriers and restraining forces reduced the number of options for coping effectively.

Animal studies by Pavlov produced experimental neuroses by the simultaneous administration of conflicting conditioned stimuli and also by training discriminatory behaviors and then increasing the discriminatory demands to difficult or impossible levels.

Other human research indicated some responses to such difficult or impossible conflict situations, ranging from hostile-aggressive fantasies of toddlers observed by Bach, to later Lewinian studies. Such defenses included encysting, fixation on unreal belief systems to cope with unfulfilled expectations and cognitive dissonances, or outright denial.

In studies of schizophrenic communication, Gregory Bateson found that some order existed in the apparently disorganized messages, with a structure designed to deal with their difficulty of perceiving communications context. Suspecting ill will, and unable to discriminate ill will from good, they tended to withdraw from communication entirely and to dismiss attempts at contact as trivial.

Bateson postulated a childhood exposure to contradictory parental injunctions as the root of such behavior. Such double-bind situations with important others, without clearcut punishment, reward or expectation cues, are seen as prototypical of the CM process.

The primary survival functions of CM communications appear to be twofold: to avoid or delay open aggression and conflict, and to protect oneself against rejection. Bateson envisioned metaphor as such a CM device: "The convenient thing about a metaphor is that it leaves it up to the other . . . to see an accusation in the statement . . . or to ignore it."

One may observe at least six ancillary functions of CM:

1. The delay provided by CM is commonly a delay of confrontation, allowing time needed to plan, adjust or find solutions in conflict.

2. The paradoxical nature of CM double messages permits withdrawal from or denial of aggression.

3. The unclarity of CM communication permits testing, to see how much resistance or counter-aggression might be generated and determine what can be tolerated.

4. In certain instances, the concealed and indirect aggressions of CM can produce a degree of change, or at least a distancing which reduces tension, without risking the more effective open demand for change.

5. As observed in the text, CM tends to evoke responses to itself (in what is described as the *CM spiral*) rather than to the actual demand for change. And this spiral of exchange may displace the change-aggression to safer ground.

6. Through CM messages, options for change may be rehearsed in relative safety, while the relationship is kept static rather than labile. Rituals may be established thereby, which are nonthreatening, but which permit changes to be previewed. In this manner, CM helps deal with the common fear that change secured might be change for the worse.

By ordering and analyzing CM material, we have been able to undertand the processes involved. But the why and when of instigation remain reasoning speculations. On the personal level, instigation of CM behavior appears to begin with:

Fear of Rejection. Such fear appears to be that open demands for change may be rejected, and the person rejected, if demands are expressed too openly, prematurely or assertively.

Difficulty or Uncertainty of Change. Dissatisfaction, without a clear sense of the source or the required change, seems to be a spur to CM, along with a concern that the partner may be locked into the status quo and resist change per se.

Preservation of Hope. CM communications may appear when rejection seems certain, has already taken place and even when open demand has been withdrawn. If the change need remains pressing, CM allows a continued, indirect expression and maintains some hope of eventual relief.

Punishment. In some instances, recognizing that change has been rejected or is impossible of hope, CM becomes a way of negative reaction. In this mode, CM creates discomfort for which responsibility can be avoided or denied; and perhaps a resulting instability helps to maintain some sense of personal power in the face of feelings of helplessness and/or defeat.

Control. The sustaining of power seems to be one key factor in CM behavior. It appears to be a way of asserting dominance while denying its existence or the wish for it. In this respect, CM behaviors may be responsive to efforts to assert independence or equality, to deprive another of freedom or authority.

Ambivalence. There is clinical evidence that CM behaviors reflect ambivalent feelings toward change. Either the right to change or its desirability may be in doubt. In this respect, CM communications may signify intrapsychic rather than interpersonal conflict, with fears of self-rejection.

Rather than being conscious stratagems for dealing with the above and related factors, it is plain that CM behaviors are unconscious adaptations to deal with the stresses of interpersonal systems. The most psychologically sophisticated individuals will resort to CM tactics which are revealed as such only in retrospect. Thus, clinically, heightened awareness of CM processes and experiences proves valuable.

CM behaviors also seem to be engendered by system-related factors. In this sense, they are more likely to occur in unstable than in stable relational situations, as a way of dealing with insecurities. As examples:

Entrances. In seeking to enter into a new system, involving work, love, friendship, a new community, the newcomer is disinclined toward open assertion of self. Similarly, the established and secure members of a system may see an entrant as a source of potential instability in what has been a stable system. CM communications become operant as individuals seek approval or acceptance, or as they assert covertly that a new entrant must not disturb a system which is stable and comfortable.

Exits. Conversely, changes threatened by the departure of an individual from a stable system may be dealt with by crazymaking. In the extreme, such exits have been known to be a key factor in spouse murder. Rejection, whether from a job, a team or a love affair may become psychologically too threatening to be carried out or accepted openly. So CM behaviors may be invoked to force or hinder an exit, again without the assumption of responsibility.

Our experience has been that, despite the subtlety and the unconscious nature of CM behaviors, it is not difficult to teach an awareness of the experience, whether as actor or as recipient. More than a dozen such exercises are suggested in the *Aggression Lab Manual*.

An important clinical value of such exercises is that they dramatize the worth of open and direct aggression in contrast to the mysterious and covert aggressions of CM. In the use of demonstration rituals, we find that it is easy to invoke the almost universal CM skills—and then to expose their real nature. Similarly, it is not hard to demonstrate the CM aspects of interpersonal convention, from the insincere "How are you?" to the meaningless "Let's get together for lunch—sometime," and the endless statements of "I would, but I can't." Such examples are commonplace in every culture as testimony to virtually universal fears that asserting demands for change produces fears of rejecting or of being rejected. And the management of either aspect of rejection (as suggested in *Pairing* and in *Intimate Enemy*) becomes a valuable tool in dealing with crazymaking, by teaching that rejection of a single demand or behavior does not imply total rejection.

At a deeper level, however, professionals should be warned that the exploration of crazymaking—without appropriate professional guidance—may have all the emotional toxicity of crazymaking itself. Interpretive debriefing, following crazymaking exercises and experiences, is needed. There must be an accepting tolerance of those who cannot participate in revealing CM rituals (perhaps 5 percent of clients). And there must be some support also for those who become overinvolved, along with careful interpretation of CM games as they relate to real-life situations.

The awareness of CM behaviors, and the attempt to unravel their devious complexities, are not without hazards. Persons on the Bach Institute staff have encountered serious personal difficulties while trying to unravel the mechanisms. The authors of this book have not explored the subject with impunity. The pathogenicity of crazymaking is real. None of us are free from it, and its unconscious nature presents psychological hazards for ourselves and for the laity which cannot be ignored or taken lightly. Yet a constructive awareness of CM processes can be inherently productive of growth. As with virtually all psychological discomforts, the crazymaking experience can be a valuable tool for growth.

Of value in teaching recognition of the crazymaking experience is the following checklist:

1. Feeling temporarily thrown off balance and momentarily unable to right oneself.

2. Feeling lost, not knowing where to turn, searching aimlessly.

3. Being caught off guard.

4. Feeling disconnected, confused, disoriented.

5. Feeling off balance, as if the rug had been pulled from under one's feet.

6. Receiving double messages but somehow unable or fearful to ask for clarification.

7. Feeling generally "bugged" by the simple presence of a person.

8. The discovery that one was mistaken in one's evaluation of where one stood or what it was all about.

9. Feeling totally unprepared for a broken promise or unfulfilled expectation.

10. Experiencing the shattering of an important "dream."

11. Where one assumed goodwill, ill will *seems* to prevail.

12. One feels pushed around, not in control of one's own direction.

13. Unable to get off redundantly spinning circles of thoughts.

14. What seemed clear becomes muddled.

15. An uneasy, weird feeling of emptiness.

16. A strong wish to get away, yet feeling unable to move, as if frozen.

17. One is befuddled, not able to attack the problem.

18. Feeling vaguely suspicious that something is wrong.

19. Feeling that one's subjective world has become chaotic.

20. The situation seems subtly permeated with unknown and uncontrollable factors. No simple solution is in sight.

21. Ambivalence: simultaneous feeling of aggression and docility.

22. Feeling that, I must be doing something wrong.

23. Losing one's basic values, feeling that everything one strives for, believes in and thinks "is crazy."

24. "I don't know what got into me. I am making a fool of myself."

There are, as well, some notable differences between feelings experienced by the agent of CM and those of recipients, to wit:

Agent	versus	Target
Planning how to proceed		Passive waiting, anticipatory stress
Secret excitement		Defensive laughter
Feeling important and strong		Restricted and weak
Sexual or power fantasies of being served		Masochistic excitement —what will he/she do to me?
Inventive, creative, trying out ideas		Dependent, trying to become mechanical, routinized
Imposing ever clearer structure		Confused, disoriented
Enjoys power-impact on target		Fearful of exploitation and embarrassment
Conflict over domineering behavior		Scheming countermeasures
Fearful of rebellion, becomes stricter		Increased resistance to being pushed
Would go on a little bit longer		Cannot wait for quitting time
Stressful anticipation of retaliation		Uplifted by thoughts of vengeance after role reversal
High and energized at the end		Exhausted but glad it's over

Properly understood, crazymaking can be a valuable

source of information to the therapist and to either person in a relationship. It can, notably, suggest the needs for appropriate change. So the object is not to extinguish CM behaviors, but rather to reduce the immediate pain and to try to elicit the underlying meanings, the aggressions which need to be asserted openly and clearly. If the object of crazymaking is change, then the therapeutic need is to make the demands for change manifest, so that they may be negotiated and, to some extent, can proceed.

Above all, perhaps, crazymaking is testimony to the ceaseless need for change in virtually all relationships. Its recognition signals an awareness of discomfort and imbalance. As with all behaviors, crazymaking is a valuable clue. What we do and say becomes an indicator, no matter how veiled, of what we are and what we wish.

The split messages of crazymaking becomes a doubly valuable clue for the teacher and the therapist. For, appropriately understood, they can tell us not only what is most wished, but what is most feared. And in the true understanding of these painful entities lies a way toward growth and intimacy—a way that does not fear the conflict that is ordinary in human relationships, but uses it as a guidepost to an understanding, both of ourselves and of the relationships that keep us from the intrinsic madness of isolation and loneliness.

APPENDIX II

Some Further Notes For Student, Teacher And Therapist

Throughout the text, we have noted that the phenomenon of crazymaking is virtually infinite in its variety, and that there is thus no hope of making anything like a complete glossary of CM patterns. For this and other reasons, the phenomenon also resists the making of a true classification system or anything more than a rather loose typology, which we have attempted to do, for example, by viewing CM patterns in terms of violations of the rights of sanity.

The truth is that CM patterns are exponentially more varied even than we have suggested. For one cannot hope to understand them without taking into account a further variety of contexts. These contexts may vary endlessly in situational and relational respects, as well as in the contexts of personality and of individual expression. But not only may the same crazymaking words have entirely different psychological meanings in different contexts of the moment, one must also consider what we might call the historical context. On the most obvious level, this means taking into consideration the personal and relational history which precedes the behavior. But somewhat more subtle, and demanding an awareness on the part of the theorist or therapist, is the fact that CM is intrinsic to all important relationships. Thus it is part of the history of all such relationships. And thus, to some extent, CM behaviors are in part responsive to the old "stings" of these relationships, to an underlying (though often slow-moving) crazymaking spiral.

It should never be forgotten that what we are really trying to understand is the nature of the aggression that is being expressed indirectly, and the nature of the barrier of fear that inhibits direct expression of demands for change. If we remember always to establish the context of CM, in a number of ways, before attempting to draw conclusions, we can find in the concept and in the mechanism of the process valuable clues to guide understanding and therapy.

As an example, the authors believe that there is a very valuable therapeutic purpose to be served by asking the question about any important other, "How does (he, she, it) drive you crazy?" Or, "How would you (describe, categorize, give a name to) this pattern?" Or, "What kind of crazymaking pattern most upsets you?" And, "Can you give me a recent example of that pattern, and tell me who uses it?" There is projective value here.

Why These Further Notes

In an effort to provide a personal and more simplified insight into the mechanisms of CM, the authors have consciously delimited the reader's perceptions of the experience. This is, in part, to avoid having the book become crazymaking in itself, both by *overloading* with information and by creating what could become a paranoid sort of suspicion of intimates.

However, for the serious student and the professional, it is felt that there should be some additional explication of the variables; also some additional indications of major categories of CM experiences and patterns taken from clinical experience. As an example, in preparing the text, the authors felt that it was important to explain that not all aggression (particularly, not that aggression that was merely an expression of assertions for impact or change) was hostile. However, it was believed that to incorporate further variations of aggression goals would only be confusing, and through doubt might actually heighten fears of aggressive behavior, whether one's own or those of another.

Some of these more sensitive, and important, areas of CM behavior which have been omitted from the text are indicated below, in the understanding that the professional is likely to require them for understanding and application:

I

Some Variations of the Nature and Purpose of Aggression

In the main text, we have differentiated between only two primary kinds of aggression—*Impact-type and Hostile-type*. However, in considering the modes of aggression, we have observed that it is useful, both theoretically and therapeutically, to take into account four additional types of aggression:

1. Indirect, or Passive-Type Aggression

It may be misinterpreted that all indirect or passive-type aggression is expressed as crazymaking. While it may be argued, by the furthest extension of definition, that all CM behavior represents indirect or passive-type aggression the converse is not necessarily so.

In a broad sense, CM is a kind of archetype of indirectly expressed aggression. But in another sense it is not necessarily always true that crazymaking derives from a fear of expressing aggressive demands for change or other aggressive feelings in an indirect way. Consider, for example, the status of play-type aggression (qv), such as teasing.

Therapeutically or theoretically, it is our clinical finding that it is not always necessary to identify the precise nature or derivation of the fear that presents a barrier to openly assertive demand. Rather, the therapeutic conversion of seeming passivity and of indirection into open expression, with some understanding of the pathologies of sadism.

3. Instrumental-type Aggression

This may be defined as the use of aggressive energy to achieve a goal. For example, Freud considered an aggressive wish of the male to dominate the female as intrinsic and biologically useful to sexual purposes. We would caution that it is easy to make assumptions of instrumental-type aggression, and hard to prove them. One must be careful not to use such assumptions as escapes from difficulties of relational analysis.

4. Play-type Aggression

Aggression incorporated into fantasy and play can be a harmless entertainment, may signify repressed or concealed relational problems or be a combination of both. Henri Bergson's line, "When one laughs, one shows one's teeth," should not be taken as a constant; it is not always true. Here is another example of the need, in looking at crazymaking communications, to consider all contexts of the situation, relationship, etc.

For depth understanding of CM behaviors, this more refined system of aggression types (beyond that suggested in the main text of merely differentiating Impact Aggression or Hostile Aggression [qv]) has proven very helpful. It can be valuable in trying to determine the nature of *Aggression Phobia* (which consists of such behaviors as lead to the withdrawal from open, direct expressions of aggression). That is, by understanding the nature of the aggressive behavior which is avoided, we may be helped to comprehend the nature of the individual's fear, and also the nature of such CM processes as may have become operant in a relationship.

The Creative Aggression System is a conceptualization of aggressive processes. The fundamental objectives of its application to human behavior center about the conversion of patterns of H-type Aggression to those of I-type Aggression. That is, one seeks to achieve acceptance and expression of inpulses toward open, change-making assertions—and to minimize thus the crazymaking effects of indirect expression, with its hostilities and the probability of eliciting hostile response. Application of the *CAG system* is a primary antidote to CM.

II

The Love-Crazy Syndrome

This is an important source of CM behaviors and their pathological effects. Freud has suggested that the perceptions and effects of being in love are commonly psychotic in character—since magical, unrealistic characteristics tend to be assigned to the loved person and the relationship, and tend to be sustained by persisting denials of any conflicting reality.

It has been proposed that such magic and unreality derive from the infant's perceptions of parental love—and the wish that love relationships in adulthood shall mirror these perceptions of a loving person who is unfailing and unconditional in the giving and welcoming of love, in the manner of the mother.

Therapeutically, of course, such beliefs evoke great (and sadly, often very effective) resistances to the work of the therapist. The challenge to confront the adult realities of love—the conditional nature of all relationships and the necessity to test the realities and to establish a relational *quid pro quo*—can evoke endless ego-defensive behaviors, even to the leaving of therapy in order to deny realities and to sustain the warm magic of the happy complacency of the infant. All the forces of hysteria and all the terrors of separation anxiety support the resistance to psychological truth.

In this context, it is clear, "Love" is the ideal greenhouse for the nurture of CM. For the motivation to sustain the love-crazy state can easily serve as a barrier to any aggressive impulse, force repression and lead to the later emergence of aggressions in symbolic, conflicted and dualistic ways. Such repression is fueled further by two inimical, clashing psychological forces: (1) the adaptational requirements of life, which call for constant change and (2) the requirement of the love-crazy state for what is virtually a rigid status quo.

So it is that crazymaking can become the subversive handmaiden of love—and in our culture, which tends to picture love as a constant, a state of unconditional feeling and binding, a CM component is a virtual certainty.

In therapeutic terms, it may be important to differentiate the love-crazy state in its nonrealistic, aggression-phobic and change-phobic totality, and the love-crazy *component* which invades virtually all love relationships. In the following analysis, we describe the natural history of the totality, but the component aspect should also be considered.

There are three phases to the state:
1. The distant fantasy
2. The *all-electric trip*
3. The illusions and disillusions of the exit

Each phase is supported by CM behaviors, which tend to support the natural evolution, and to hasten it. For the CM factor leads ultimately toward both inner and relational confrontations with reality, and stimulates ego defenses. With each, the challenge to the therapist is to elicit reality-testing behaviors and consequent evaluations.

In the light of what we have seen about CM, much that concerns these phases should be clear, in terms of their relationship to crazymaking patterns and processes.

Phase I. This is essentially a phase of fantasy formation, the fantasy being one of a potential, ideal relationship. In this sense, the initial behavior is self-generated. There is the self-creation of what may well be a false expectation, either that a magic partner will be found or that some individual about whom one has little information or with whom one has only a minimal relationship would be an ideal lover. The behavior is typified by the infatuations (often with celebrities) of adolescents.

The failure to test reality is notable. However, it

should be noted further that such fantasies may also be encouraged subtly by another, perhaps as a real participant in a parallel fantasy, or perhaps even as a kind of teasing to evoke wanting and admiration. An example might be the lady next door who, noticing that the male of the neighboring house is mowing his lawn, decides to take a sunbath.

Such illusions, whether one-sided or mutual, commonly go untested. The rejection risk is great, since there is almost always an underlying perception that the fantasy has little or no documentary basis. Phase II may never come.

Phase II.

In this phase, enough risk has been taken so that the fantasy is actually acknowledged. Impact has been sought and received. The "all-electric trip" has begun (as we have described in *Pairing*). And it is certain to eventuate in crazymaking experiences. These may be minimized or even largely prevented by one of four conditions.

A. Mutuality

One-sidedness is one of the main hazards of the love-crazy experience, since it creates the CM precursor of a very great imbalance of power. As we have seen, such imbalances are likely to trigger CM behaviors.

B. Recognition of the Temporary State

Because such relationships are largely fantasy-based, they can withstand the pressures of a continually impinging reality only so long. Recognition that the excitement is real, but that it has strong fantasy coloration and is unlikely to persist, helps to prevent false expectations. The situation is analogous to that of the viewer of a fantasy movie, who enjoys the fantasy, identifies, feels deeply about it, but understands that sooner or later the lights will go on, that the fantasy has offered valuable respite, but will not probably change life's realities.

C. Willingness to Exit

To continue our movie metaphor, the partners must not be like the child who is unwilling to leave when the film runs out. If the myth of the pair is one of an unending fantasy state, some bitter CM behavior lies ahead for one or both. (See Phase III, below.) To prevent crazymaking, both partners must be willing to assert and/or accept the wish of the other to leave.

D. Willingness to Relinquish Fantasy for Reality

To preserve such a relationship, the majority of the fantasy must be sacrificed so that change can be permitted and the constant wish for change accepted. It is the repression of the wish for change which eventually exhausts the partners with denial, and with the creation of elaborate psychological mechanisms to avoid all aggressive impulses. The fate of such repression and avoidance has been made clear enough.

Perhaps above all, the partners must recognize that the relationship can appear to be a kind of magical gift of the gods, free of all conflict, effort or negotiation; but that this is fantasy. Communications skills must be acquired and the need for real communication accepted.

Phase III

This phase has the highest CM component of all. For at the point at which an exit is desired by one or both, the pressure to deny (or repress) the wish is enormous. The partners, for example, may begin to play a game of *"I-don't-want-to-stop; you-do."* Baiting, setups and innumerable other tactics come into bitter, painful play, in order to deny the responsibility for asserting exit wishes.

The double message, "I-want-to-leave-you; I-want-to-stay-with-you" is perhaps the most murderous crazymaking of all. Literally. The resistance to fantasy-destruction or the sharpness of the sting can actually be so great that partners can kill, as suggested by interviews with seventy-four actual spouse-killers. Conversely, the pressures of sustaining a fantasy relationship that has been shredded by reality can be so great that some will kill to escape.

Some CM Aspects of Phases II and III

A. One-sidedness

We have mentioned this hazard above, together with

the power-balance crazymaking that is likely to be employed either to (1) enjoy the adulation and slavishness without being fully engaged in the relationship or (2) to bind the desired other with dependency patterns. As shown in the text, either is likely to spur counter-crazymaking.

B. The Emotional Roller-Coaster

The intense experience of trying to live out a powerful fantasy can be exhausting and frightening. Euphoria and sexual excitement alternate with anxieties of separation and rejection, and with depression. Small bits of reality become wicked stings in the CM spiral which may reflect the changes of mood and the denial of all but the positive.

He: (*After sex*) God, that was good!

She: Did your wife ever do that for you?

C. Walking on Eggs

The denial of reality generates a constant underlying tension, since conflict, rejection and aggression become more threatening and denial and repression more needed. Thus both partners become guarded, open communications become dangerous, and initial spontaneity dies. The partners feel constrained, generating CM responses.

D. The Clinging Vine

The need for continuing confirmation of the love-crazy state is great. The demand for confirmation is not only from the other, but also from oneself. There may be an actual competition to prove involvement, super-adequacy, super-trust. Failure to please or be pleased becomes a disaster, heightening the tension and demand. Again, real feelings must be denied in this confirmation, and CM is the inevitable result.

E. Surrender of Perception

The demand for consonance, with unendingly shared values and wishes, denies any wish for change or any polarization. Consequently, there tends to be a surrender of one's own values and perspectives in favor of those of the other, and of the fantasy. Whether self-generated or imposed, such demands tend to lead toward CM patterns. For, as has been shown in the text, the surrender of individual perspective can be a surrender of identity.

F. Stasis

The requirement for dynamic interaction as the sustenance of all valid relationships is well known. And as has been suggested, the love-crazy state does not easily admit of change, only of confirmation of the status quo. What is illusory is the excitement (often self-generated) of the all-electric relationship. In fact, the demand for stasis rules out the truly interactive, replacing it with repetitive rituals, which may even include pseudo-conflicts which must result in a return to the status quo. Sexual and other communication becomes stereotyped and impoverished for want of real (and possibly conflicting) input. In general, the demands of such fights consist of demands to maintain a static institution, not to change.

G. Isolation

A very common component of these relationships is their tendency to preserve isolation, which may mean nothing more than that the partners are preserving their fantasy from the disruptive intrusions of reality, often as represented by other people. Isolation also tends to generate a morbid dependency, with a discomfort that leads to repressed or denied demands for change, in order to be released from the stifling duality, from the trap.

H. Preoccupation

From the foregoing, it is easily seen that the demands of the electric magic, with their narrow foci of dependency, continually confirm and enhance the role of the fantasy other as a kind of sole-source emotional supplier. With such dependency typically comes a demand for more and more frequent input of information of the magical other. These demands can, and usually do, become onerous. ("I called you at ten last night; where were you?" "You were still out to lunch at three o'clock; with whom?" Etc.)

The burdensome demands of sustaining the all-electric fantasy in the face of real lives and real wishes for change are emotionally depleting. The stasis is boring. Clinical observation suggests that the crazy-making which is inevitable finally must overcome the satisfactions of the fantasy, usually within about five to six months, unless distance limits the frequency of exposure to reality by limiting the number of contacts.

As we have implied above, any of the CM impositions upon the love-crazy state may be turned to use in seeking exit. (And as indicated in the main text, there is the pathology that uses CM-prone situations for the exercise of sadistic impulses. The latter are characterized by the spinning of romantic illusions, which are then suddenly broken by abrupt and unsuspected exit maneuvers. As, "Honey, you're a great girl" (post-orgasmically) "but we're going to have to let you go."). Happily, such sadists are rare.

Among nonsadists, the therapist needs to be aware of how the would-be exiter from a love-crazy relationship takes on (largely by unconscious motivation) the sadistic semblance. Elaborate constructs of behavior are developed to deny the intent to exit, to attribute the need to exit to external circumstance or to the behavior of the other, to prepare other resorts to replace the relationship from which the exit is made and to pay off the guilt which derives—usually by good works and often in the seeming interest of the partner who is to be left. In the latter case, generous gifts, especially tender lovemaking or especially extravagant promises of faith and avowals of gratitude may actually be CM warning signs, an unavailing sugar-coating for the blow to come.

The objects of such CM exit behaviors become candidates for therapy with a dismaying frequency.

III

Sexual Crazymaking

Insights into the patterns and processes of crazy-making have proven to be a valuable asset in dealing with the deceptive arena of sexuality. It has long been known to therapists that sexual interactions are among the most dramatically informative sources of symbolic information about individuals and relationships. But precisely because sexual interactions are so powerfully rife with meaning, and seem to have so overt a character, some interpretive difficulties arise, especially:

A. The therapist or theorist may overread the data, particularly by leaping to conclusions about such common factors as the anorgasmic state in women or the prematurity of men. For example, to conclude that the anorgasmic woman is emotionally immature or non-accepting of the feminine role seems presumptive, and is denied by careful study of the case. We commonly see a progression from entirely competent sexual function to failures which too often are glibly classified as "impotence" of one kind or another. Are we thus to assume that many people regress from maturity? We think not.

B. Whether the therapist is right or wrong in quickly made assumptions about sexual problems (which we see as a kind of stereotyping), so fraught is the sexual context with powerful wishes, fears and angers that it commonly becomes a walled center of resistances, repressions, denials and ego defenses. In other words, when sexual difficulty is dealt with as an integral factor of the personality (although often it may not be), we hold that threats and anxieties are produced more often than there are returns to functional competence.

Analogously, if a patient says, "I don't dance well; I love the music and I feel the impulse, but then I trip over my own feet," we are likely to deal with this matter on a functional basis. We are not so therapeutically naive that we leap to relate this failure to fundamentals of the person; we do not say, "Well, of course—look at your relationship with your father. How can you dance until you deal with your anger for your father?" To do so would be to condition this poor person to a recall of parental problems every time the band strikes up. Yet delicate though we may mean to be in dealing with sexual problems, by envisioning them as integral to the personality, we may do far more harm than good.

The Sexual Communication

With our understanding of crazymaking, we find that there are alternatives to such interpretations of sexual problems. As has been pointed out in *The Intimate Enemy, Creative Aggression* and especially in *Pairing*, it is theoretically and therapeutically helpful to see sexual expression as one more context of communication and interaction, as an effort of intimate communication.

Especially, we see sexual expression as one of the most profound contexts of aggression, as an intimate assertion of the self in interpersonal relationships. In sex, one speaks of one's desires for intimacy (and accordingly, also for distance and for one's rights of impact, space, clear information and personal feeling) in the most dramatic possible way.

It seems to us (and is confirmed by clinical experience) that the person who cannot say, openly and directly, "I want to choose where we go for dinner," also cannot say, "I want to be on top." And we believe that such cases can be extended almost infinitely. To put it succinctly, the inability to make the felt, passionate assertion of self, out of fear of one kind or another, can generally not assert the sexual wish for change.

Moreover, just because the sexual aggression is so real, so powerful, so clear, the sexual arena becomes a strikingly dramatic field for crazymaking. Expectations, whether real or fantastic, are high. The potential for riposting to the CM sting is enormous if one wishes to return hurt for hurt. Sexual reluctance or embarrassment (often culturally inspired) becomes a commonplace of aggression phobia. The conventions of romantic love demand sexual stasis ("I always want you, and only you; I am satisfied by you and only you, and you please me always." Etc.).

Conceptualizing sexual difficulties in CM terms seems to us to be not only realistic, but also far more acceptable, than many other therapeutic interpretations. The double message says that one conforms to the sexual expectations, on the one hand, but then does not want, act or become satisfied on the other. Sexuality can encompass CM behaviors at their most impactful.

The Crazymaking Paradoxes of Sexuality

It is quite ordinary to find unacceptable paradoxes in one's sexuality, according to the CM patterns and processes. There is the wish to be close, yet the wish to be free; there is the wish to surrender and the wish to overwhelm; the wish to be gentle coupled with the wish to be aggressive; the wish to belong with the sense of rights to the space of one's own body.

The Crazymaking Sexual Code

Compounding these problems of frustrated assertion ("How can I say I don't want her tonight?") and of all the conventions of what is or is not permissible ("Your friend Tom turns me on," or even, "I wonder what it would feel like if Margaret came to bed with us") is the tendency to see sexuality as a powerfully effective place to continue the CM spiral. And making all these games covertly possible is the fact that most of us still tend to communicate our sexual wishes in a mutually developed code.

Just as we are mythologically taught to guess whether "He loves me; he loves me not" by tearing petals from a flower, we are also accustomed to *divining* "He wants me; he wants me not" from a host of coded signals. What does he/she wear to bed? What kinds of banter (sexual or nonsexual) has he/she engaged in tonight? In fear of rejection, we seek some assurance that sexual aggression will be accepted, wanted, welcomed. And we seek further assurance that once accepted, the sexual impulse will be a measure by which we please, not by which we will be accommodated, paid off, even made to feel beholden or guilty.

The trouble with these codes, among other things, is (1) like all symbolic systems, such codes are commonly not clear modes of expression; there is much room for either genuine misunderstanding or for a CM setup operation, (2) like all systems for predicting human behavior, especially rejection or acceptance, they are too rigid to reflect all the possible twists and turns of response (the brief but sedate cotton nightgown might indicate acceptance of a sleepy, gentle kind, yet sexual stimuli might change this to a highly aggressive demand) and (3) the rigidity and potential deceptiveness of such codes does not permit prediction of nuances: "Yes, I did mean you could go ahead, but I have to be in a certain mood to do *that*."

In brief, sexual codes and interpretations of probable response offer a hotbed of CM potential—especially involving the hazards of Divining; Mind reading, Mind ripping and Mind raping; Accommodation and Collusion; Derailing; CM exits and more. Even the presumption that the sexual impulse seeks satisfaction does not always hold, and not solely because of inability. True, as one popular author puts it, "Any woman *can*." But the question is, does she really want to, or do the parameters of CM patterns make it more satisfying still to withhold response? Perhaps above all, reason says that sexual partners ought to be able to say what they want of one another, clearly, and thus gain permission to enter one another's bodily space with relaxed confidence. That most do not do so is testimony to the almost pandemic fears of sexual assertion, and the reservation of the sexual ground for CM purposes.

The authors believe, and have some clinical evidence to substantiate, that analysis of sexual dysfunction according to CM principles is a useful diagnostic tool and also a most workable and relatively nontoxic way to give patient or client an understanding of their sexual psychodynamics. As much as sexual function can be dealt with psychodynamically in theory, and psychotherapeutically in practice, so much can CM principles be envisioned and applied to the enlightenment inherent in their understanding. Most commonly, the CM spiral becomes the poor-sex spiral.

It can be valuable (and the dynamics need hardly be spelled out) to understand such CM patterns as "I'll-show-you; I-won't-come," or, "You-turn-me-on-so-much-that-I-can't-keep-from-coming-fast.'' Such patterns are ideal grist for the human mill of dualistic communication. The use of sex for CM mechanisms becomes clearer when the *sexual context* is considered and made clear to both therapist and client.

Sexual context is perhaps best understood by looking at the modern trend toward what we call *Sport-Sex*. If we bear in mind that sexual behaviors are modes of communication, then we have a better chance of interpreting with some accuracy what is being said. And in so considering *Sport-Sex*, we can see that there is an inherent double message; for here is an acting out physically of the search for intimacy, with a denial that true intimacy is wanted. This is an inherently CM paradox: ''I want to be intimate with you, but not intimate.''

What is primarily operant in *Sport-Sex* is *Segmentalization*, that is, dealing with a person as a function of that person. As suggested early in the text, Segmentalizing is commonplace, but in order not to be a CM behavior, it requires mutual agreement to such limitation, as in the case of the gasoline-station attendant and the customer. The CM potential of this behavior, however, is implicit when one partner imposes upon it, or is led to impose, a perspective of a broader relationship, as of caring or of false future expectations.

Perhaps the essential message for the psychologist in the CM aspects of sexuality lies in the making explicit that which convention and rejection fears make implicit in the act. Especially, if the act is not to be an intimate one in the eyes of either or both partners, but merely a segmentalized game or release, both need to be aware of the case—and both need to agree. Otherwise there is inherently a crazymaking double message which can do psychological damage.

In general, we may surmise that the wide-ranging CM implications of sexuality can be dealt with best only if the nature of the act and the relationship is defined by open assertions of the meaning of the physical gestures. The authors feel that there is a paradoxical new kind of sexual Victorianism, sustained by the avoidance of open aggression, in which one may *do* anything, but is commonly forbidden to say what one wants to do or be direct about the purpose or the context of feeling and personal meaning. As long as these latter factors are *assumed* to belong to one cultural convention or another, they are more than likely to lead to CM experiences.

IV

Self-Crazymaking

The sophisticated reader is likely to have discerned, throughout the text, a recurrence of self-generated CM behaviors. The subject of Self-Crazymaking has a range at least as broad as the interactive CM, which is the main subject of this book. Our notes here are intended only to confirm the awareness of the phenomenon and to counsel that this factor not be ignored in analyzing or attempting to manage CM behaviors and experiences.

Bondage, a CM pattern of a fundamental kind, is perhaps the most Self-CM-free formulation. The CM factor here is that ordinary aggressions must be repressed in order to continue a relationship that is perceived as mandatory. Examples may be the mother-child relationship, or perhaps the state of the husband who feels bound to an unsatisfying and even wounding marriage, but cannot bear to sacrifice his valued parental role, which would be necessary were the marriage terminated.

Yet even in *Bondage*, which is implicitly a CM situation, the self-generated aspects cannot be ignored. Is the *Bondage* real? Would aggressions for change really force a break and the total loss of the relationship, or be intolerable to the other? Objectivity is difficult here, and inner images can control.

In other CM behaviors, self-generation is almost certainly an important factor. It cannot be ignored.

Bugging is an exemplary pattern of the latter case. This is a recurrence of apparently unmotivated CM behaviors. It is a common resort of people who either demand or resist dependency, often because they are trying to establish a kind of centricity which the other is not willing either to grant or to confirm. *Bugging* is frequently a testing behavior, or it may be a continuing response to a situation to which one feels bound.

It is not hard to see that in a true *Bugging* pattern of chronic annoyance there must be some CM-self-generation on one part or the other.

As is so often the case in psychology, extremes of *Bugging* and *Bondage* ultimately appear as mirror-images of one another, with a common linkage. Without some comprehension of the Self-CM phenomenon, such connections may not be clearly established, as in the formulation: "He bugs me; I feel bound." What we have said of *Carrot-Dangling, Collusion* and *CM Exits* suggest some commonplace experiences that are self-generated in some part.

Plainly, illusions which require denials of reality and suppressions of aggressive feeling imply a component of Self-made CM fantasy, as in the case of *Love-Crazy* Phase I, the undocumented infatuation from a distance. Indeed, probably any of the CM patterns that we have described imply some Self-CM.

However, we envision a Self-CM which is entirely *sui generis*. The concept begins with inevitable conflicts of the inner self. It continues with internalization of superogatory images (perhaps a more modern and functional way to interpret Freud's concept of the superego). In either the psychoanalytic case or in the case of today's psychotherapist (who looks more at process than at unconscious roots of character development), the Self-CM conception has been found to be functionally useful. And to the therapeutic client, such a concept is more easily acceptable and less loaded with unconscious resistance than is the traditional concern with parental internalization.

Two Major Patterns of Self-CM

Briefly, two tendencies of Self-CM need to be recognized by therapist, theorist and the CM-wounded individual:

   A. Victimological cooperation

That is, a tendency to accept, and perhaps collude with, CM processes that are instigated by others, and

   B. Sui-Generis CM

That is, painful processes which originate in, and through, the self.

The matter of victimological cooperation may be seen in almost any of the CM patterns presented in the text. It is merely, in perhaps a somewhat simplistic sense, saying, "You are not entirely wrong or without justification in invading my rights of space, feeling, impact or information. I yield—not perhaps without a sense of the CM sting—but accepting your right to deprive me of what I do not think I can, or should, keep to my own."

The *sui generis* aspect is different. It is represented by such questions as, "I know better; why did I do it?" "Why did you set yourself up to be hurt?" Etc.

Within the CM concept is a means by which the therapist can point out how the fear to assert what one wishes to assert results in a double message to the self. To point out such behaviors as matters of needlessly feared barriers to true self-assertion is an easy therapeutic device that can alert the client without laying upon the client a self-image of ignorance, foolishness or perversity. The inner conflict is as real as the relational one. The inner enemy is as formidable a psychological foe as is the most manipulative associate.

Some Functional Aspects of Self-CM

Although any CM pattern has a Self-CM component, we shall note here only a few of the clear indications.

A. Setup Operations. One cannot be engaged in such ploys without obstinate beliefs in contradiction of reality—whether beliefs of worthiness or of magical resolution.

B. Overloading. Frequently, people overload themselves—taking on more than they can do, burdening themselves because they fear that the partial rejection of a "No" will mean total rejection of a person. The fantasies of unexpressed aggression may lead to doing what one is not ready to do.

C. Derailing. It is a common human device, when faced with any unpleasant reality that is difficult to manage, to replace it with some other manageable reality. For example, if one is overweight, one may not wish to deal with the food sacrifices that must be made to lose weight. So one may buy unreasonable books, products or ideas instead, read them faithfully and act upon the unrealistic promise rather than upon the inwardly known reality.

D. Self-Made Spirals. Preoccupation with other than the known main objects can lead us away from our goals that are difficult to achieve. The great novel may not be written, but how can we pass up watching the seventy-eighth in some 160 baseball contests which lead to the pennant?

There are many such diversions and illusory distractions. Unclear about what we want, or where we are going, we set up double-binds for ourselves. By playing self-analyst, we spend our time and energy in speculating, rationalizing and interpreting, rather than acting.

Rather than deal with uncomfortable realities, we encyst. Or, in the same context, we divert and mystify ourselves. We cannot deal with reality, so we impose intellectual and analytic barriers in the false belief that we are only trying to "find" ourselves; thus we may experiment in needless, even self-destructive ways.

A final hazard, which misdirects in the search for a way out of CM behaviors, is to fall into exaggerated beliefs (countenanced by unthinking, popular literature), that we are all, or at least ought to be, autonomous, entirely self-stimulating, self-gratifying or self-realizing.

This pop-psychological literature suggests, in contradistinction to all of the responsible professional literature, that what may be considered as CM experiences are to be explained and managed as though they originated only in the self.

Nothing could be more naive or far from the truth. Indeed, the attempt to deal with Self-CM without the consideration of interactions with others, we find, is doomed to failure. Conversely, it is by engaging, understanding and acting upon the feared aggressions in interactions that we find the most ready acceptance of psychological reality.

For if there is a barrier, a damper of some kind within the self that denies and frustrates the assertions of self, then it cannot be seen clearly or managed openly except by dealing with it in the interactive context. One is helpless, or nearly so, in dealing with one's own denials. One can manage, negotiate, talk and think about interactions with others.

We believe that (as expressed in the psychoanalytic literature of "working through") the barriers imposed by the self are amenable to change and removal best when one deals with them in terms of relational experience. Spurred by the fundamental qualities of human aggression, frustrated by the self-directed or other-directed inhibitions of internalization, or of the introjection of the CM experience, the realities of crazymaking are best seen as changes of relating, not as changes of the seemingly integral self.

BIBLIOGRAPHY

Albee, E., *Who's Afraid of Virginia Woolf?* New York: Atheneum, 1962.

Alberti, R., ed., *Assertiveness*. San Luis Obispo, CA: Impact, 1977.

Bach, G. R., "Constructive Aggression in Growth Groups." In A. Jacobs, ed., *The Group as an Agent of Change*. New York: Behavioral Publications, 1974.

———, "Creative Exits—Fight Therapy for Divorcées." In V. Franks and V. Burtle, *Women in Therapy*. New York: Brunner/Mazel, 1974.

———, "Fusion: Aggression in the Service of Eros—Sexual Liberation Through Compassionate Aggression." In G. R. Bach and H. Goldberg, *Creative Aggression*.

———, *Intensive Group Psychotherapy*. New York: Ronald Press, 1954.

———, "Pathological Aspects of Therapeutic Groups." In *Group Psychotherapy*, August 1956, 133–148.

———, "Sex and Aggression—Fair Fight Therapy for Lovers." Unpublished lectures and lab exercises. Taped by the Inst. Adv. Human Behavior: Stanford, October 1978.

———, "Spouse Murder." In *Journal of Contemporary Psychotherapy*, 1979.

———, *Young Children's Play Fantasies*. Washington, DC: Am. Psych. Assoc., Monograph, 1944.

———, R. Bach, and S. Harrison, *Guide to Pairing Effectiveness*. Los Angeles: Bach Institute. In preparation.

———, and Y. Bernard, *Aggression Lab—the Fair Fighting Training Manual*. Dubuque, Iowa: Kendall–Hunt, 1971.

————, and R. Deutsch, *Pairing*. New York: Wyden-McKay, 1970; Avon, 1971.

————, and H. Goldberg, *Creative Aggression*. New York: Doubleday, 1974; Avon, 1975.

————, and H. Molter, *Psychoboom*. Düsseldorf: Diederichs, 1976.

————, and L. Nicholson, *The Cradle of Crazymaking*. *Voices*, Vol. 12, no. 4, issue 46, 1976/77.

————, and L. Tolbert, "Who Cares?" Book manuscript in preparation. To be published by Delacorte Press (New York) in 1980.

————, and P. Wyden, *The Intimate Enemy*. New York: Morrow, 1968; Avon, 1970.

Bateson, G., *Steps Towards an Ecology of Mind*. New York: Ballantine, 1972.

————, et al., "Towards a Theory of Schizophrenia." In *Behavioral Sciences*, Vol. 1, 1956.

————, and G. R. Bach, "Chatting About Crazymaking." Privately tape-recorded in 1976/1977. Unpublished.

————, and J. Ruesch, *Communication*. New York: Norton, 1951.

Beier, E. G., "Beneficial Aggression." In *Journal of Communication*, Vol. 27:3, summer, 1977.

————, *People Reading*. New York: Warner Books, 1975.

Berger, M., ed., *Beyond the Double Bind*. New York: Bruner-Mazel, 1978.

Fadiman, J., and D. Kewman, eds., *Exploring Madness*. Monterey, CA: Brooks-Cole, 1974.

Feshbach, S., "Aggression and Sex-Research Results—Updated." Personal communication, 1978/1979.

————, et al., "Sexual Arousal and Aggression." In *Journal of Social Issues*, 1978.

Freud, S., "Die endliche und die unendliche Analyse" In *Gesammelte Werke*, Vol. XVI, Werke aus den Jahren 1932–1939, 59–99. London: Imago, 1950.

Fry, W. F., *Sweet Madness*. Palo Alto: Pacific Books, 1973.

Goldberg, H., *The Hazards of Being Male*. New York: Nash, 1976; Signet, 1977.

————, *The New Male: From Self-Destruction to Self-Care*. New York: Morrow, 1979.

————, and R. T. Lewis, *Money Madness*. New York: Morrow, 1978.

Grinder, J., and R. Bandler, *The Structure of Magic*. Palo

Alto: Science and Behavior Books, Vol. I, 1975; Vol. II, 1976.

Haley, J., "Ideas Which Handicap Therapists." In *Journal of Communication*, Vol. 27:3, summer, 1977.

Lewin, K., *Principles of Topological Psychology*. New York: McGraw Hill, 1936.

———, *Resolving Social Conflicts*. New York: Harper & Row, 1948.

Laing, R. D., *The Politics of Experience*. New York: Ballantine, 1967.

Lasch, C., *The Culture of Narcissism*. New York: Norton, 1979.

Nicholson, and L. L. Torbet, *How to Fight with Your Kids and Win!* New York: Harcourt Brace Jovanovich, 1979.

de Rivera, J., *Field Theory as Human Science, Contributions of Lewin's Berlin Group*. New York: Gardner Press, 1976.

Stoller, R., *Sexual Excitement*. Pantheon Books, 1979.

Wanderer, Z., and T. Cabot, *Letting Go!* New York: Putnam, 1978.

Watzlawick, P., et al., *Pragmatics of Human Communication*. New York: Norton, 1976.

INDEX